IMAGES
of America

MEXICANS IN NORTH CENTRAL WASHINGTON

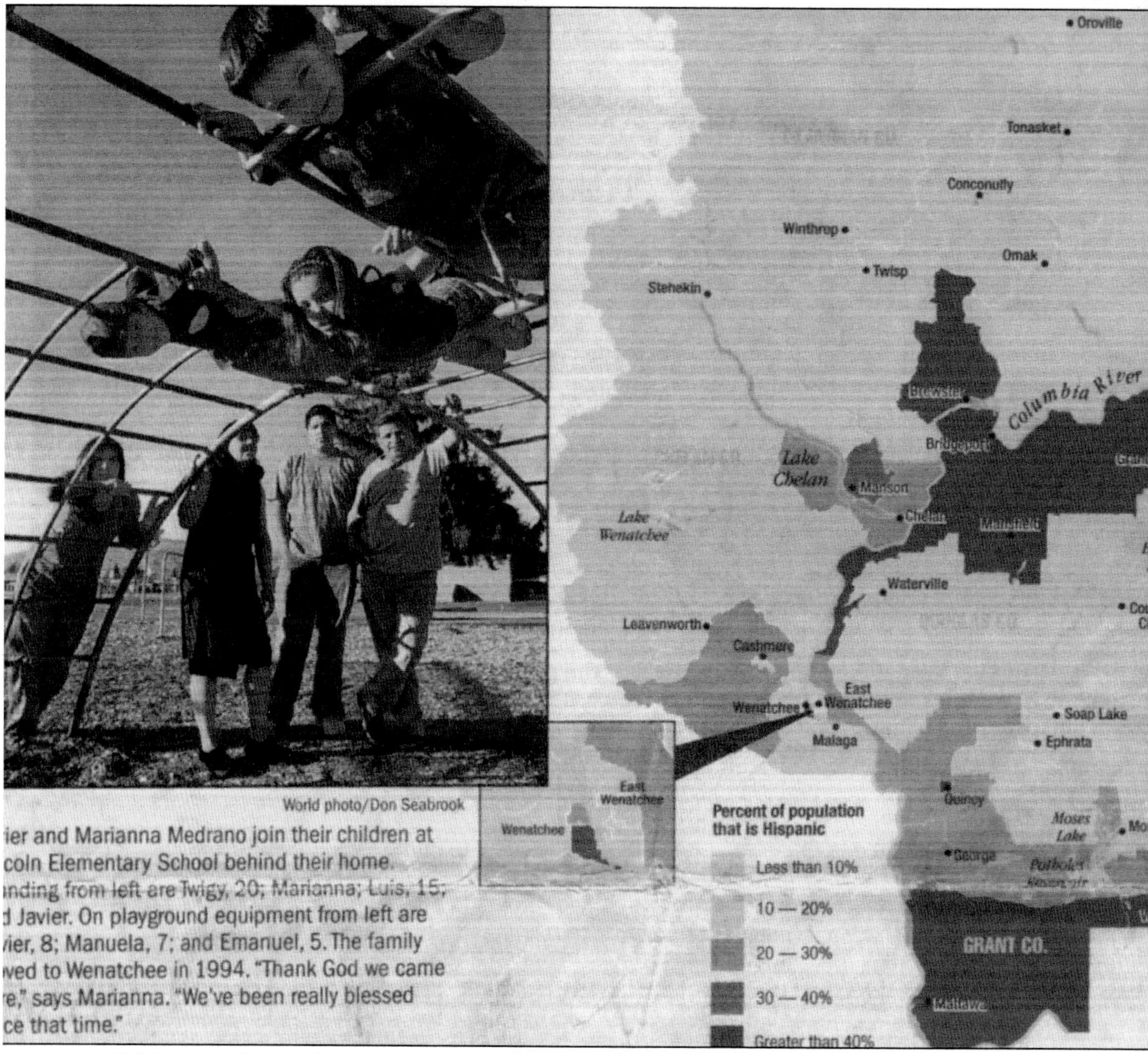

This map shows the percentage and geographical location of Hispanics in North Central Washington. (Courtesy *Wenatchee World*.)

ON THE COVER: This photograph was taken in 1966 of a fourth-grade class at Pioneer Elementary School in Quincy, Washington. (Courtesy Garces family.)

IMAGES
of America

MEXICANS IN NORTH CENTRAL WASHINGTON

Jerry Garcia

ARCADIA
PUBLISHING

ISBN 978-0-7385-4879-1

Published by Arcadia Publishing
Charleston, South Carolina

Printed in the United States of America

Library of Congress Catalog Card Number: 2006938510

For all general information contact Arcadia Publishing at:
Telephone 843-853-2070
Fax 843-853-0044
E-mail sales@arcadiapublishing.com
For customer service and orders:
Toll-Free 1-888-313-2665

Visit us on the Internet at www.arcadiapublishing.com

Para mi madre, Gloria, y mi hermana, Yolanda,
dos mujeres con muchísima fuerza.

Contents

ACKNOWLEDGMENTS

I want to thank Arcadia Publishing and my editor Julie Albright for the opportunity to put this project together. My initiation to the history of Mexicans in North Central Washington (NCW) came first from growing up in this region but, more importantly, from the Mexican elders and pioneers of Quincy. A heartfelt *gracias* goes to those early pioneers who helped me piece things together: Benito Alamillo, Raymond Ambriz, Sipriano Barrera, Juan Antonio Callardo, Ruben R. Camacho, Guadalupe Cruz, Roberto D. Garcia, Ruben D. Garcia, Jesse Gonzales, Ramiro Hinojosa, Bernie and Diane Jaramillo, Roberto Luna, Andres Martinez, Javier Noriega, Manuel and Rita Puente, Alicia Garces, Baldemar Garces, and Felipe Ybarra. And a special thanks goes to Dora Sanchez Treviño, who provided great insight to the Chicana experience in NCW.

A project like this cannot be completed without the support from the community and their input. A special thank-you goes to Mark Behler, curator at the Wenatchee Valley Museum, who generously provided access and permission to reprint photographs from a wonderful collection at the museum. I am also very grateful to Jim Tiffany, managing editor of the region's Spanish-language newspaper, *El Mundo*, who provided numerous photographs on the Mexican community in Wenatchee and historical background. I want to acknowledge Washington State University Special Collections and the Washington State Archives. I am also deeply indebted to the *Wenatchee World* and two of its employees, Don Seabrook, photograph editor at the *Wenatchee World*, and Linda Barta, the librarian. The *Wenatchee World* provided access and permission to use numerous photographs from their newspaper, without which this project would not have been completed. Don Seabrook and Linda Barta each spent time from their daily schedule searching for photographs, and I am deeply grateful for their support. Finally I send a thank-you to all those individuals depicted in this book. Your courage and strength to leave your homeland for one thousands of miles away speaks to your determination to make a better life for your children, your families, and yourself.

INTRODUCTION

This book depicts the history of Mexicans in North Central Washington (NCW). This region includes the counties of Chelan, Douglas, Grant, and Okanogan. In the contemporary period, Mexicans reside in almost every community in the region, but this was not the case in the past. The majority of the communities discussed and portrayed in this book are those that the earliest Mexican pioneers chose to reside in because of economic opportunities. Those communities include Wenatchee, Quincy, Moses Lake, Royal City, Warden, and Brewster. This volume also includes places like Othello, located in Adams County and adjacent to NCW. Othello is included because it shares historical roots with communities such as Quincy, Moses Lake, and Warden, and it is part of the Columbia Basin.

The modern movement of Mexicans to the Northwest begins in the 19th century. According to Carlos Maldonado and Gilberto Garcia in *Chicanos in the Pacific Northwest*, during this early period, Mexicans arrived from California as hired mule drivers in the mule trade transportation industry in eastern Washington, because of their expertise and skill, during the 1860s. This makes Mexicans some of the earliest settlers in the region. However, the settling of large numbers of Mexicans in the Northwest had its beginning in the early 20th century. In general, Mexican immigration to the Pacific Northwest follows some of the same contours as the national pattern. The impact of the Mexican Revolution from 1910 to 1920 reverberated well into the Northwest. With thousands of Mexicans being pushed and pulled into the United States by the turbulent period of the revolution, jobs along the border region became scarce and competitive. This in turn created an expansion of the Mexican diaspora that reached beyond the Southwest to include the Pacific Northwest in search of employment. As agriculture expanded in the early 20th century in the Northwest, Mexican labor recruitment accelerated. This expansion was due in part to the development of dams and canals that brought irrigation to such places as the Yakima Valley. Many of the first arrivals during this period were foreign-born Mexicans. These workers came to Washington to work in agriculture, picking hops and blocking sugar beets, and in the fruit industry. This period also saw the railroad industry employing an increasing number of Mexicans in Washington.

In 1930, Washington officially reported 562 persons born in Mexico or having parents born in Mexico. The Great Depression of the 1930s and the subsequent large-scale deportation drives that affected Mexicans in other regions of the country had little effect on the small Mexican population in Washington. The only known wide-scale instance of deportation of Mexicans in Washington occurred when McNeil Island Federal Penitentiary released 90 Mexicans on the condition of their repatriation back to Mexico. As the Great Depression subsided and World War II commenced in Europe, agriculture production became paramount and labor critical.

According to the U.S. Census, by the beginning of the 1940s, the Mexican American population of Washington stood at approximately 2,400. The Mexican population increased considerably during and after World War II. For instance, as the United States entered World War II, the immigration restrictions in place a decade earlier eased as the war caused labor shortages throughout the

American West. Nonetheless, a reliable source of labor eluded NCW, and every fall, this region fell into a panic over a lack of workers. Thus, under a bilateral agreement between the United States and Mexico, NCW became the beneficiary of thousands of imported Mexican nationals known as *braceros* from approximately 1943 to 1947. This period represents the arrival of the first large-scale movement of Mexicans into NCW. Communities such as Wenatchee, Quincy, Moses Lake, and Okanogan each utilized Mexican bracero workers to harvest their crops.

The migration of Mexican Americans created the impetus for permanent Mexican communities. The Moses Lake Army Airfield received Mexican American airmen and soldiers. The region experienced an influx of Mexican American migrants who moved up from the Yakima Valley. Although the bracero program all but ended for the region by 1947 because of the prohibitive cost, one exception is the braceros brought in as a result of the Korean War in the 1950s, when some were recruited into small regions of the Northwest such as the Columbia Basin. For some regions in NCW, the ending of the bracero program represented the end of significant numbers of Mexicans in their communities until the 1970s and 1980s. Wenatchee, the largest community in NCW, followed this pattern after using some of the largest numbers of braceros for a fruit industry reliant on outside labor during World War II. Thus, for places like Wenatchee, Okanogan, Brewster, and Bridgeport during the fall harvest, thousands of Mexicans returned to the NCW but quickly returned to their place of origin after the picking was completed. Wenatchee and other similar communities maintained small Mexican enclaves until the late 20th century. This was mainly due to a lack of available year-round work.

The post–World War II movement of Mexicans into NCW was primarily U.S. citizens of Mexican ancestry coming from south Texas, the Midwest, the Rocky Mountain region, and to a lesser extent California. Irrigation once again played an important role during this era. Completed in 1942, Grand Coulee Dam focused on generating electricity to aid the war effort, but postwar production prioritized irrigation through the development and completion of the Columbia Basin Irrigation Project. Water first reached the Columbia Basin region in 1952, and in the subsequent decades, over 500,000 acres have come under production. The large number of labor-intensive crops put into production ensured a steady need and stream of laborers into the region. This development explains why communities such as Quincy, Warden, Othello, and Moses Lake established significant Mexican communities earlier than other regions of NCW. These areas developed a diverse agriculture economy as early as the 1940s, and by the end of that decade, Mexican Americans began to arrive into the area. For example, Jesse Gonzales and his family came to Quincy in 1948 and is the earliest Mexican American family known to have made Quincy their permanent residence. Born in 1929 and raised in Lubbock, Texas, Gonzales left Texas in 1930 with his family to follow the sugar beet crops, which took them to Wyoming and Montana before they eventually settled in the Yakima Valley in the early 1940s. The four generations of the Jose Hernandez family from Moses Lake can trace their roots to the region to 1954. The family of Juan and Natalia Garcia, who originally came from the northern regions of Mexico and crossed into Texas at mid-century, also are representative of this early migration. After following established migration routes that took them to Arizona, Colorado, Wyoming, and Montana, this family finally settled in Quincy in the late 1950s. The development of the Columbia Basin Irrigation project played an undeniable role in attracting ethnic Mexicans to NCW.

By the late 1950s and early 1960s, well-established Mexican communities were visible in NCW. Not only had the population increased significantly during these decades thanks to the migration of Mexican Americans and the non-renewal of the guest worker program in 1964, but the Mexican community began to integrate itself, and clear signs of social and cultural life appeared in many forms. NCW, with a history of Mexican labor in the region and a persistent need for it, continued to attract not only Mexican American labor but also Mexican immigrants. Thus, the coalescing of these two groups had a profound impact on the region. As a critical mass of ethnic Mexicans emerged during this period, the community began to move outward, rather than remaining isolated. One of the first signs was the inauguration of the annual Mexican fiesta, with the earliest celebrated in Quincy in 1957. Similar celebrations occurred in Wenatchee and

Moses Lake. Most of these Mexican fiestas had a connection to the Catholic Church whereby any proceeds from the celebration were donated to the church. Social organizations such as Latin American Associations sprang up in Quincy, Othello, and Moses Lake, which organized Mexican dances and other social events. As these Mexican communities began to empower themselves, political organizations emerged, such as the Progressive League of United Mexican Americans (PLUMA) in 1967 that addressed issues affecting the Mexican community with chapters in Quincy, Moses Lake, Othello, and Warden. In 1968, the Mexican American Federation (MAF) was created with chapters throughout Washington, including Moses Lake. The MAF eventually morphed into the Washington State Commission on Hispanic Affairs in 1971. Head-start and migrant education programs were established in efforts to integrate Mexican children into the school system. Mexican Americans in NCW also participated in national affairs emerging in the late 1960s and early 1970s.

The Chicano (Mexican American) civil rights movement also emerged during this era and reverberated through the NCW region. By the late 1960s and early 1970s, the Mexican population of NCW had increased to represent approximately 10 percent of some of the counties such as Grant. However, Chelan, Douglas, and Okanogan continued to see only minimal gains and the Mexican population in those areas remained mostly transient. Yet in communities such as Quincy, Moses Lake, and Othello, the Mexican population was large enough and so politicized that various individuals and groups were directly involved with the Chicano movement. For example, Andres Martinez of Quincy, a longtime civil rights activist, was the state of Washington national delegate to La Raza Unida Party's national convention held in El Paso, Texas, in 1972. In 1973, a group of individuals from the Columbia Basin organized a picketing campaign against Safeway stores for the United Farm Workers grape boycott. And that same year, PLUMA entered a float in the Apple Blossom Parade in Wenatchee with the theme of "Chicanos from Aztlan," embracing the ideology and symbolism of the national Chicano movement. By the end of the 1970s and early 1980s, early signs of a demographic shift were appearing.

By the beginning of the 1980s, the Mexican population in NCW can be characterized as primarily Mexican American, with a small movement of Mexicans directly from Mexico or seasonal workers converging on the region during the fall harvest. Two developments during this period dramatically shifted the population, repercussions of which continue to be felt in the contemporary period. First, NCW as a whole is one of the largest agricultural zones in the nation. In 1980, Washington ranked first in the nation in the production of apples and other fruits. During the 1980s, the region began to increase production in a variety of labor-intensive crops but significantly in the apple industry. This intensification resonated throughout the industry and increased the number of year-round laborers to maintain the industry from the fields to the packing sheds. As year-round work became available, family and social networks spread the word, which put the Mexican population in NCW on a trajectory toward record-setting numbers by the end of the century. Wenatchee's Mexican community is an excellent example of this trajectory. At the beginning of the 1980s, the Mexican population of Wenatchee represented 2.2 percent of the city's population. Second, during the early 1980s, immigration became a national debate thanks to a rise in nativism directed towards undocumented workers entering the country and working in industries that became reliant on their labor. The result of this debate was the implementation of the 1986 Immigration Reform and Control Act (IRCA). Embedded within this new immigration policy was a program allowing undocumented workers to become "legal" residents by meeting certain conditions. As a result, thousands of Mexicans in NCW came forward to apply for legal residency.

By 1990, approximately 5,600 of those individuals resided in Chelan, Douglas, and Grant Counties. Although IRCA had a short-term effect in deterring the movement of undocumented Mexicans into the United States, by the 1990s, the clandestine movement had picked up once again. Three major factors contributed to this. First, the disparity in wages between those earned in Mexico and the United States makes the 2,000-mile journey economically viable. Second, the fruit industry of NCW has become dependent on this type of labor in order to pick the thousands of acres of apples, cherries, peaches, pears, and apricots. Third, by the beginning of the 1990s, family networks were well in place in the region, which facilitated the movement of family members and established a strong support base. Thus, by the early 1990s, each of the counties in NCW had Hispanic populations ranging from 10 to 18 percent of the population, with certain communities being much larger. However, the largest increases were still yet to come.

The explosion of the Mexican community from the 1990s to the present in NCW follows the phenomenon that is occurring at the national level and is facilitated by entrepreneurial opportunities, the lure of family members, and an agriculture industry that remains heavily reliant on Mexican labor. From approximately the 1980s, the increase in the Mexican community in NCW has been fueled by Mexican immigrants. This movement has dramatically altered the landscape of NCW. The impact of this increase in the Mexican population is felt in almost every facet of daily life, from the development of new schools to the opening of literally dozens of Mexican-owned businesses in the region. A large portion of the Mexican community is no longer employed in agriculture. A very visible professional class has emerged in almost every community in NCW.

In conclusion, the history of Mexicans in North Central Washington can be traced to the arrival of contract laborers from Mexico during the World War II period. This was followed by the arrival of Mexican American migrants, who created the first permanent Mexican communities in the region. As the Mexican American population reached a plateau by the end of the 1970s, the population as a whole began to increase from the movement of Mexicans coming directly from Mexico during the 1980s. From 1990 to 2000, NCW recorded a 140 percent increase in its Hispanic population, mostly of Mexican origin! Currently Hispanics make up over 21 percent of Wenatchee's population; 65 percent of Quincy's population; over 25 percent of Moses Lake's population; 60 percent of Brewster's population; 90 percent of Mattawa's population; 65 percent of Bridgeport's population; and 78 percent of Royal City's population.

One

Early Settlers

North Central Washington was home to a number of different tribes. In the Wenatchee area, the most prominent were the Salish Indians. The Wenatchi band (P'squosa is the original name), a division of the Salish clan, lived at the confluence of the Wenatchee River and Icicle Creek. In 1855, the Wenatchi Indians were offered a reservation under the terms of the Yakama Treaty with hunting and fishing rights, but it has yet to be honored. Today many of the Wenatchis live on the Colville and Yakama Reservations. Another Salish clan is the Sinkiuse, who lived along the Columbia Plateau. Chief Moses (his Americanized name) was in charge of this tribe during the late 19th century, and the city of Moses Lake is named after him. The first large contingent of white settlers began to arrive shortly after the 1850s. When Washington became a state in 1889, it already had a substantial number of white residents, and in 1891, Wenatchee had a population of 108. In 1893, Wenatchee was officially incorporated. By the beginning of the 20th century, Wenatchee was growing and becoming well known for its emerging apple industry. The photographs in this section portray some of the early settlers, including some of the first Mexican Americans in the region.

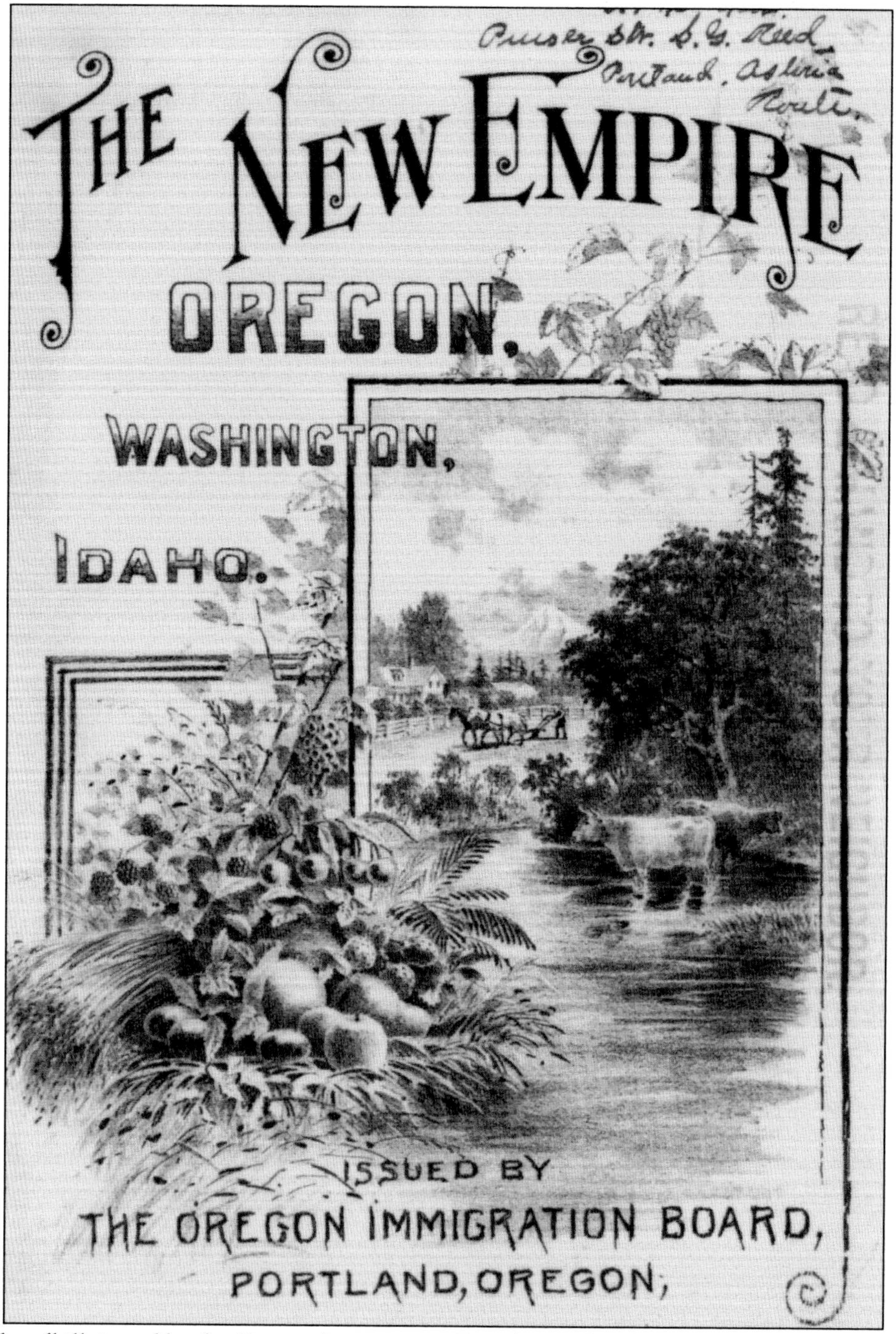

This handbill, issued by the Oregon Immigration Board, circulated throughout the Midwest and eastern part of the United States in an attempt to entice individuals to the Pacific Northwest. This is an excellent example showing a romantic image of a region with abundant fruit, grains, land, and plenty of water. However, many early settlers encountered a region that was dry, inhospitable, and difficult to grow crops in until the Columbia was diverted for irrigation in the 1930s and 1940s. (Courtesy Washington State Archives.)

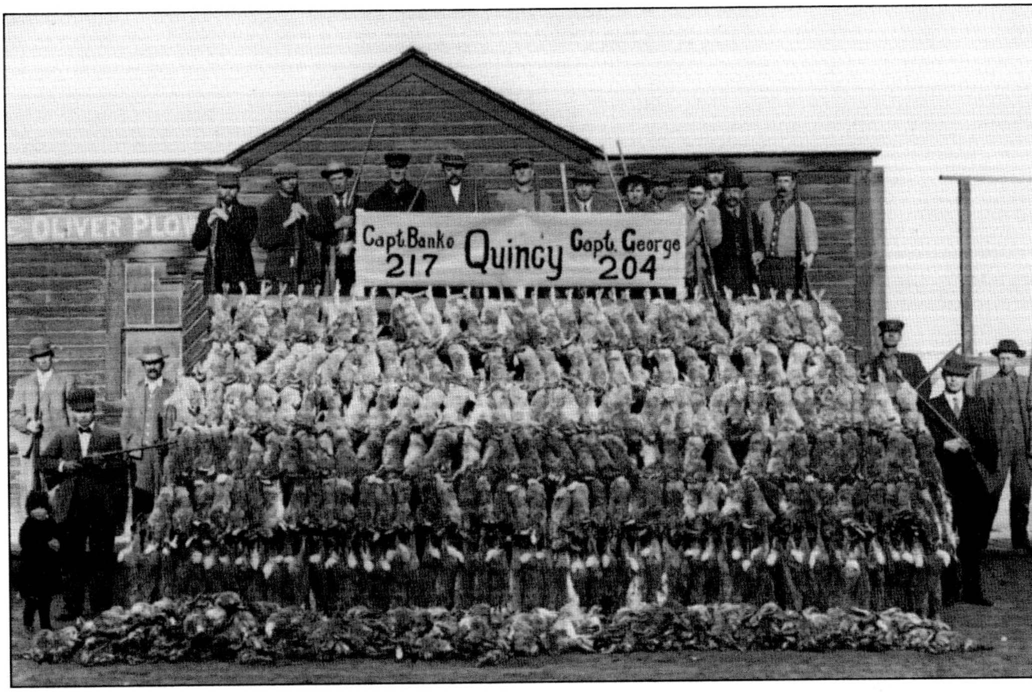

Quincy, founded by European immigrants, was incorporated in 1907. When the Great Depression struck in the 1930s, many of its inhabitants fled the area and, for a period, the region resembled the dust bowl areas of the Midwest with abandoned farms and very dry conditions. Besides suffering from droughts, communities such as Quincy had to deal with animals that ate or damaged crops. The above photograph depicts one of the many jackrabbit hunts that occurred in Quincy. The jackrabbit is Quincy High School's mascot. The below image is of Quincy as it looked in the early 20th century. (Courtesy Washington State University.)

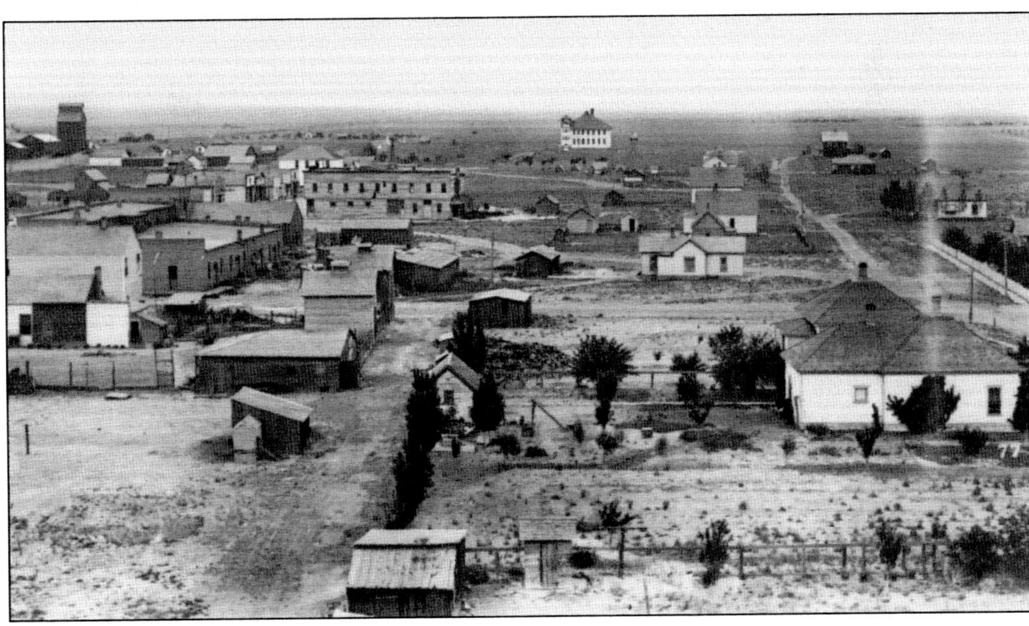

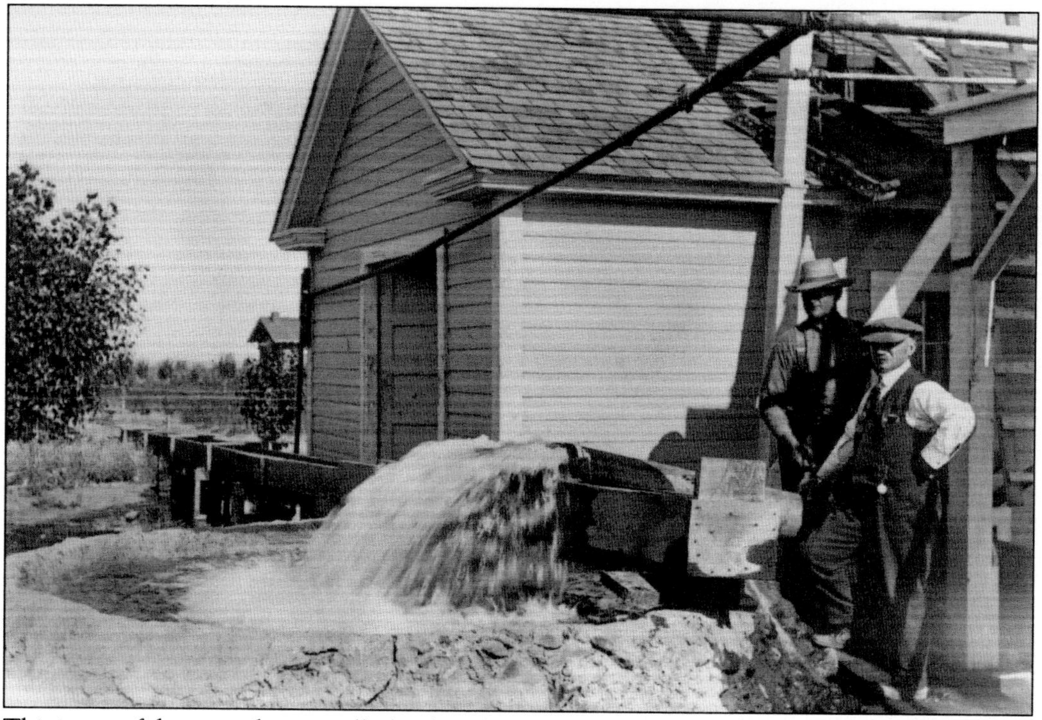

This is one of the groundwater wells developed in and around the Columbia Basin *c.* 1910 and long before the arrival of water from the Columbia River. Irrigation water from the Columbia Basin Project didn't arrive until the early 1950s. Prior to that, a variety of schemes and proposals were developed in attempts to make the region fertile. The German immigrants below in the Quincy Valley were some of the first settlers to NCW. (Courtesy Washington State University.)

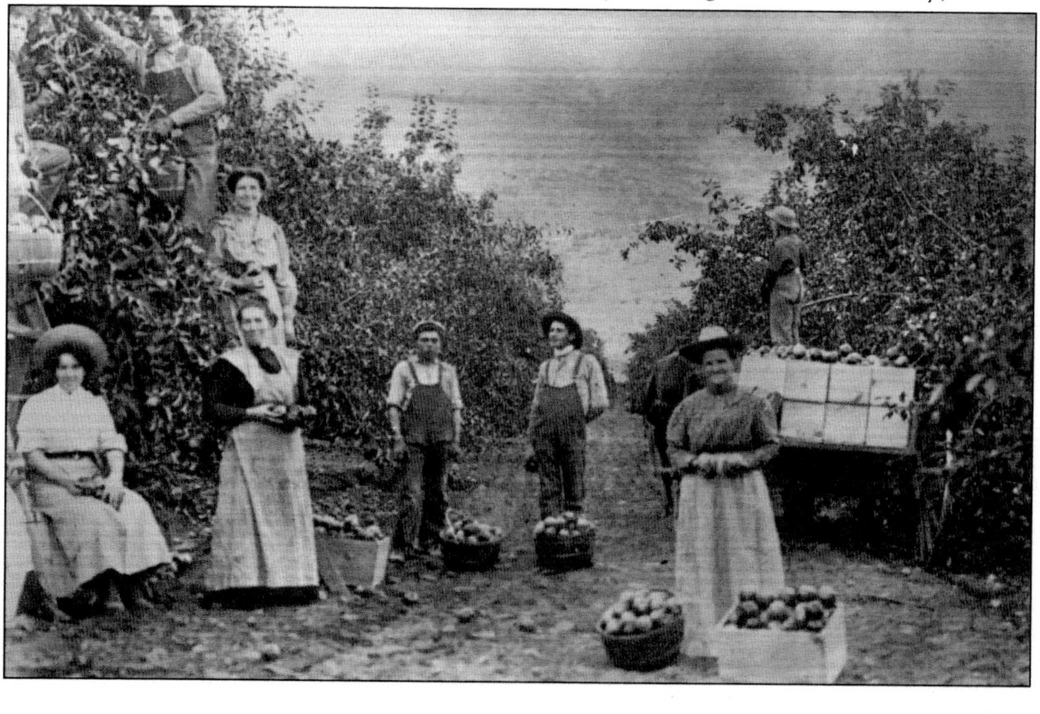

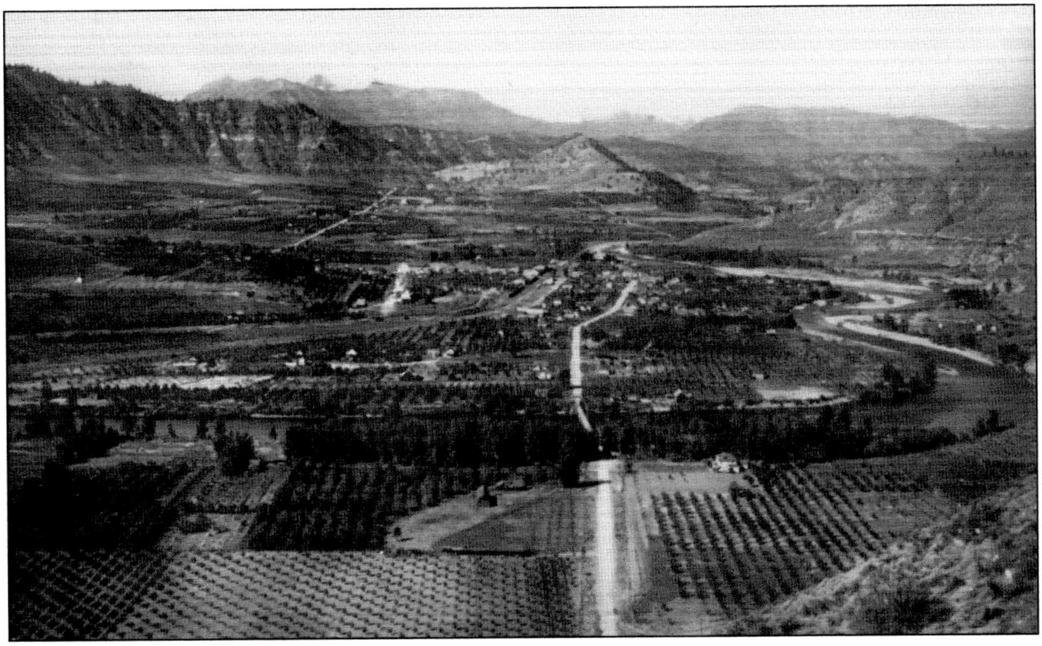

This panoramic view of Wenatchee shows why Native Americans, Europeans, and contemporary residents are drawn to the region. Not only did Wenatchee have the potential for economic success, but its location at the foothills of the Cascades, straddling the Columbia River, and the region's natural beauty captivated individuals. The depiction of Wenatchee's main avenue provides an excellent example of the community's development. Wenatchee Avenue remains the city's main business district. (Courtesy Wenatchee Valley Museum.)

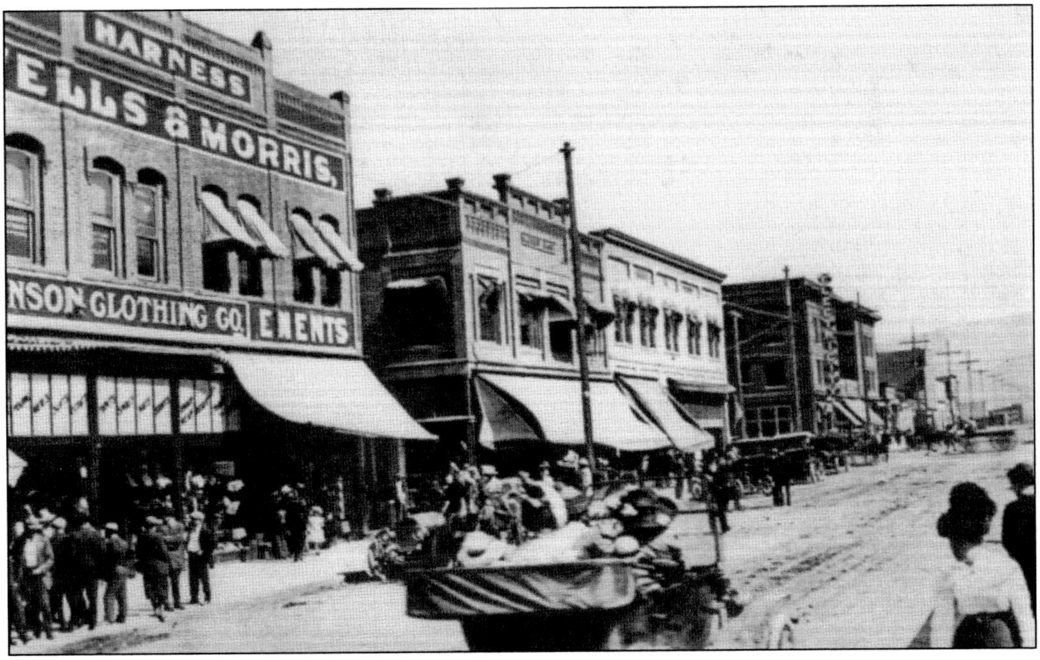

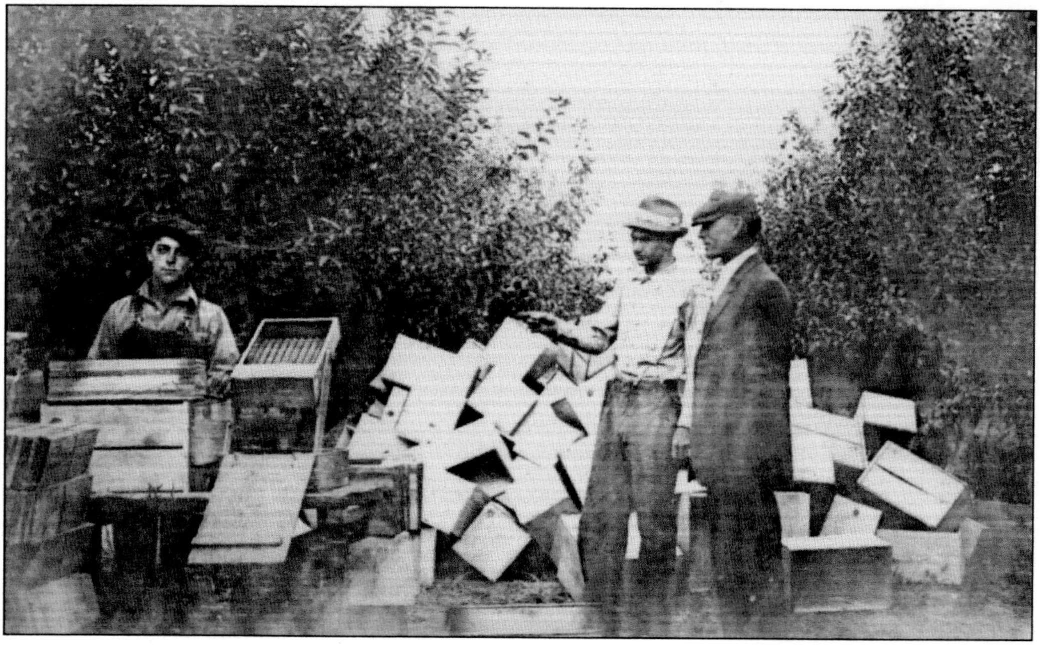

In the early 20th century, most of the labor was performed by immigrants. The photograph above depicts a picking and packing crew at Sunset Orchards. The bottom photograph depicts Native Americans working in the orchards. Wenatchee and the surrounding region were once dominated by the Salish linguistic family of Native American tribes until the late 19th century. The 1910 census counted only 52 Native Americans in the Wenatchee area. Today barely one percent of the population of Chelan County and the city of Wenatchee is Native American. (Courtesy Wenatchee Valley Museum.)

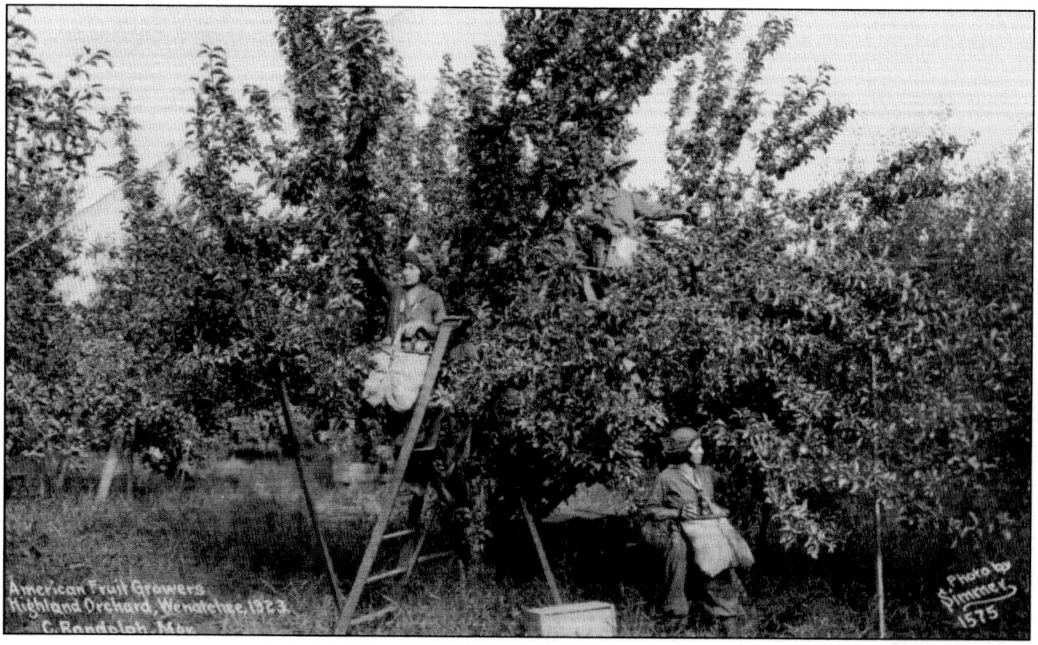

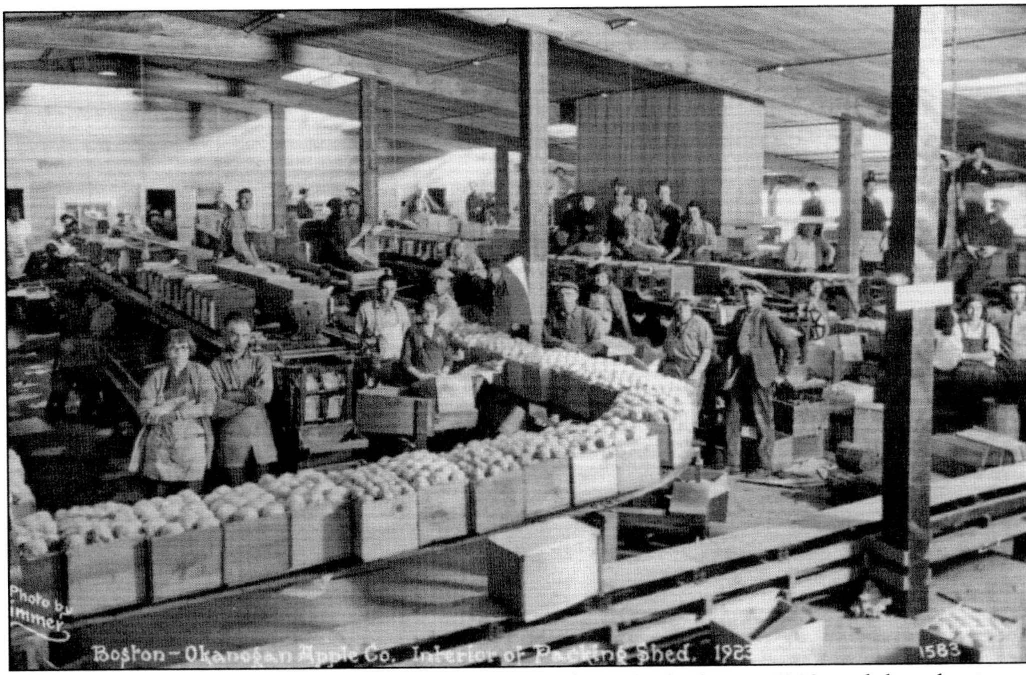

The top photograph shows the interior of an apple packing shed taken in 1923, and the other image was taken in 1926 depicting workers boxing apples at American Fruit Growers in Wenatchee. A contemporary facility looks very similar to the one here, albeit with modernization, but the basic principles of packing apples remain the same. In fact, the major difference in the contemporary period is the faces of the workers. Today many of those faces are of individuals of Mexican ancestry. (Courtesy Wenatchee Valley Museum.)

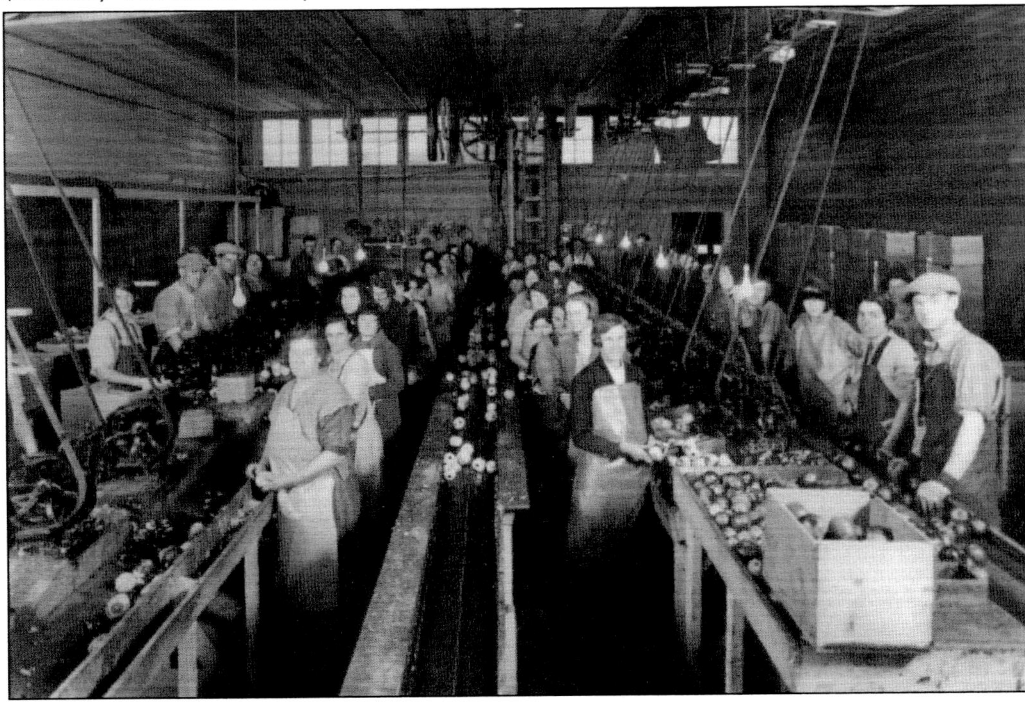

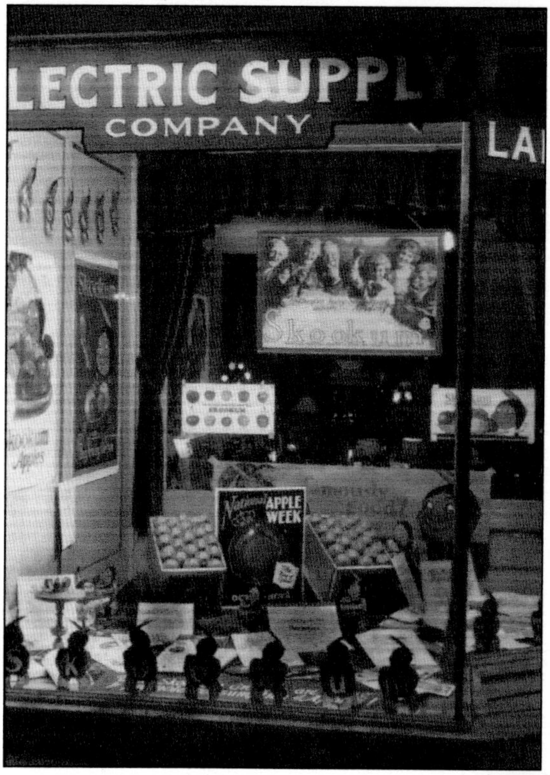

The photograph at left depicts a store along Wenatchee Avenue. The apple industry, even in its formative years, understood the importance of advertising. Here a number of themes are used to sell apples. One is the wholesomeness of the apple, depicted by an extended family enjoying the taste. The other is the commodification of indigenous culture. In this photograph, the "happy Indian" image stereotype is used to sell apples. Who could resist buying apples from the three lovely ladies below? An obvious posed photograph, possibly of Apple Blossom princesses appearing to pick apples, contrasts the beauty of the female figures with the apples. (Courtesy Wenatchee Valley Museum.)

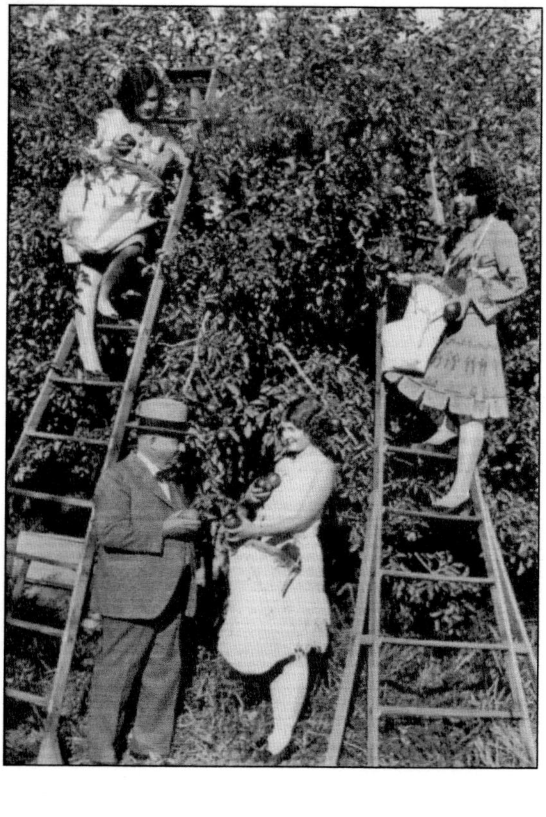

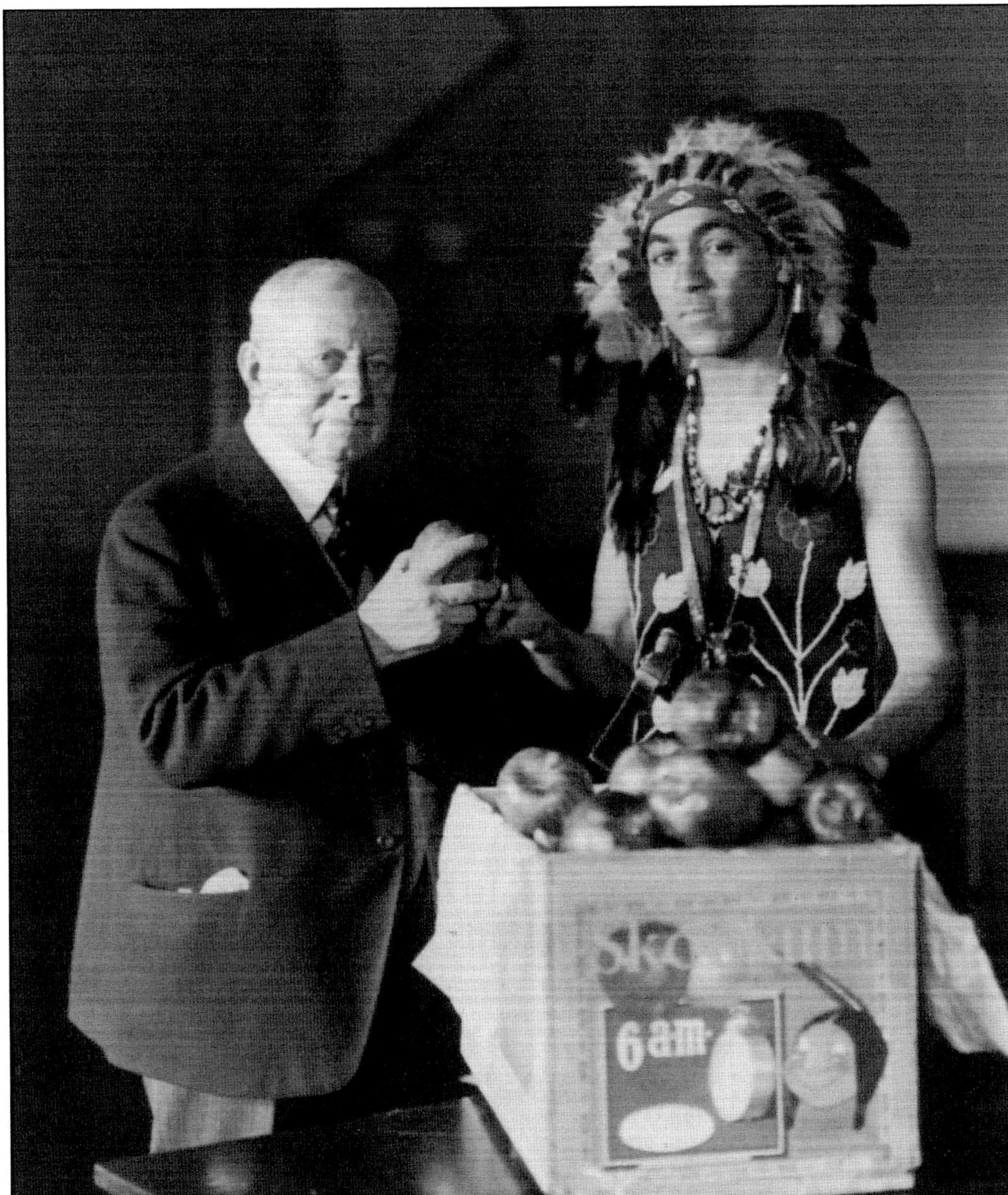

In the early years of advertising NCW apples, Native Americans played a prominent role. These roles ranged from depictions on boxes and handbills to advertisements in newspapers, but the industry also used "real" Native Americans to promote the NCW apples. Pictured here is Chief Kiatus Tecumseh, radio's "Tenor of Wenatchee," who promoted apples throughout the country. He is pictured presenting a box of Skookum apples to Gov. Aram J. Pothier of Rhode Island in 1928. (Courtesy Wenatchee Valley Museum.)

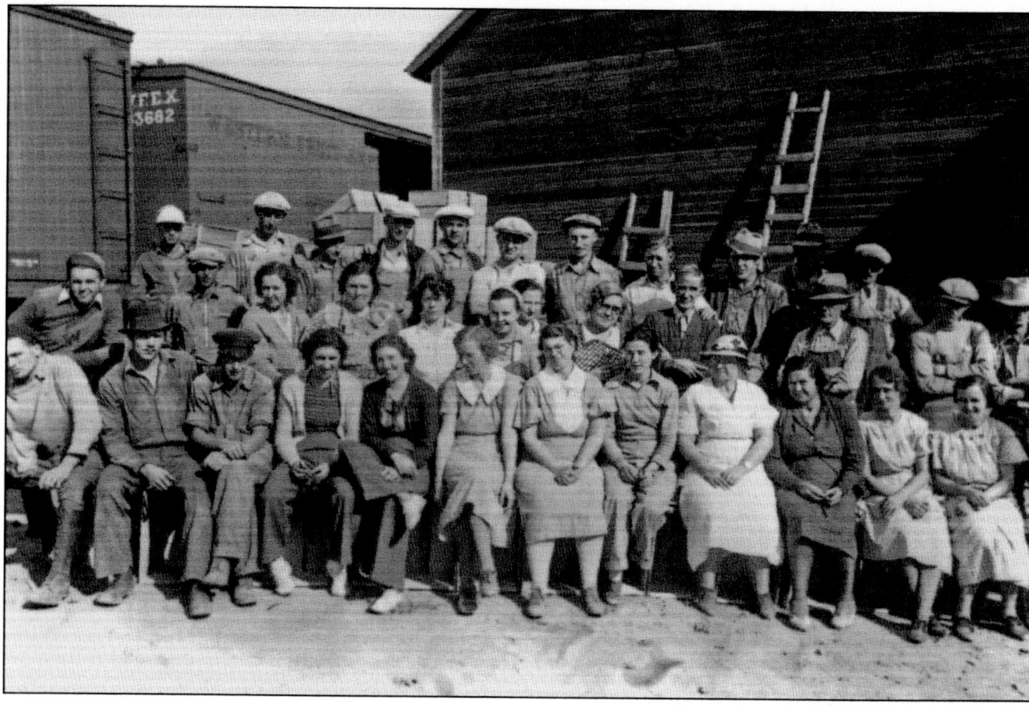

By the late 1930s, Quincy had rebounded from the drought years with groundwater providing a limited means of production. The top image shows a group of packing shed workers. The labor force shown will begin to change in less than a decade. Before the 1940s, much of the population in NCW remained homogenous. The bottom photograph also illustrates the racial background of the labor force. This picture is of a crew in Quincy appearing content, perhaps happy that they have work during the Depression years. (Courtesy Wenatchee Valley Museum.)

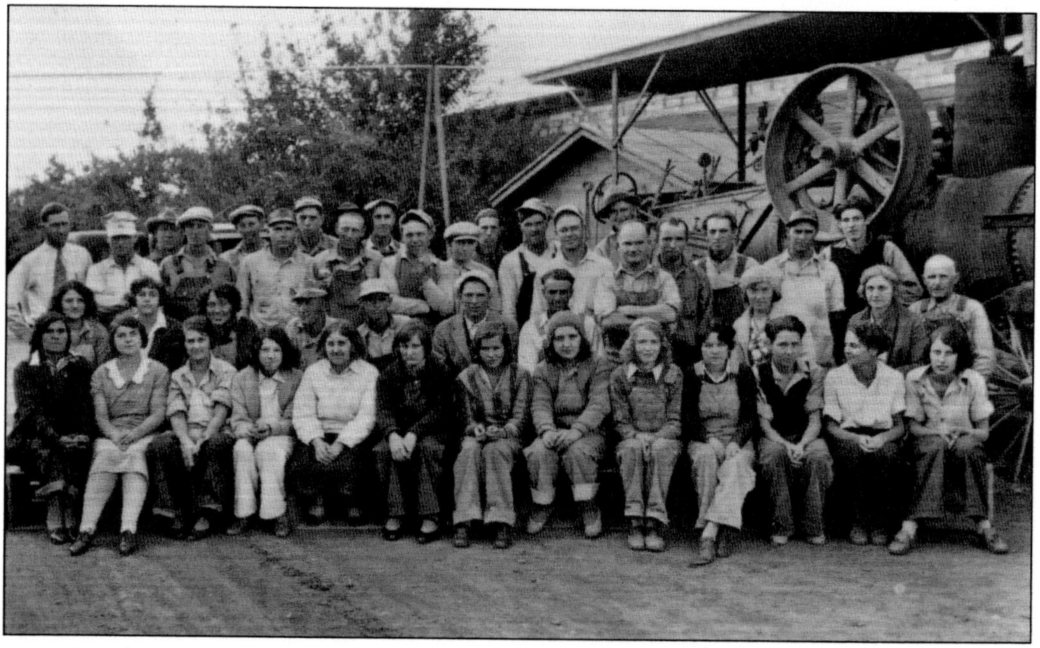

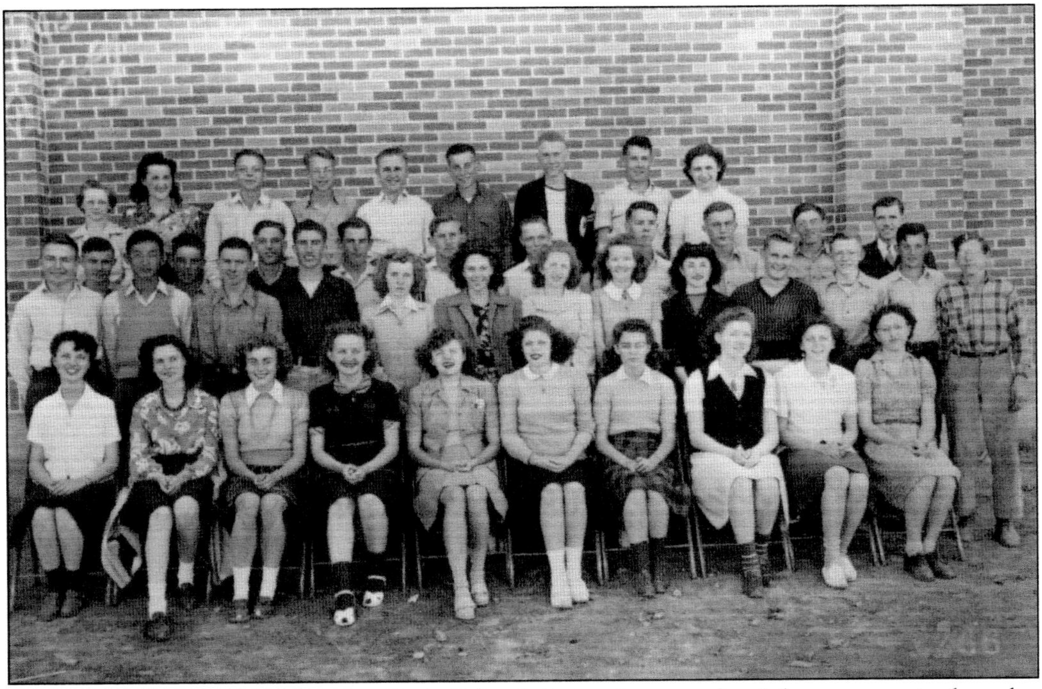

This class photograph at Quincy High School shows the growth of the community but also that, during the early 1940s, communities throughout NCW had very little racial diversity. This particular photograph does show a Japanese American in the second row. After the bombing of Pearl Harbor, Japanese Americans living along the West Coast had the option of voluntary removal. Most refused and were concentrated in camps for the duration of World War II. Many of the Mexican American families, before arriving in NCW, were migrants following the crops throughout the country. The second photograph shows Andres Martinez (top row, second from left) and his siblings housed in a migrant camp in Hoopeston, Illinois. (Above, courtesy Washington State University; below, courtesy Jerry Garcia.)

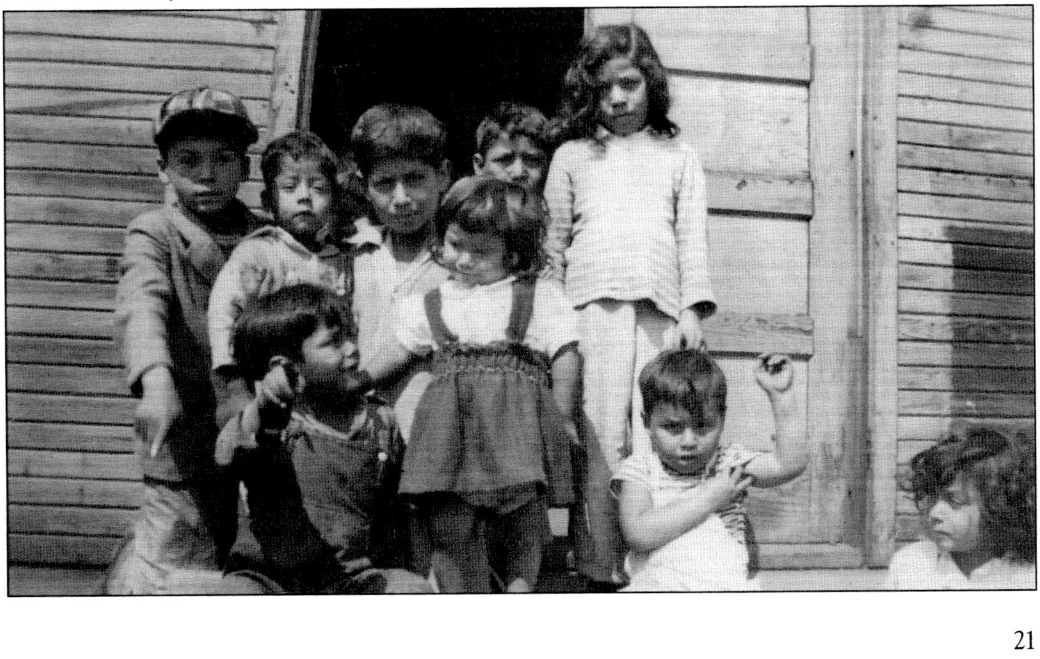

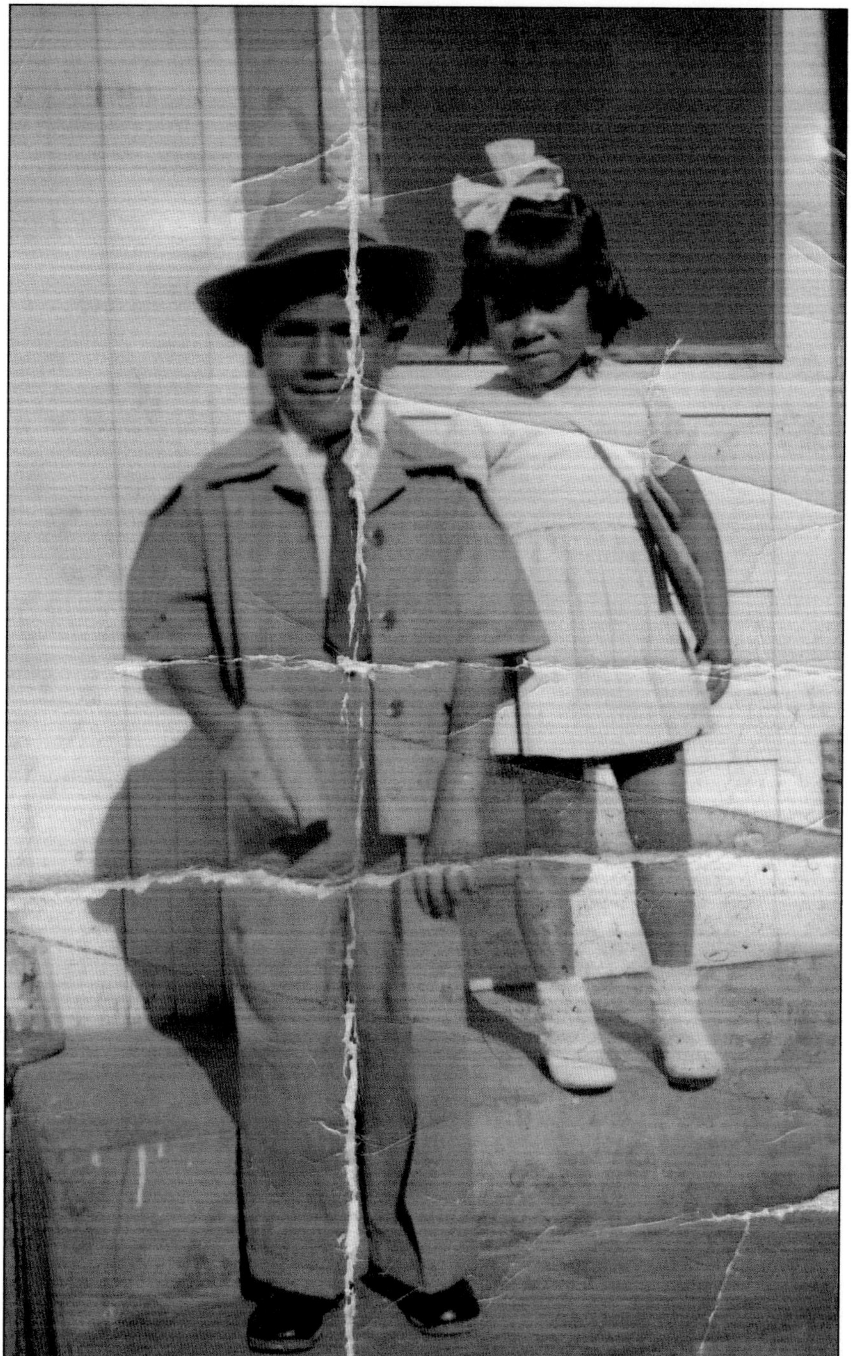

The family of Gloria Torres picked cotton in Arizona before arriving in Washington in the early 1940s. Pictured in this 1944 image is Cruz "Jerry" Torres and his sister Gloria Torres shortly before coming to Washington. For many, including Gloria Torres, who has lived continually in Washington since 1945, NCW became their home, with Texas or Arizona becoming a place to visit rather than live. The majority of the Mexican American pioneers of Quincy, Moses Lake, Othello, and Warden came from the Rio Grande Valley in south Texas. (Courtesy Jerry Garcia.)

Two

Braceros and Mexican Americans

The braceros and trailblazing Mexican American pioneers set the foundation for later generations of ethnic Mexicans to make NCW their home. Of the thousands of Mexican braceros that came to Wenatchee, Quincy, or Moses Lake, it is difficult to know just how many remained in the region. The braceros did experience forms of cultural shock ranging from the food to the climate. In general, for many of the people in NCW, this was the first time encountering individuals from Mexico. Most of the communities were very grateful for their help and attempted to accommodate their needs when possible, like celebrating Mexican Independence Day during the fall harvest.

The 1940s also represent the migration and the development of Mexican communities in NCW. It is sufficient to say that long before their arrival to the region, Mexican migrants journeyed to such places as Michigan, Minnesota, Iowa, Colorado, Arizona, Wyoming, Montana, and California. And before they arrived to NCW, they first established themselves in the Yakima Valley in communities such as Granger, Sunnyside, Toppenish, and Yakima. The family of Andres Martinez traveled throughout the Midwest during the 1930s and 1940s before arriving in the Yakima Valley and eventually the Columbia Basin. The individuals photographed in this section are considered the Mexican pioneers of NCW, and their efforts gave rise to the Mexican communities of NCW.

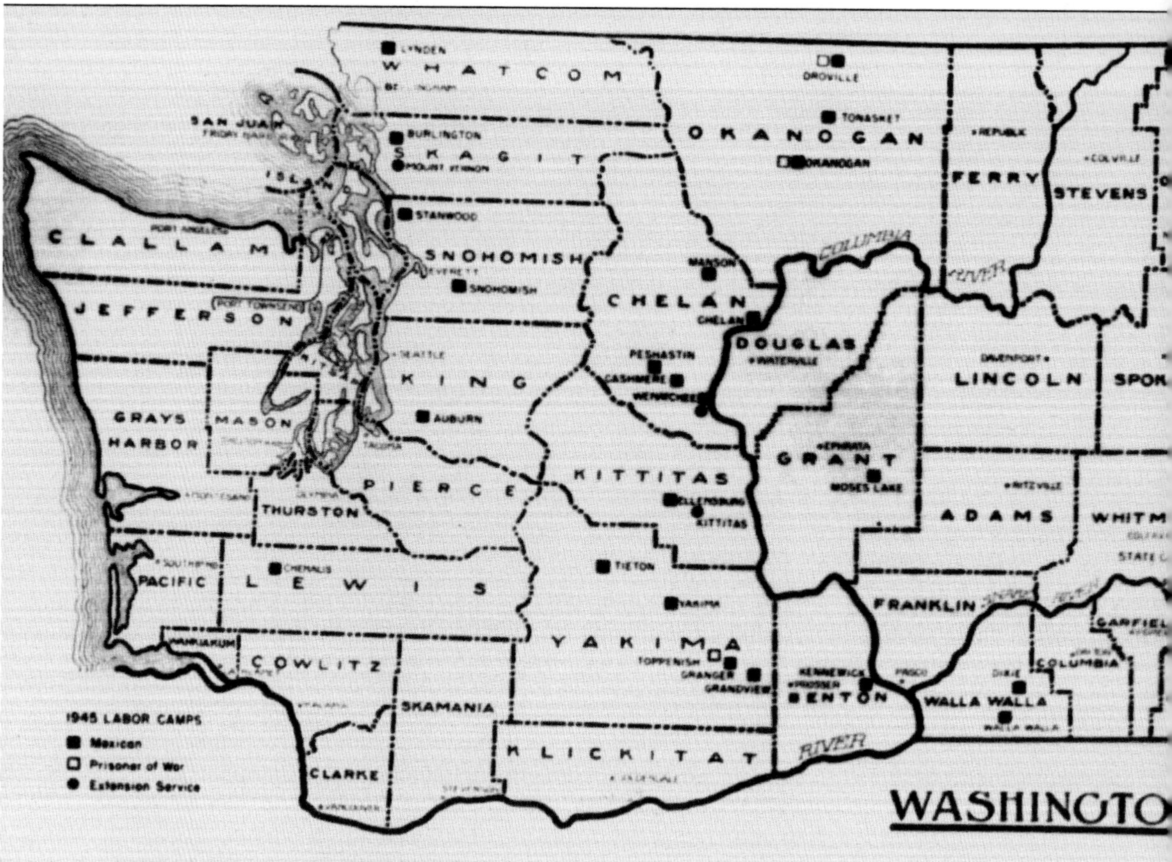

Mobilization for World War II caused a significant labor shortage in Washington, especially on the farms. Thus, by 1945, Washington utilized a variety of workers ranging from domestic workers, Mexican nationals, Mexican Americans, Japanese internees, and POW labor, primarily German. This map depicts the location of the various camps used to house Mexican and prisoner-of-war workers. Twenty-three camps were created for Mexican workers, while three existed for prisoners of war. This illustrates how Mexicans accounted for the largest foreign worker contingent in the state. The arrival of Mexicans in these communities solved many of the labor shortages, and for the first time, Mexicans had arrived into the region. (Courtesy Washington State University.)

Mexican nationals who were brought into Washington and NCW worked primarily in two areas: one, as maintenance-of-way workers for a variety of railway lines, and two, as depicted here, agricultural workers. The workers at right are harvesting hops in the Yakima Valley. The bottom photograph depicts rows of tents that housed Mexican laborers while they worked in the Wenatchee Valley. Much of the material for the labor camp came from local merchants and orchard owners. The federal government provided transportation from Mexico to the Northwest, thus economically it was an excellent option for growers to utilize Mexican nationals during the war period. (Above, courtesy National Archives; below, courtesy Washington State University.)

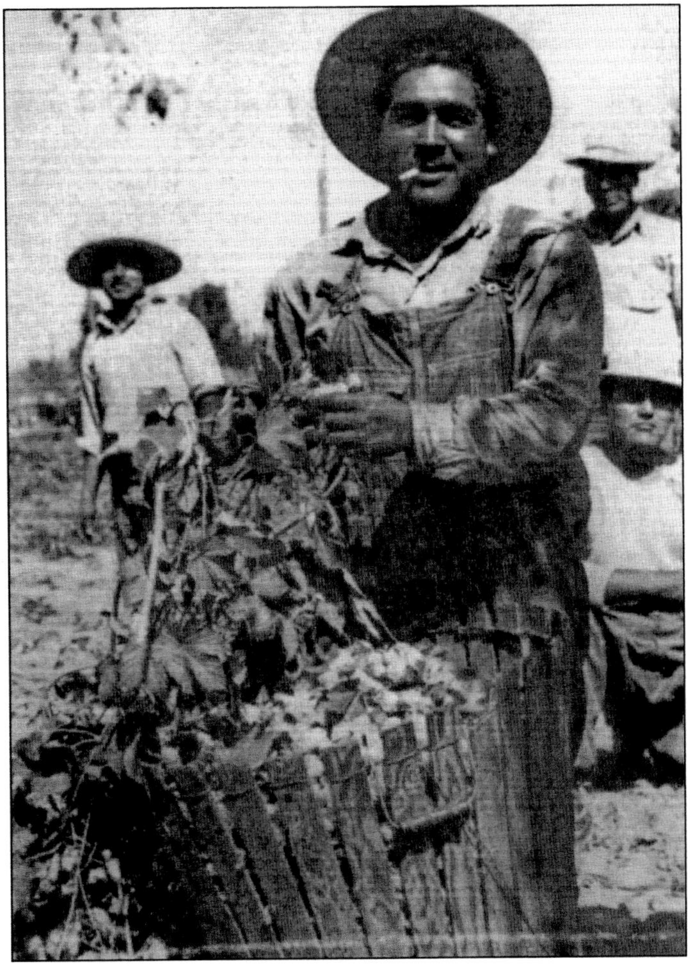

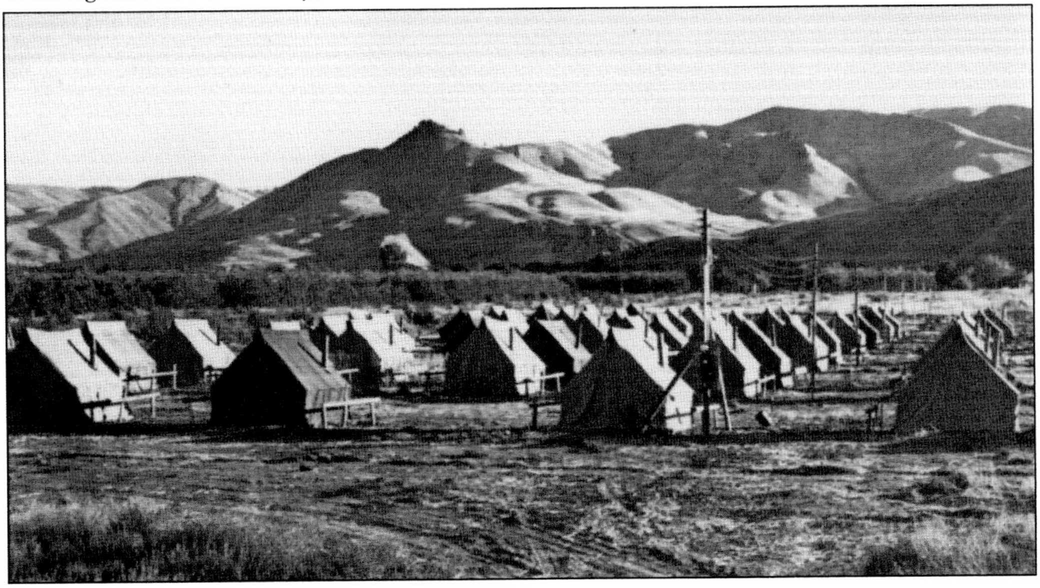

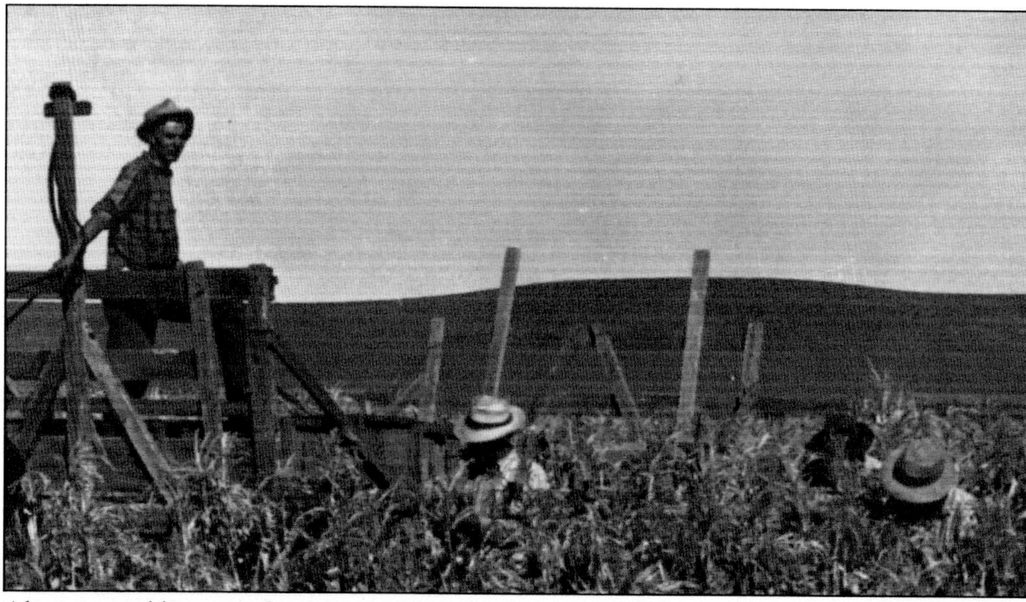

Almost invisible except for their hats, braceros are pictured here picking sweet corn with either an extension agent or foreman keeping a watchful eye on their progress. Compared to other regions of the country, Mexicans in the Pacific Northwest were treated fairly well. Nonetheless, during the war period, Mexicans complained about their treatment, wages, and food. In order to accommodate and make the braceros feel comfortable away from home, the War Manpower Commission issued a directive mandating the celebration of Mexican Independence Day on September 16. The below photograph shows a community hall in Wenatchee decorated for the celebration. (Courtesy Washington State University.)

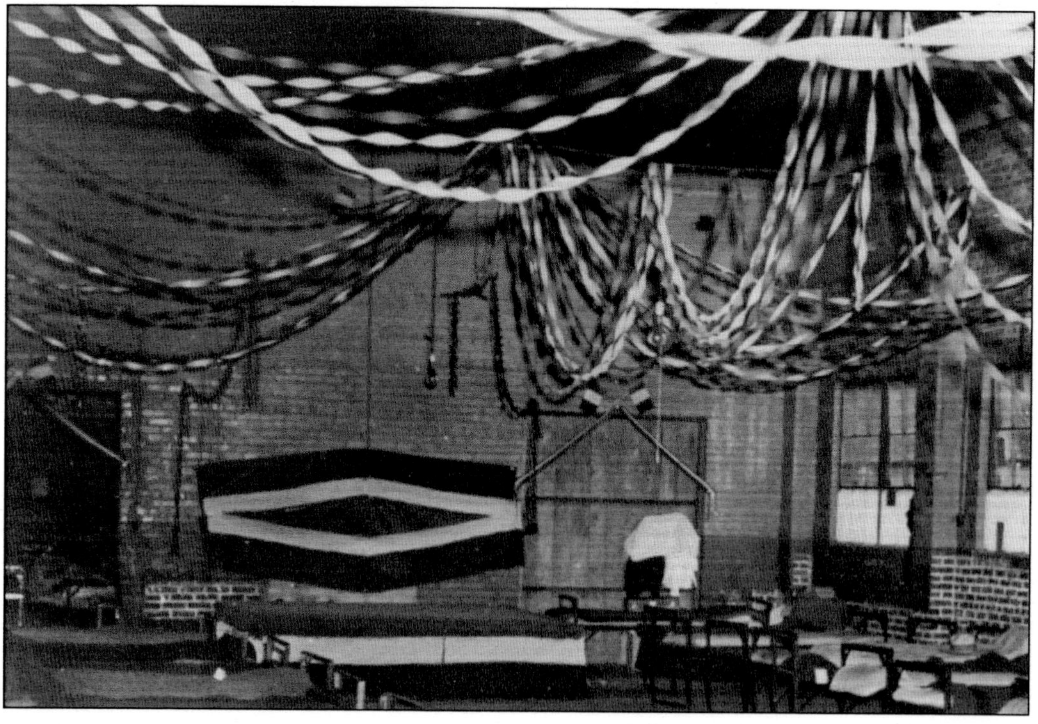

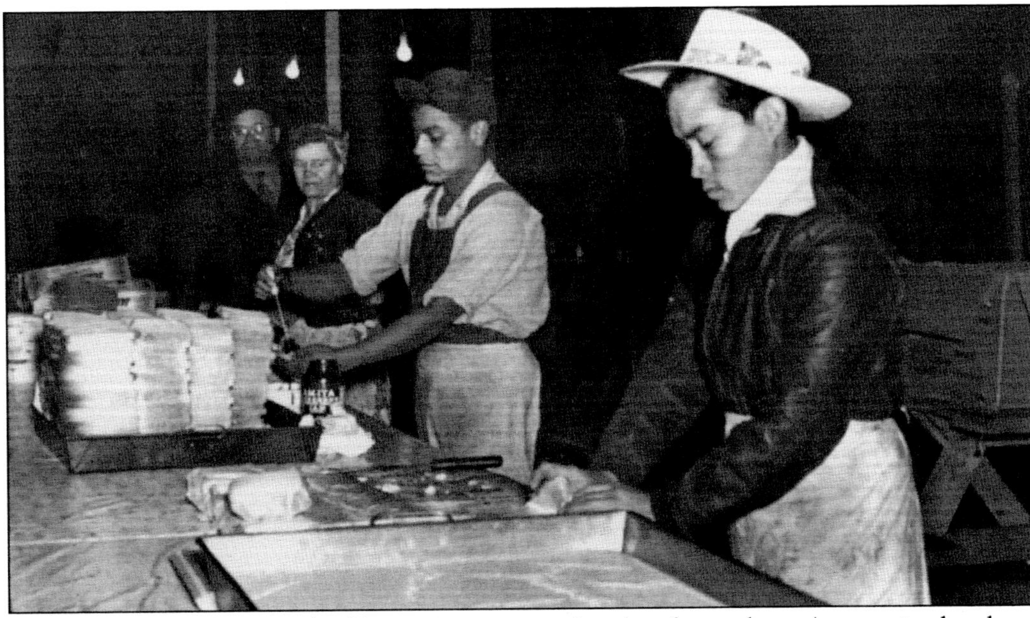

This is a typical photograph of braceros preparing lunches for workers. As seen in the above photograph, peanut butter and jelly sandwiches were not the cuisine the average Mexican national was accustomed to. In fact, so many complaints by the braceros were received that the War Manpower Commission directed all of the labor camps to make efforts to hire Mexican cooks to prepare Mexican food. Another shock encountered by braceros was the change in climate. Many braceros came from temperate zones in Mexico and had difficulty acclimating to weather. In the bottom photograph are five braceros camped at the depot in Wenatchee. Jesus Miranda, in the upper left, of Juarez, Mexico, stated, "Now they want us to go to Montana and Idaho to harvest sugar beets. This is against our will." (Above, courtesy Washington State University; below, courtesy *Wenatchee World*.)

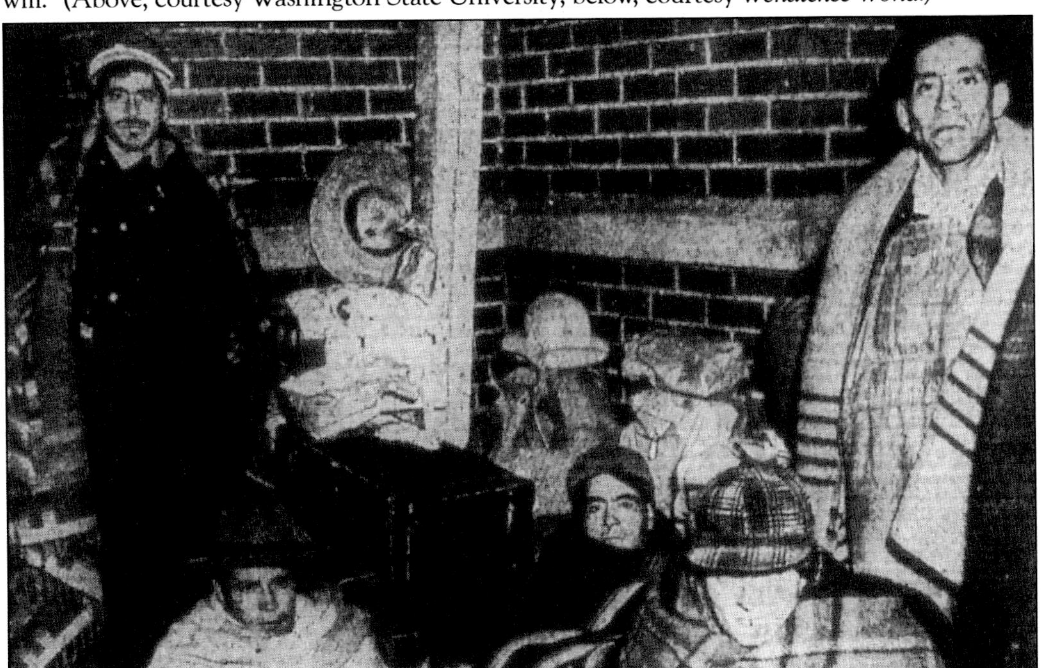

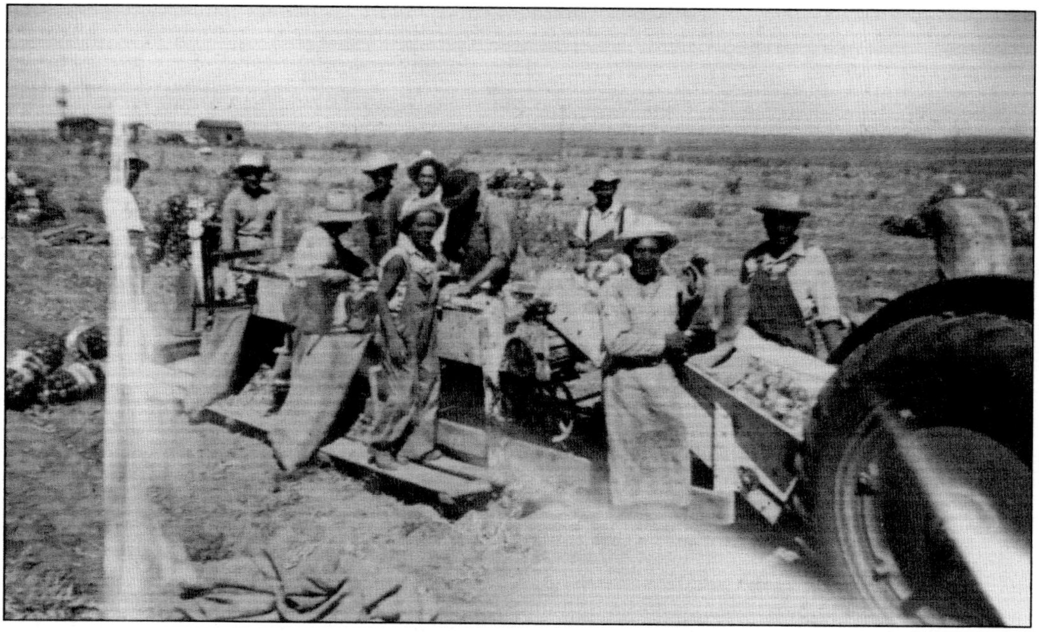

After the war period, the cost of transporting braceros from the border became prohibitive, and the program ended in the Northwest. However, there was one exception during the 1950s when grower associations of the Columbia Basin formed a fund to bring braceros during a shortage of labor. Above, this rare photograph depicts braceros working outside of Quincy. The bottom photograph depicts how Mexican Americans traveled as migrant workers from the Yakima to regions throughout NCW or used similar vehicles to carry crops to their final destination. (Above, courtesy Washington State University; below, courtesy Jerry Garcia.)

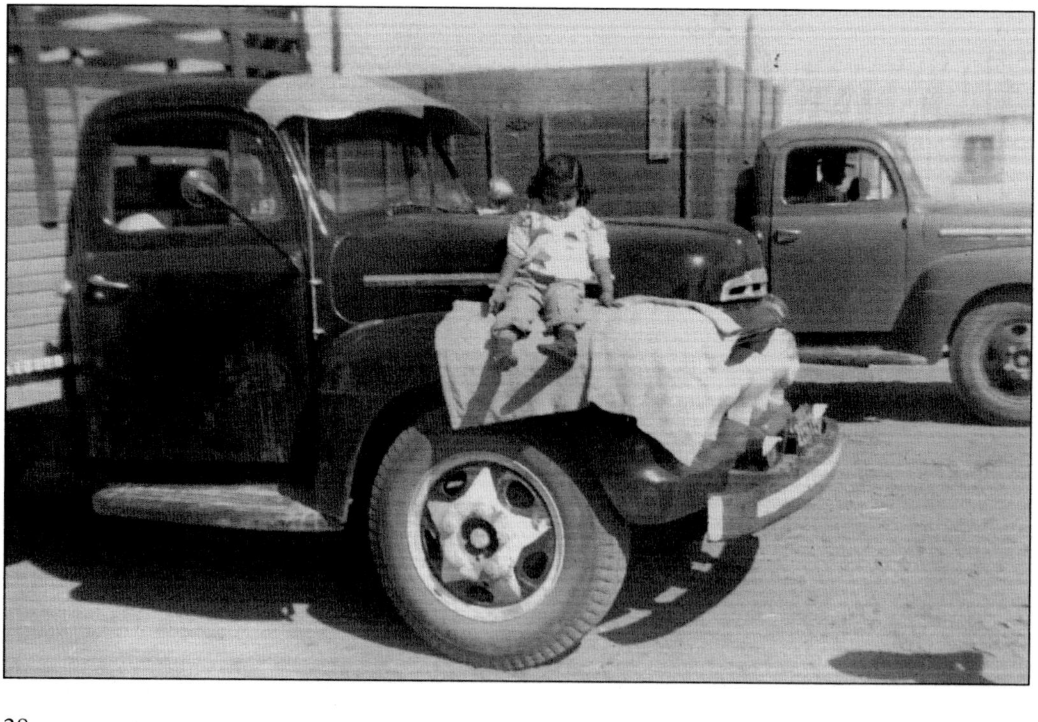

These two photographs depict Jesse Gonzales at different stages of his life. Jesse was born in 1929 in Lubbock, Texas. He first came to the Northwest in 1935 with his father, Pete, when they traveled to Montana to "bloc" beets. The Gonzaleses are considered the first Mexican American family to settle permanently in Quincy. As a young man, Jesse entered the Columbia Basin in 1948, arriving from the Yakima Valley. The photograph below shows the Gonzales family celebrating Christmas in the 1960s; from left to right are son Bill; Alvina, Jesse's wife; Jesse; and sons Frank and Tony. Jesse indicates that in the late 1940s and early 1950s, there were only about five Mexican families in the community. (Courtesy Jerry Garcia.)

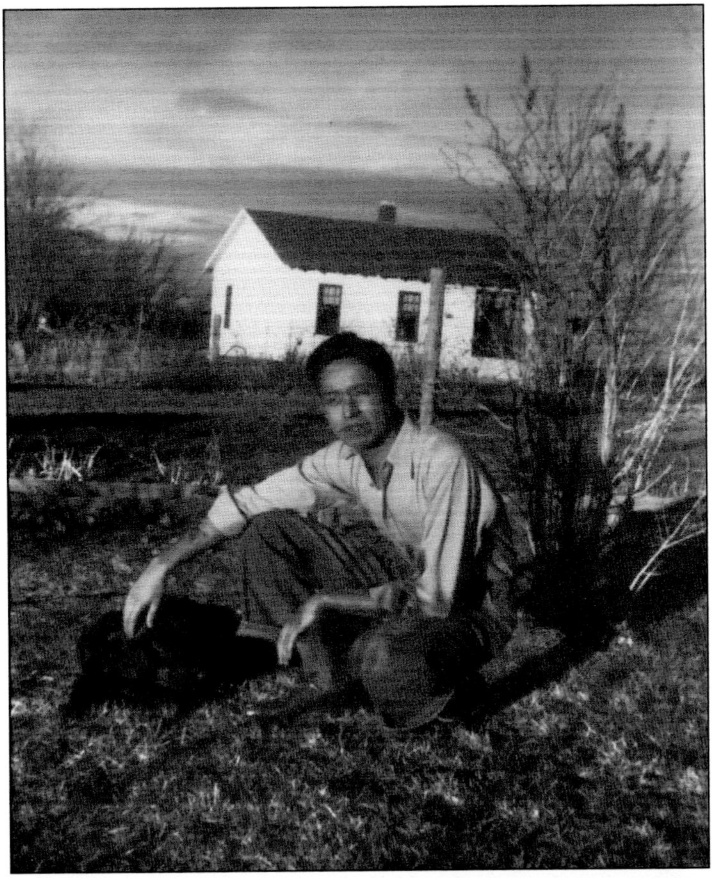

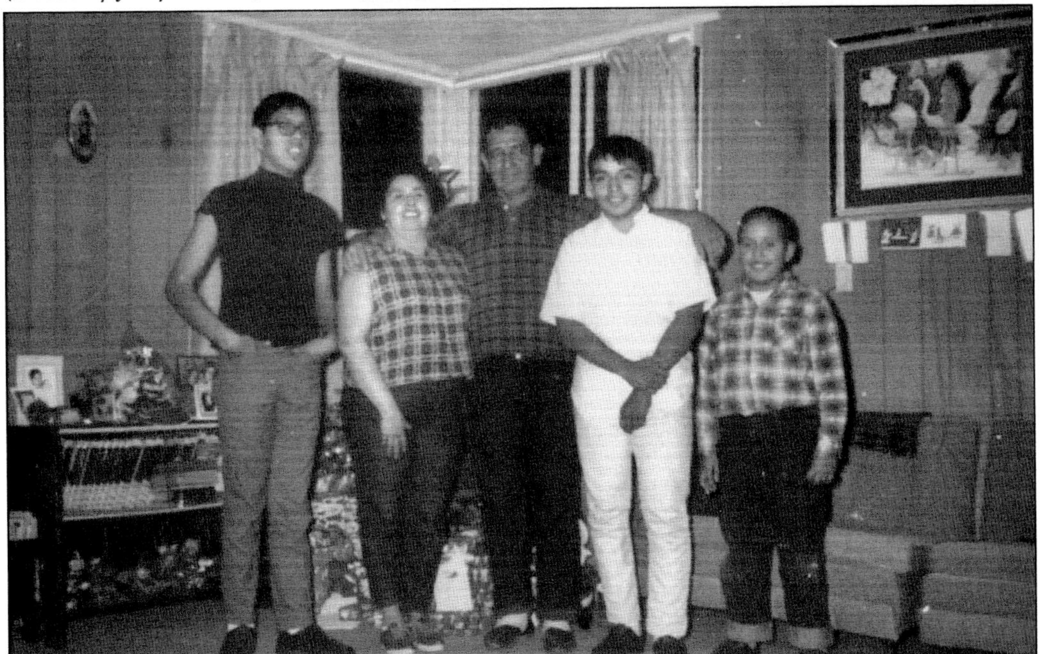

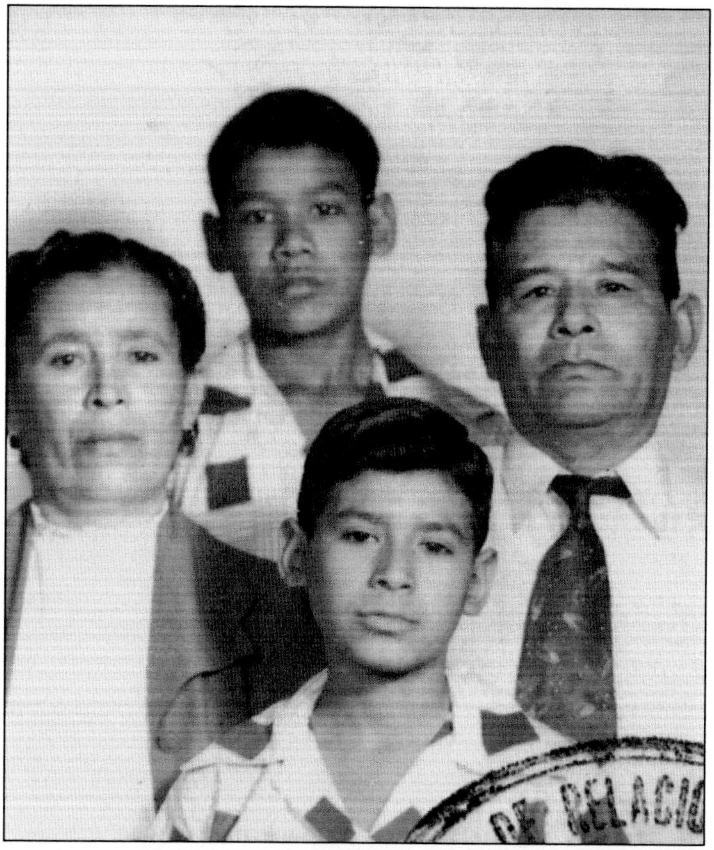

This immigration photograph is of Juan and Natalia Garcia with their two youngest children Roberto (behind) and Ruben as they entered the United States in the late 1940s. This family illustrates the movement from the Rio Grande Valley in Texas to Washington. When the family arrived in Washington in the early 1950s, their first stop was Granger in the Yakima Valley. The bottom image is of the fifth-grade class of Roosevelt School in Granger and depicts Juan and Natalia's youngest child, Ruben (third row, seventh from the left). By 1956, when year-round labor became available, the Garcia family made the Quincy Valley their permanent home. (Courtesy Jerry Garcia.)

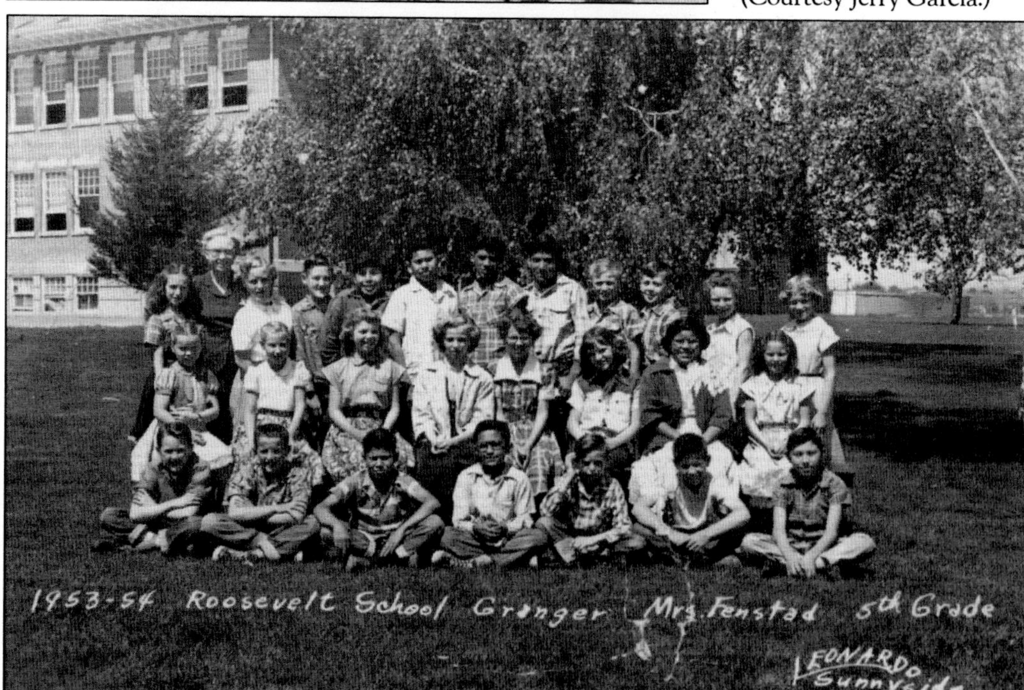

The photograph at right depicts the children of Refugio and Alicia Garces. The Garces family traveled throughout the Northwest before settling in the Columbia Basin. Many of the children of the Mexican pioneers cycled out of the fields. For the males, many followed a Garces family tradition of military service. Ricardo Garces (far left) served 20 years in the U.S. Army. Like their bracero predecessors, many Mexican Americans experienced snow for the very first time when they traveled to the Northwest. The harsh winters of the Northwest were little deterrence to the movement of Mexican Americans to the region. The bottom photograph depicts one of the early pioneers of the Columbia Basin experiencing a NCW winter for the first time. (Courtesy Garces family.)

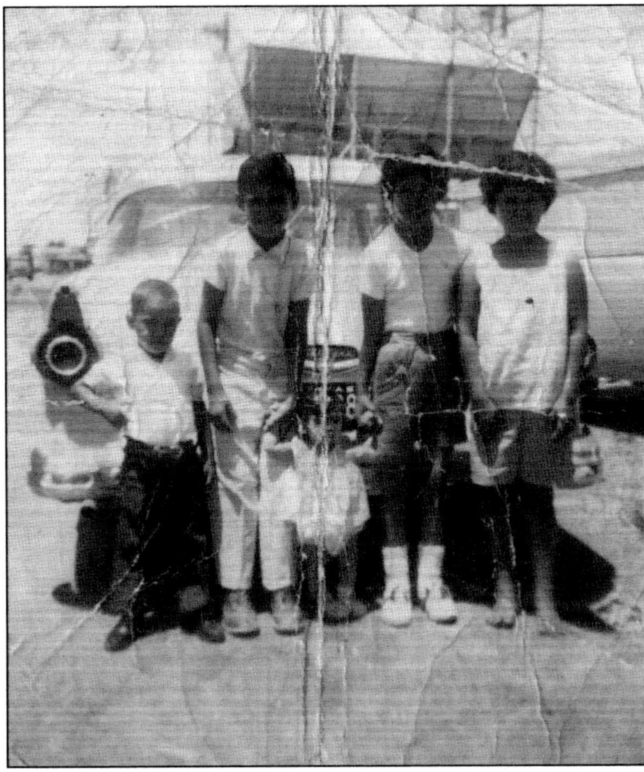

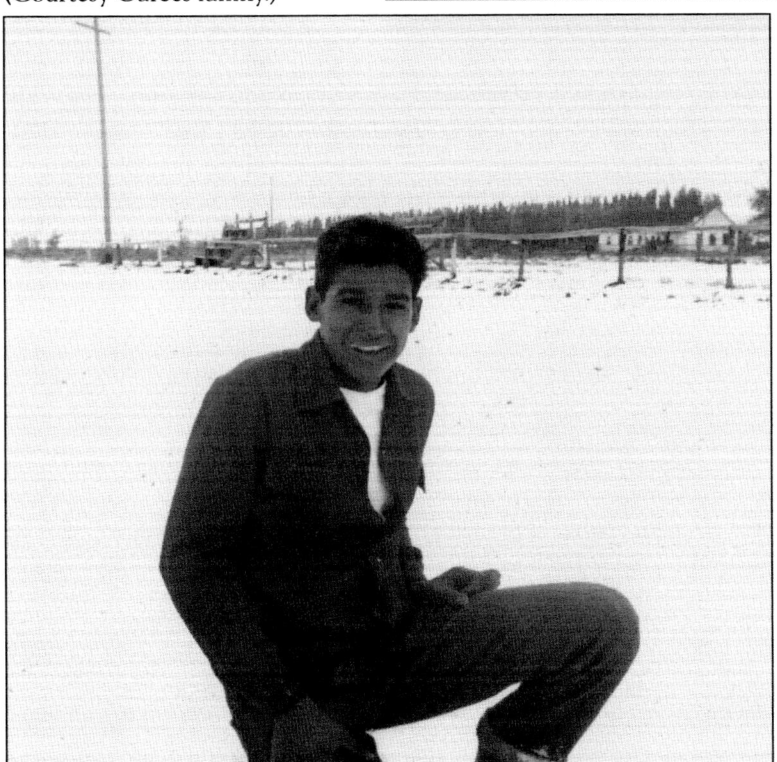

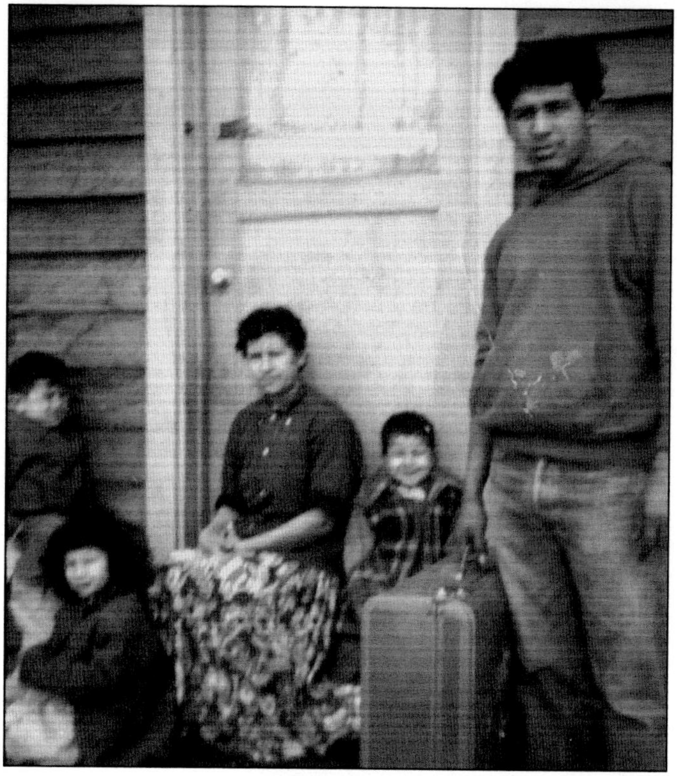

In this photograph are Rebecca Reyes and three of her children, (from left to right) Antonio Jr., Dora, and Gonzalo. At the right is her younger brother Ruben. Mexican American families traveling to the Northwest and NCW often traveled as extended families. Rebecca and her sister Dolores each married Reyes brothers, Antonio and Carlos, respectively. Together along with the Garcias, they traveled to the Northwest. Success for any ethnic group is being able to show that their labor is bearing fruit. Purchasing luxury items such as vehicles is a symbol of that success and, with it, status. In the bottom photograph, 16-year-old Ruben D. Garcia is pictured next to his new Crown Victoria on a road in NCW. (Courtesy Jerry Garcia.)

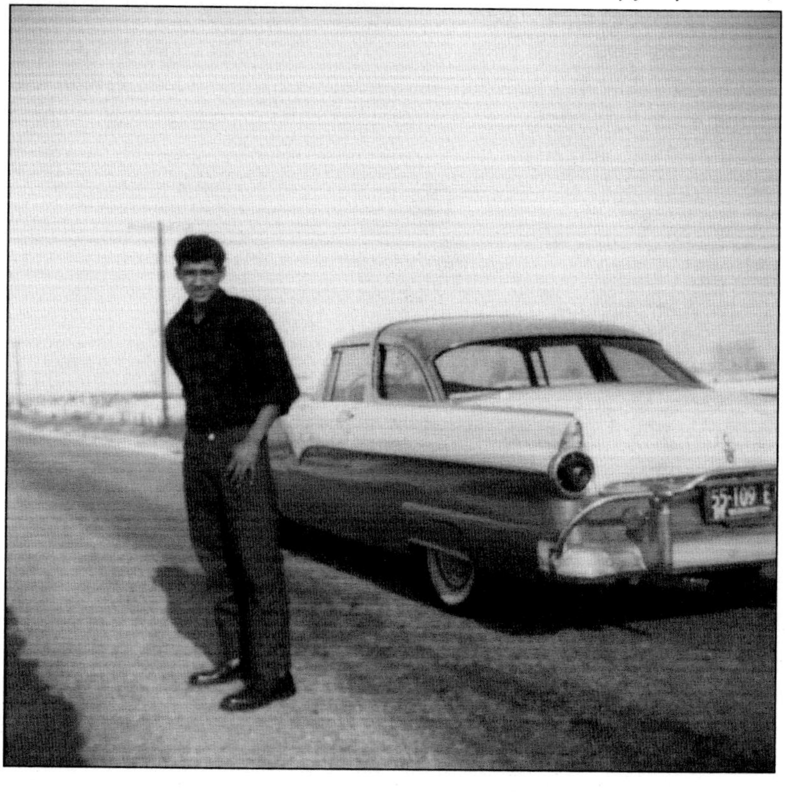

Three

WATER, MIGRATION, AND WORK

World events, changing immigration policies, and economic opportunities brought ethnic Mexicans in significant numbers by the 1940s. It should be clear that NCW started out as a rural agricultural zone, and although it has diversified some in the contemporary period, the Mexican population remains heavily employed in unskilled or semi-skilled sectors of the economy. By and large, the majority of the work performed by Mexican pioneers was directly related to agriculture or labor supporting agriculture industries such as the fruit packing plants and vegetable facilities. The Tejanos (Mexican Texans) who came to the Northwest left their homes because wages in Washington were generally much better than those paid in Texas, but they also came to escape the intense racism in certain regions of Texas.

Between the late 1940s and 1970s, as Mexicans became permanent residents of NCW, a cycle of migration also emerged. In many cases, the early pioneers and the subsequent generation cycled out of the field work and into semi-skilled positions within the agriculture industry. As one group moved out of unskilled agriculture labor, another arrived to replace it. This cycle continues in the contemporary period, but instead of a strong Mexican American migration from other regions of the United States, it has been replaced by the international movement of Mexicans. It should also be noted that some of the early pioneers had a strong entrepreneurial spirit. Many opened their own Mexican restaurants or bakeries. Others bought franchise gasoline stations, opened stores catering to the tastes of the Mexican population, or became involved with government agencies and school institutions. One savvy group attempted to establish a furniture-making industry in the early 1970s by raising capital through the selling of stocks. In the early 21st century, the Mexican community is now represented in almost every occupation. These photographs show the early spirit of the community.

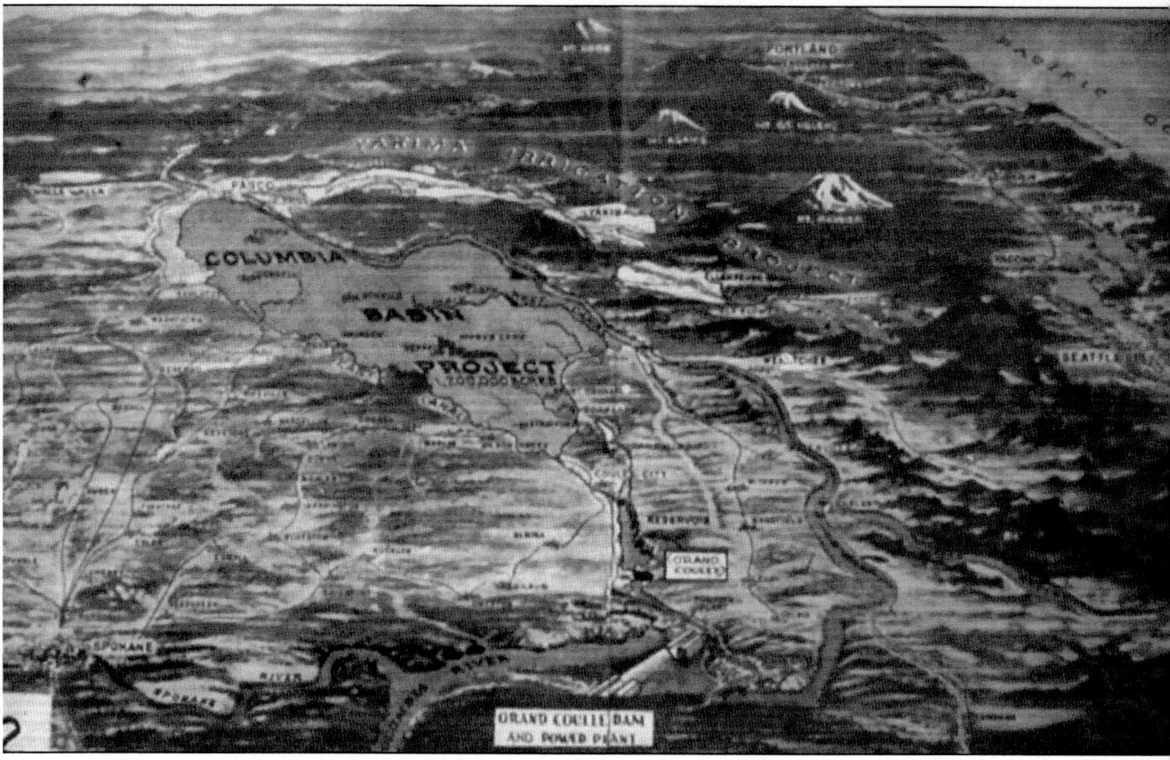

From the early days of settlement, individuals dreamed of bringing water to NCW from a variety of sources. Two simultaneous schemes emerged in the early 20th century. One scheme was the Pend Oreille "gravity" plan that proposed to bring water down from northern lakes in Idaho. The other vision was of creating a dam on the Columbia River near Grand Coulee. After investigations and a survey done in the early 1920s, on July 16, 1933, ground was broken for the construction of Grand Coulee Dam. Water first reached the Columbia Basin in 1951, and the history and demographics of the region changed forever. This map depicts the Columbia Basin Irrigation Project. (Courtesy *Wenatchee World*.)

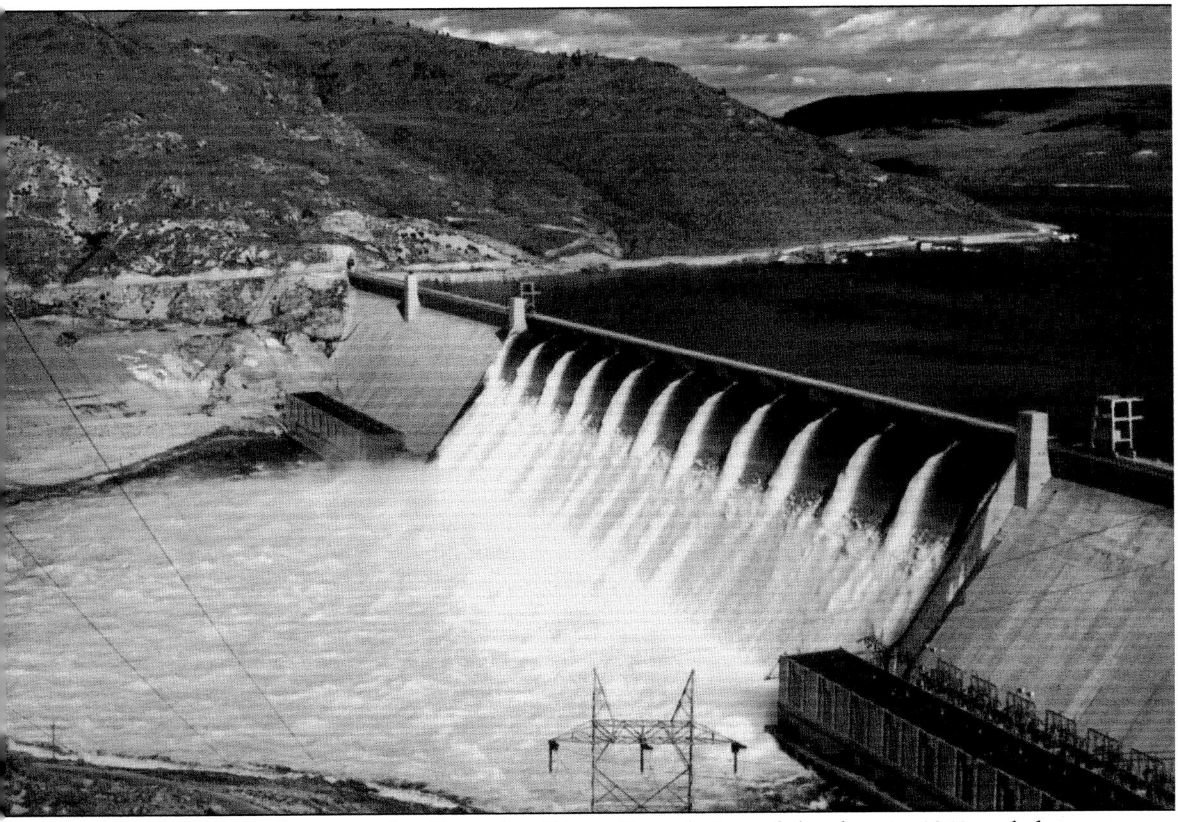

This is Grand Coulee Dam on the Columbia River. Completion of the dam in 1941 and the Columbia Basin Irrigation Project in 1952 brought water from Grand Coulee and opened up almost 500,000 acres of land for development. The public lands within the project were first offered to returning World War II veterans on a lottery basis. The conditions to qualify for the first lottery in 1948, besides veteran status, included filing a five-page application, farm experience, good character references, and a net worth of at least $3,700. (Courtesy Wenatchee Valley Museum.)

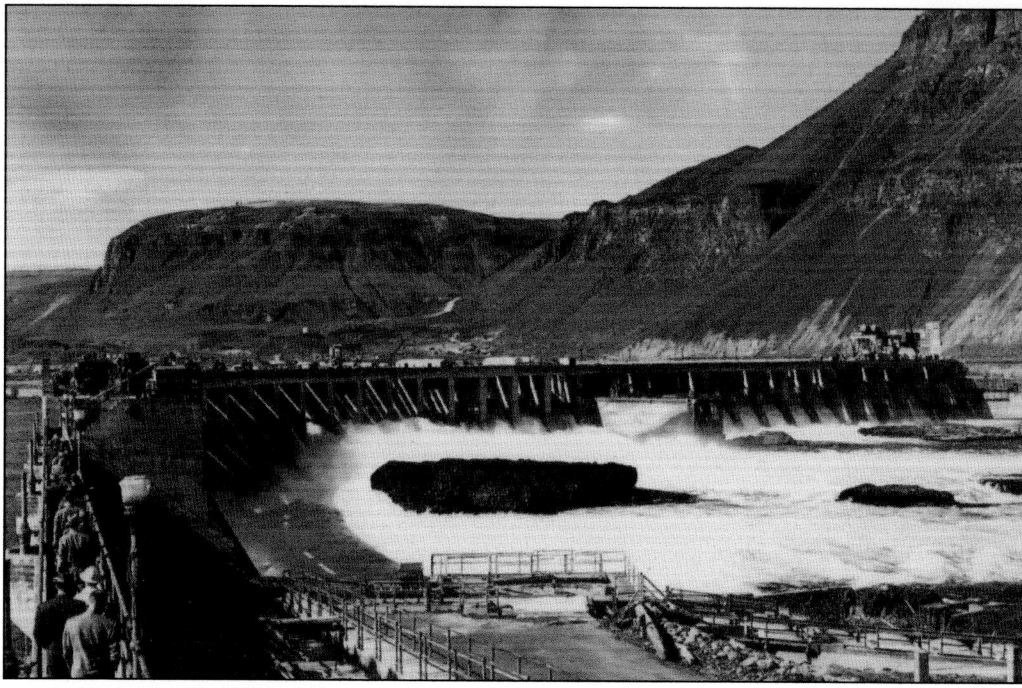

Construction of Rock Island Dam began in 1930, and its first powerhouse was completed in 1933, becoming the first dam to span the Columbia. This dam is located near Wenatchee. Construction of Grand Coulee Dam, below, began in the 1930s. The extensive network of canals, tunnels, reservoirs, and pumping plants that make up the Columbia Basin Irrigation project currently provide water to over half a million acres. This photograph depicts the construction of one of the main canals. (Courtesy Wenatchee Valley Museum.)

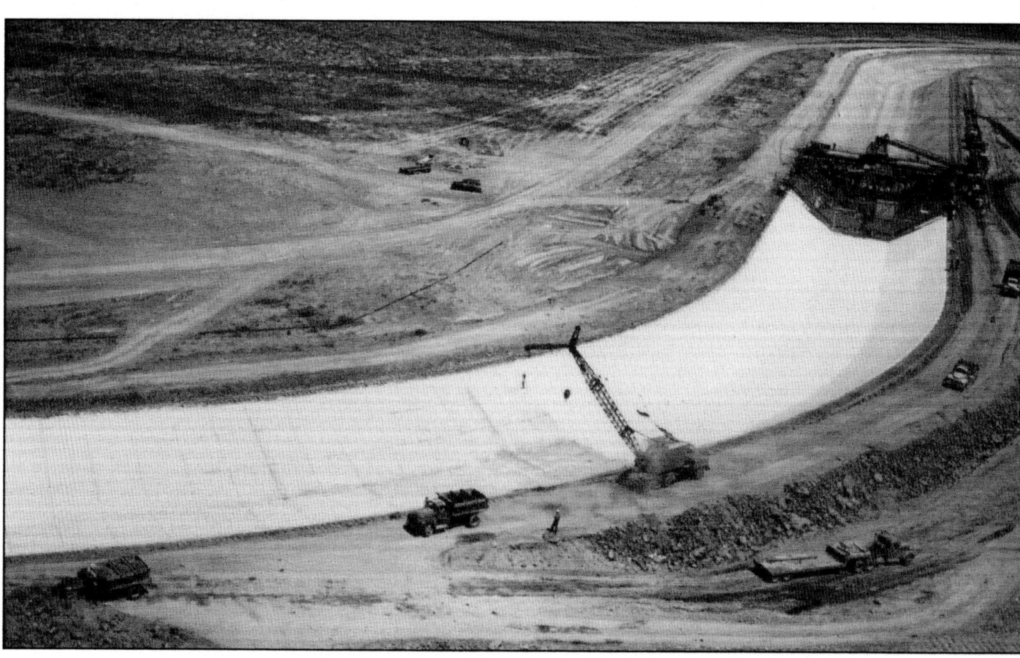

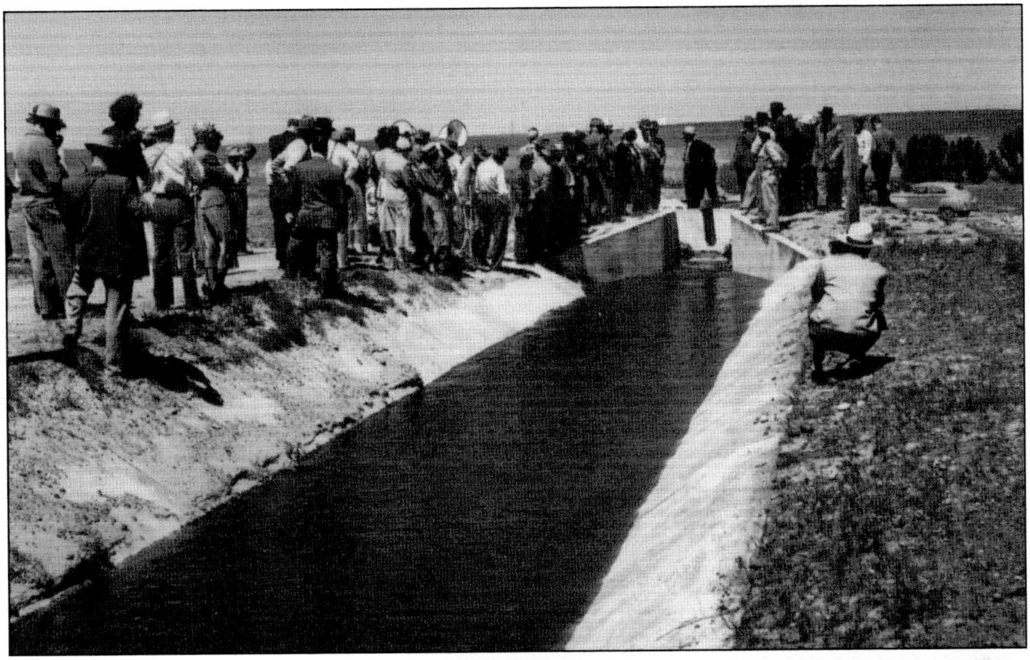

Columbia Basin farmers, media, and government officials celebrate the arrival of the first water from the Columbia Basin Project in 1951. The arrival of this water meant the survival of many communities in the region, including such places as Quincy, Moses Lake, and Othello. The impact is easily seen as before and after photographs are spliced together, showing sagebrush before the water and fertile lands and crops after. A decade after the arrival of water, over half a million acres were in production. (Courtesy Wenatchee Valley Museum.)

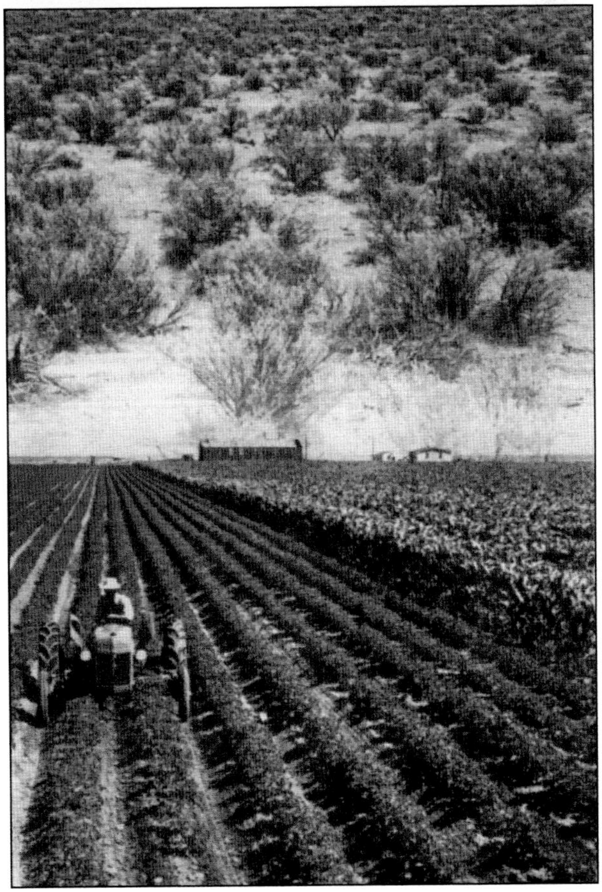

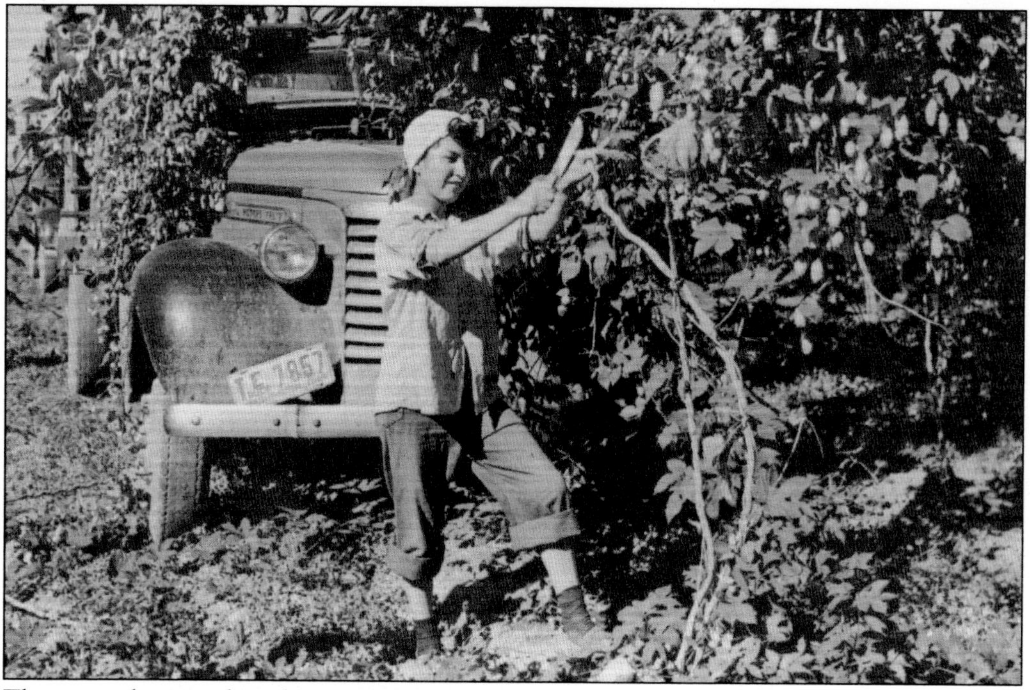

These two photographs, taken in 1945, depict two of the thousands of Mexican American women who helped the war effort in Washington. The crop that these two workers are harvesting and cleaning are hops from the Golding Hop Farms of John I. Haas, Inc., one of the major agriculture commodities of Washington and, among other things, used to make beer. Many of the Mexican pioneers of the Columbia Basin came directly from the Yakima Valley. (Courtesy Washington State University.)

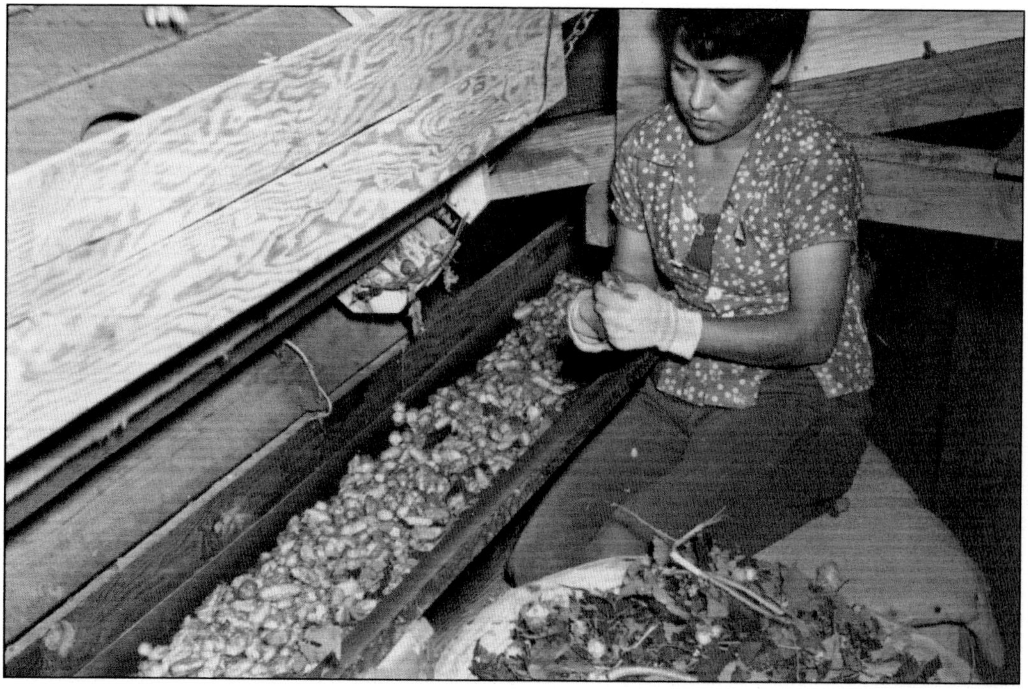

The photograph at right is of Alicia Garces and three of her children. From left to right are Ludivina, Nora, Alicia, and Elvia taking a break from work and having a cool drink. The crop in the background is very recognizable as hops because of the poles and wired configuration, which hops need to grow. The Garces family eventually made Quincy their permanent home. According to Mexican pioneer Jesse Gonzales, one of the few crops that grew consistently in the Columbia Basin in dry conditions was peas. The below image is of Mexican Americans and Anglos "vining" peas in Quincy during the late 1940s. (Above, courtesy Garces family; below, courtesy Jerry Garcia.)

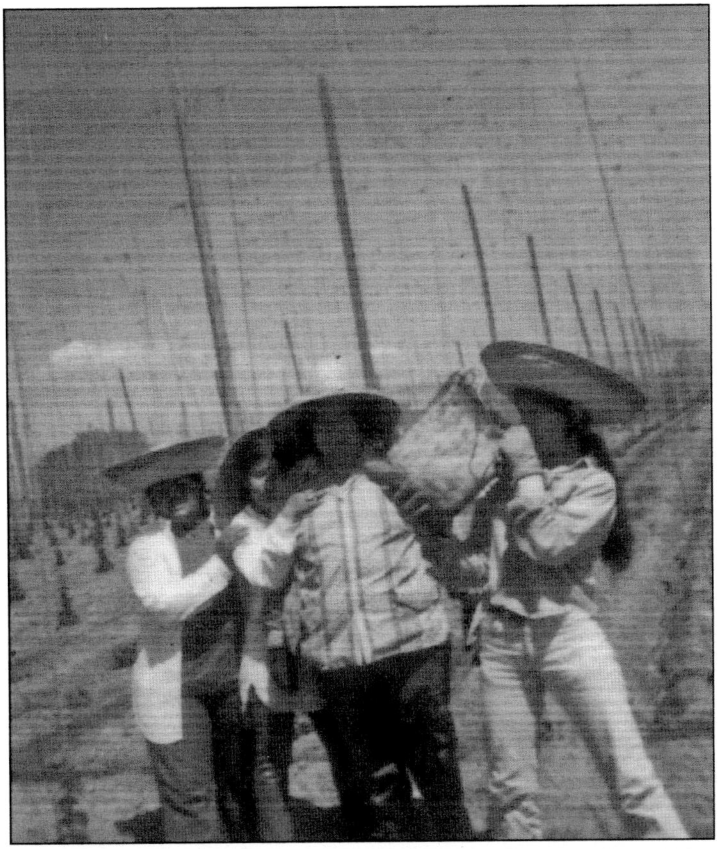

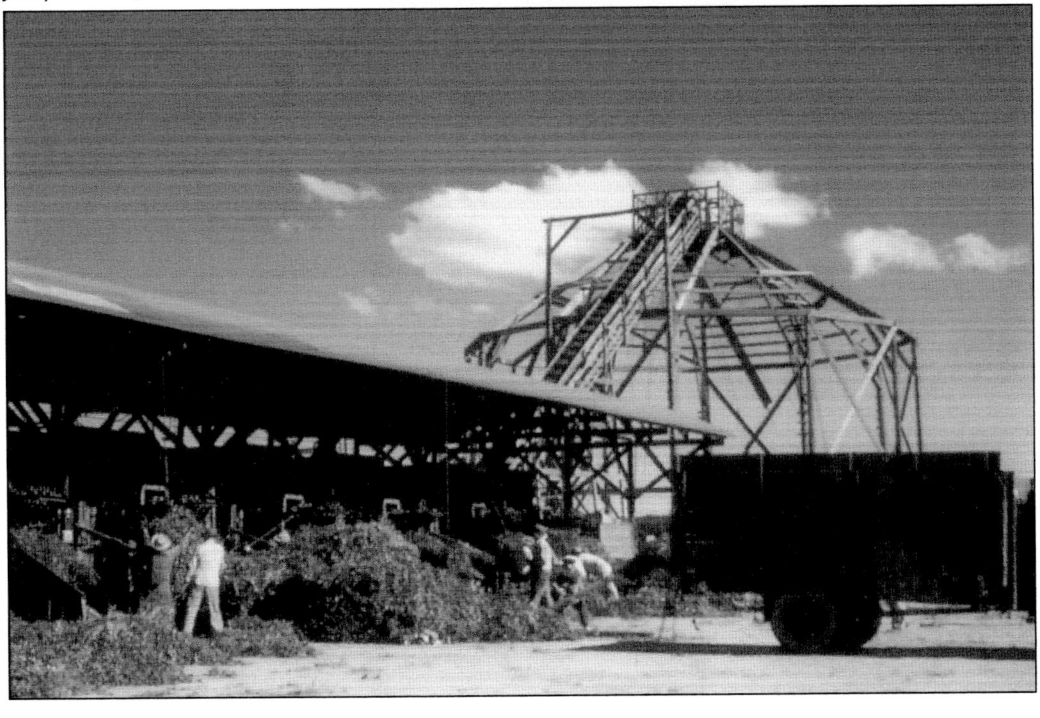

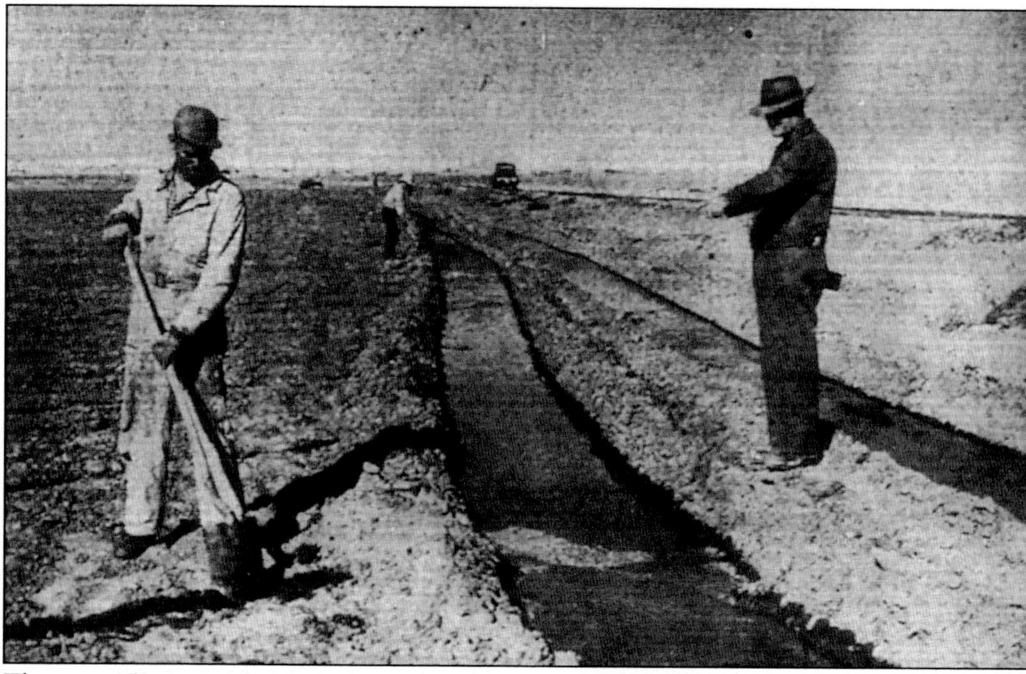

This is a 1952 image of water arriving regularly into the Columbia Basin. This farm near Moses Lake was owned by Arlene Harwood Wadkins. Her brother Everett Harwood is at the left with the shovel. Lester Harwood, at the right and directing operations, is the father of both Arlene and Everett. (Courtesy *Wenatchee World*.)

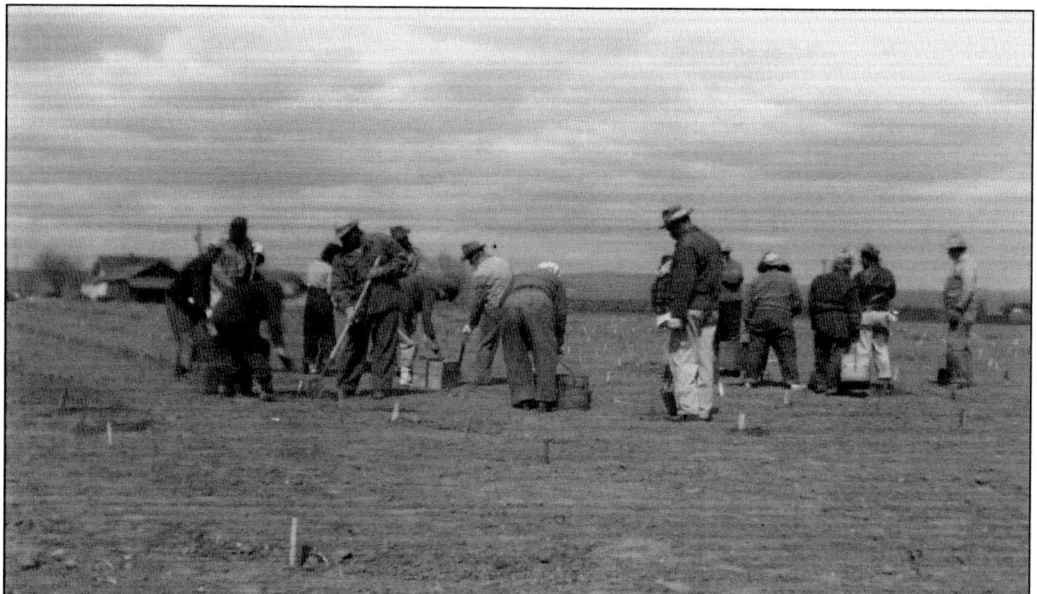

This 1952 photograph is a rare image of a Mexican American crew working in Quincy in 1952, shortly after the arrival of water. The workers include both men and women, but it is unknown what crop they are working. This photograph provides clear evidence of the emerging Mexican American community in the region and the impact water had in pulling in these early settlers. (Courtesy Jerry Garcia.)

Some Mexican Americans went into private business and attempted to carve out a living by catering to the larger community. In the photograph at right, taken in 1968, are the owners of a Mexican drive-in located in Winchester, just outside of Quincy. The owners, Narciso and Amada Medrano with Mrs. John Martinez (left), are shown in the kitchen preparing tacos, tostadas, enchiladas, refritos, and menudo. The bottom image was taken in 1971. On the left is Armando Castro working on a seed-cutting operation in one of Quincy's potato processing plants. Mexican Americans in the early 1970s were almost entirely employed in agriculture and its related industries. (Courtesy *Wenatchee World*.)

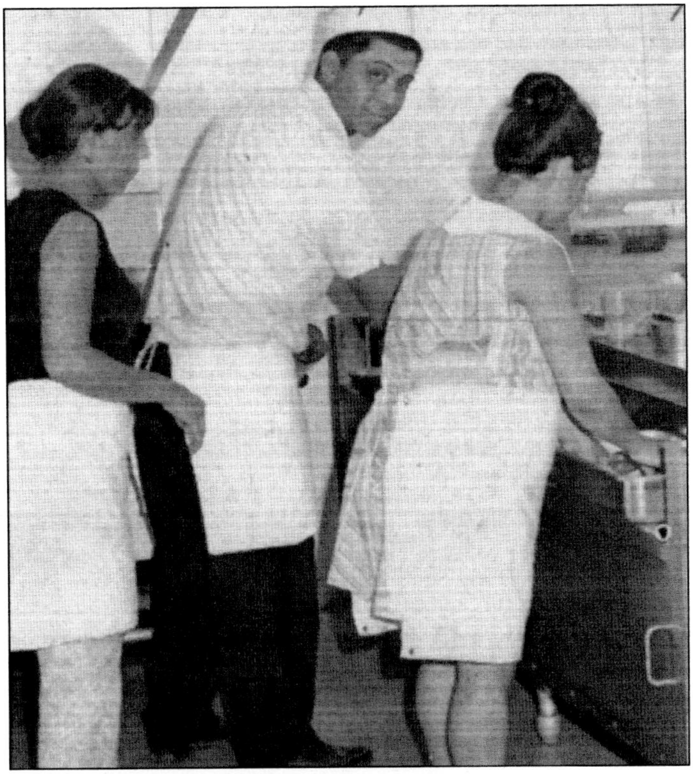

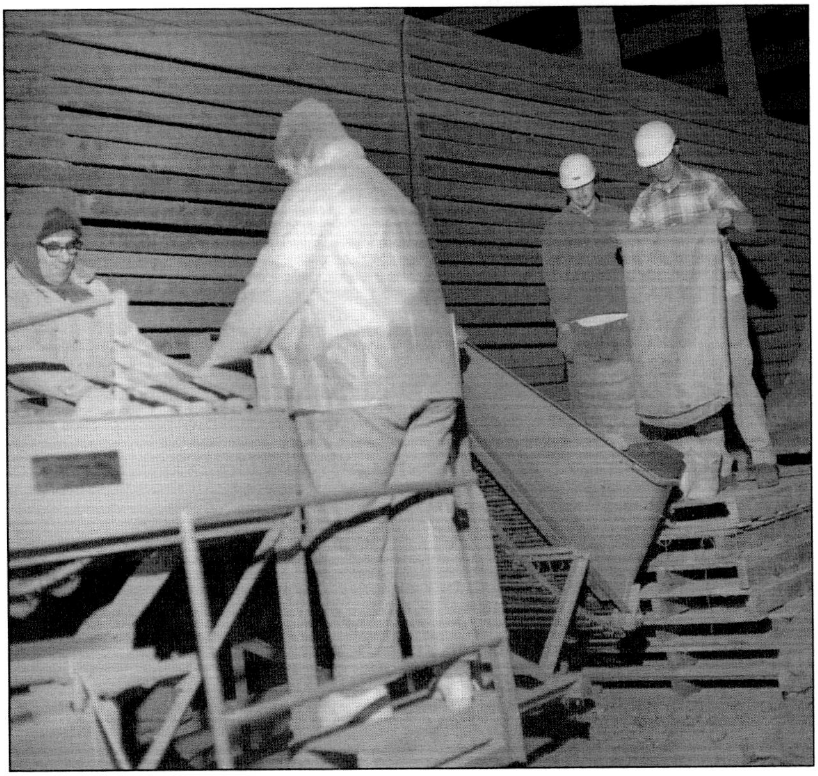

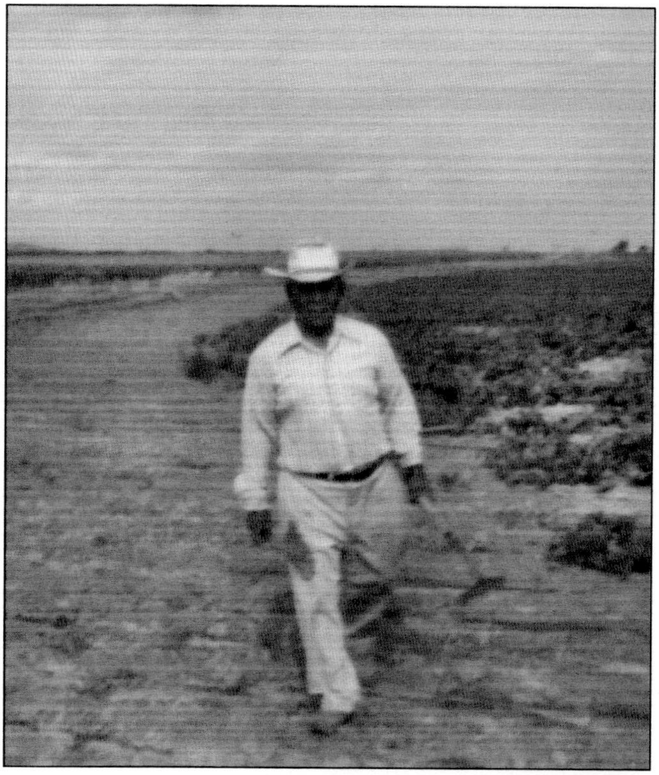

Don Juan H. Garcia brought his family to Washington in 1953. The photograph at left was taken c. 1978 and shows Don Juan in his 70s with a hoe in his hand ready to attack the beet fields. Don Juan, as an elder, instilled a strong work ethic in his children and extended family, which numbered over 200 in Quincy at the time of his death in 1989. In the second photograph are three generations of Mexican Americans in the Columbia Basin. The image was taken in the late 1970s; from left to right are Santos Villegas, Rene Villegas, Felicitas Garcia, Rosalinda Garcia (standing), Isabel Muñoz, Roberto Garcia Jr. (in front), Gloria Garcia, and Ruben Garcia Jr. Note the Chicano power sign exhibited by Rosalinda Garcia. (Courtesy Jerry Garcia.)

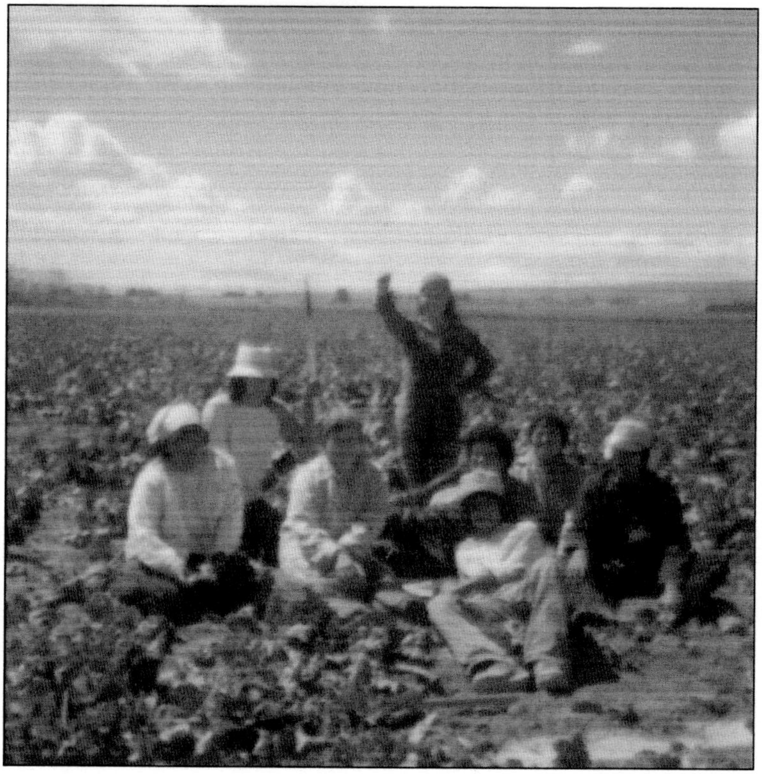

This photograph taken in the late 1970s depicts Gloria Garcia (left) and Rebecca Reyes trying to look their best while taking a break from thinning apples. When this photograph was taken, Rebecca and Gloria were sisters-in-law and often worked together as a form of solidarity and companionship. The bottom image is of Emma Hinojosa picking apples. When this picture was taken in the late 1970s, the majority of the apple picking crews were of Mexican ancestry. By this period, the region had become dependent on the permanent and transient Mexican migrant labor that came to the area. (Courtesy Jerry Garcia.)

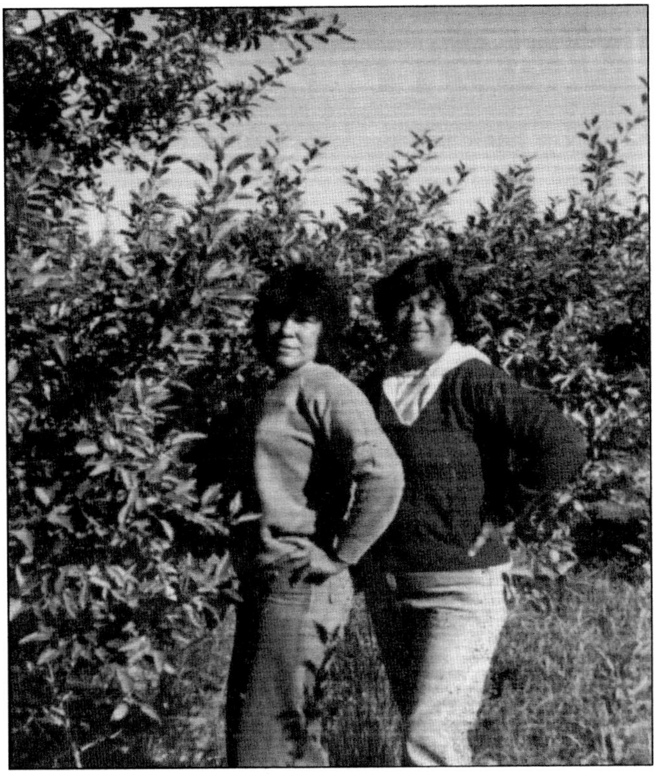

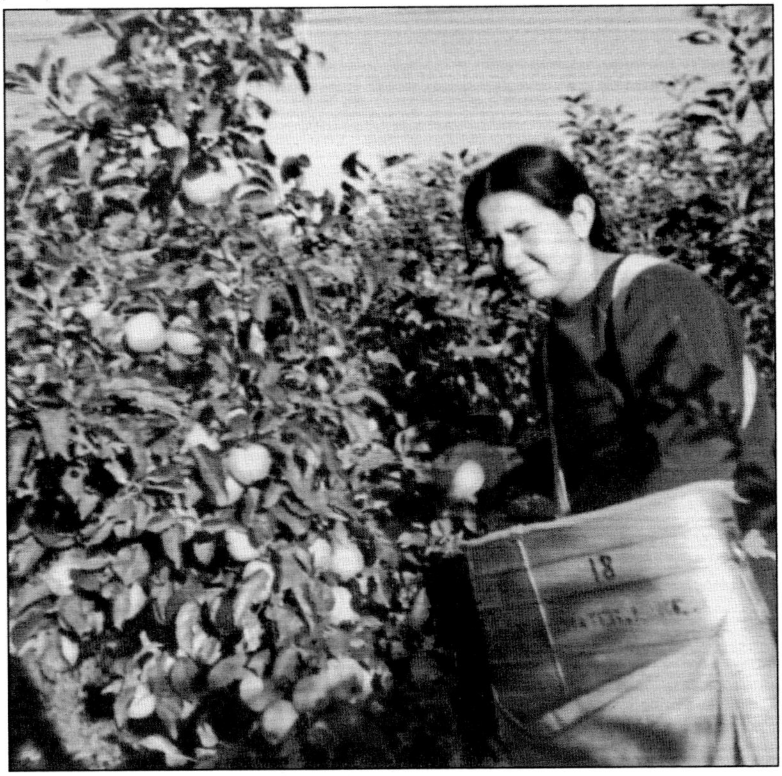

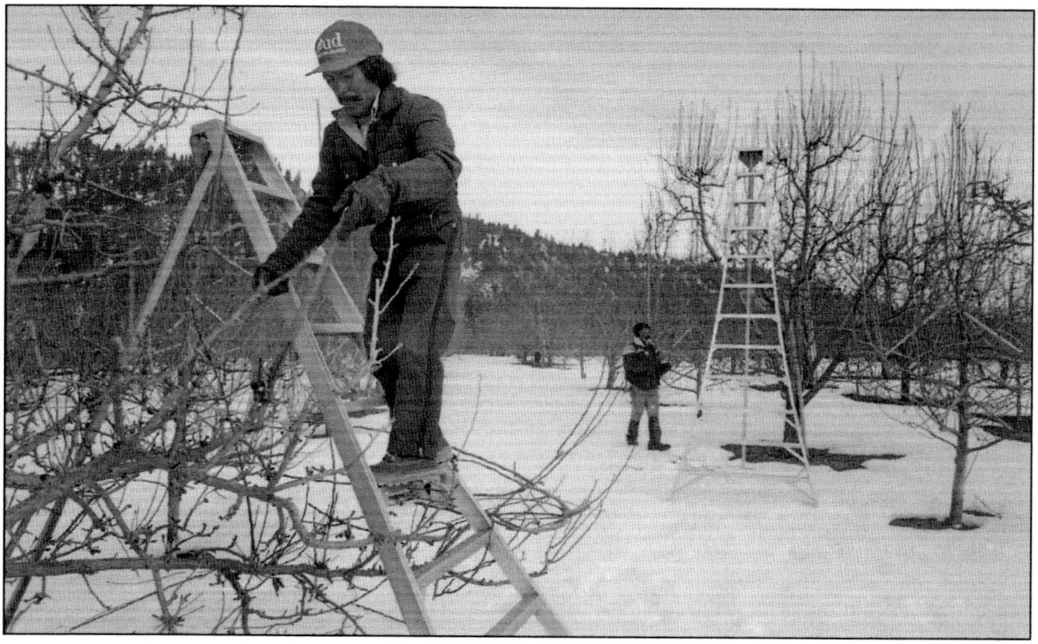

Over the last 50 years of the 20th century, the racial and ethnic makeup of the labor force in agriculture became the domain of ethnic Mexicans. Pictured above in 1987 is Efren Rosario pruning trees. Efren, who first came to Washington in 1974, supervised a crew of workers year-round in Peshastin. When this photograph was taken, his wife, Tarcila, and two children, Nayley and Jair, were with him. Below is Juana Sarmiento picking cherries in the Wenatchee area. Mexican women make up a large portion of the agriculture labor in NCW. Mexican women dominate the packing sheds throughout the region. (Courtesy *Wenatchee World*.)

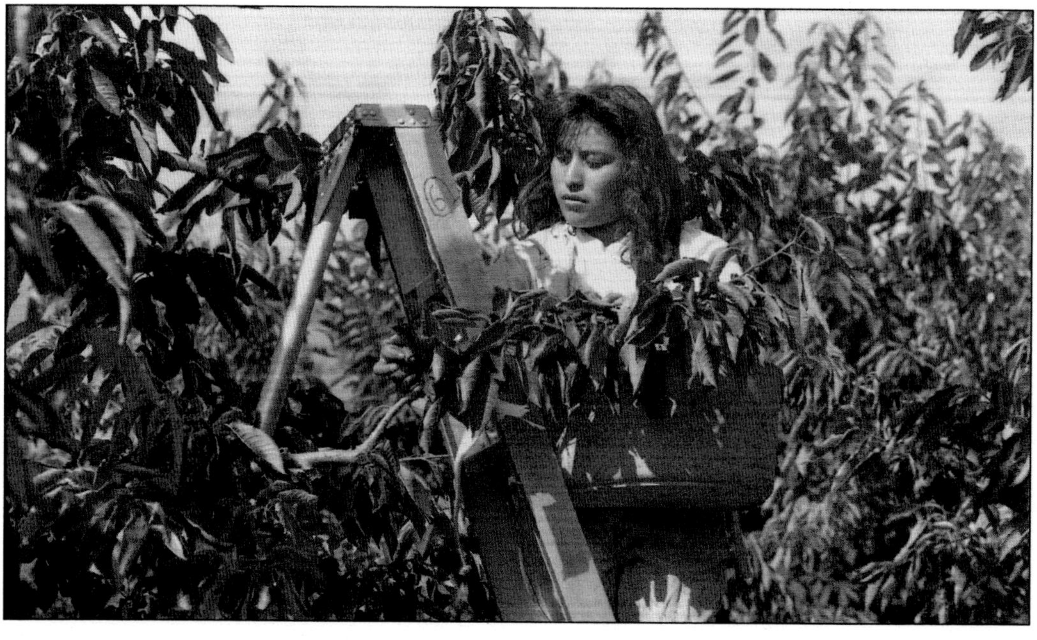

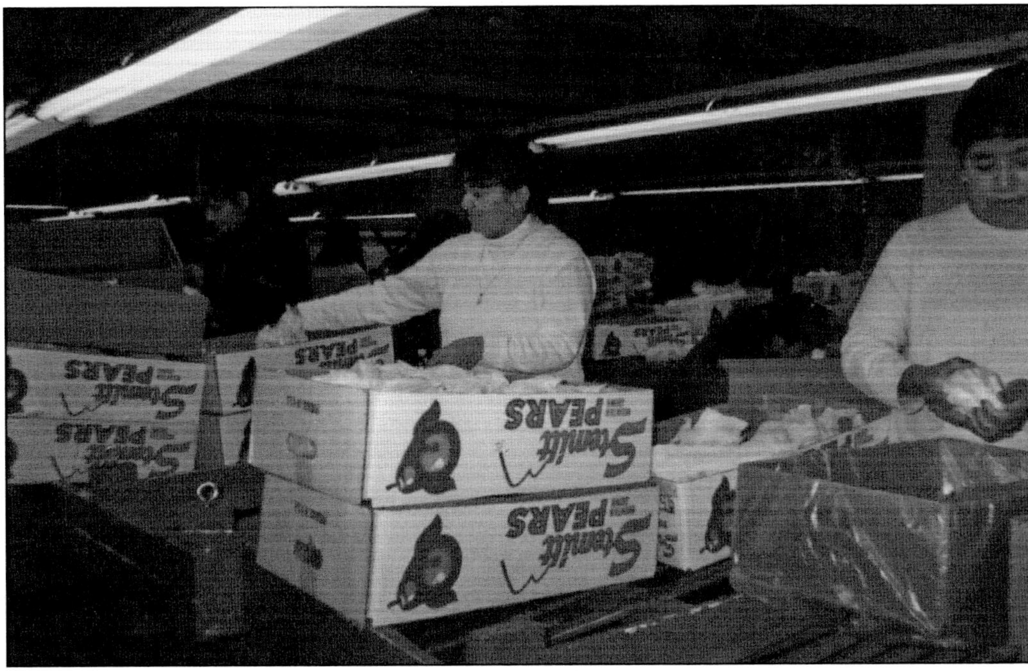

These two photographs taken in the early 21st century inside a Stemilt Growers facility in Wenatchee show the contemporary labor force within this industry. First, it is primarily Mexican women either sorting cherries or packing pears. Second, the political economy of NCW has forced many of the growers in the region not only to be reliant on a Mexican labor force, but many are advocates of liberal immigration policies due to the makeup of their labor force. (Courtesy Jerry Garcia.)

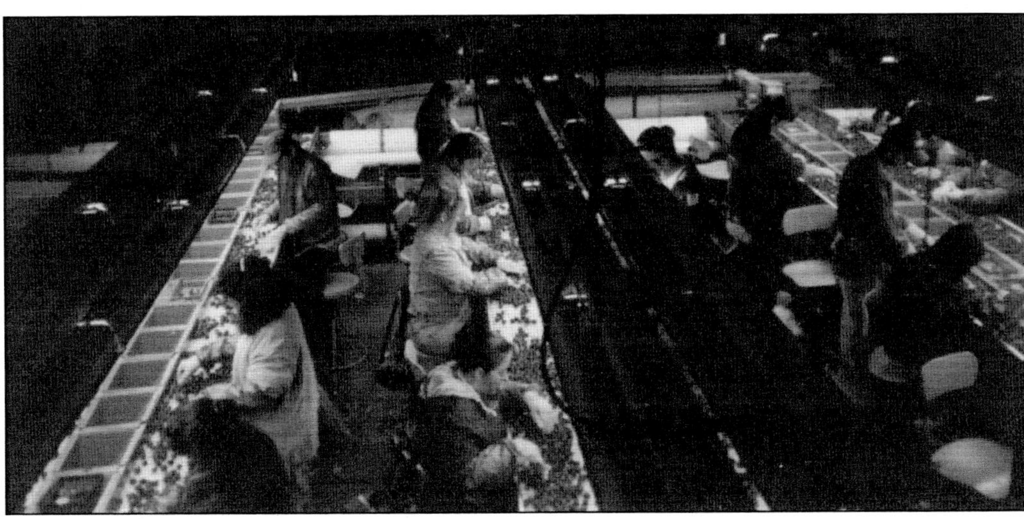

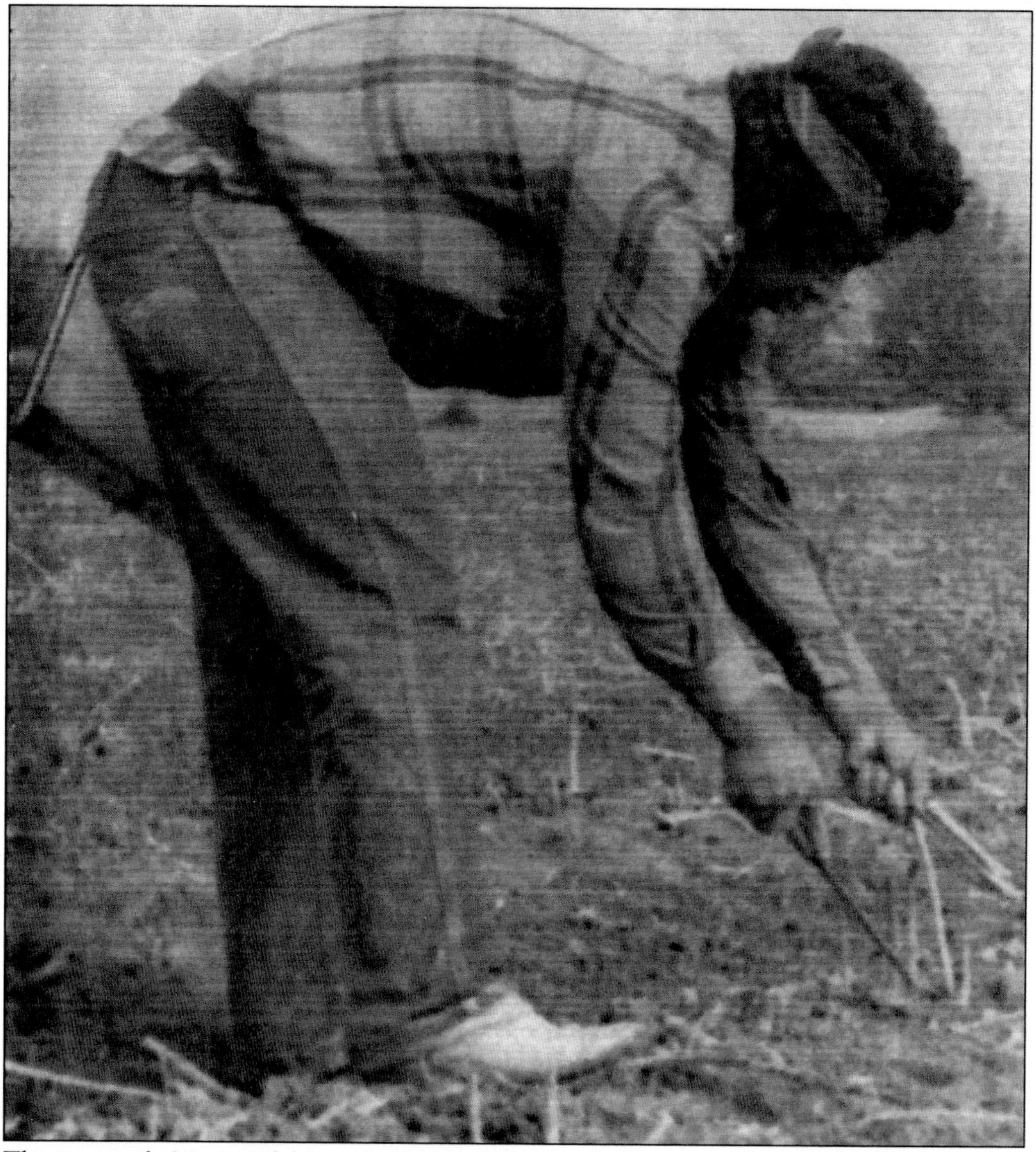

This image of a Mexican laborer cutting asparagus in the Columbia Basin, taken in 1992, shows that transient and stoop labor continues in the region. One of the unseen and seldom discussed effects of stoop labor is back injury and chronic pain from long periods of being bent over. Stoop labor was most common with the use of *el cortito*, the short-handle hoe utilized primarily in the thinning and "blocking" of beets. This hoe also symbolized the demeaning and feudal conditions of farm labor. It was not until the late 20th century that this dreaded symbol was outlawed. (Courtesy *Quincy Post-Register*.)

Four

FAMILY AND COMMUNITY LIFE

For most of its modern history, North Central Washington has been homogenous and primarily white. Its original inhabitants, the Native Americans, because of broken treaties and promises, have been reduced to small bands or scattered to other reservations. NCW simply has not been a place African Americans have gravitated to in large numbers during the 20th century, thus their presence in the region is small. The Asians, primarily of Japanese ancestry, arrived because of the impact of World War II, but their population has remained constant and small. The Mexican pioneers that arrived in NCW were the vanguard that eventually ethnically changed the region. The photographs depicted here show how the Mexican community not only worked together, but came together during times of celebration and need. A birthday becomes a community affair. A Mexican wedding or baptism not only reinforces and celebrates religion, but underlines the importance of Mexican culture with the practice of *compradazgo* (god-parenting) which creates deeper bonds between family and nonfamily members within the Mexican community.

The photographs in this section also depict resistance. A uniqueness regarding the Mexican communities in NCW is their ability to maintain Mexican traditions and customs far from their place of origin. Considering that these early pioneers trekked over 1,000 miles from either the Southwest or Mexico and somehow managed to maintain large elements of the Mexican culture speaks to the resiliency of the culture itself. Yet, as some pictures will attest, these Mexican pioneers also displayed deep patriotic furor towards the United States and upheld some of the strongest traditions of the American way of life. In the final analysis, most of the families depicted in these photographs remained in NCW, became pillars of the community, participated in all facets of community life, and instilled a sense of family and community when it was needed the most.

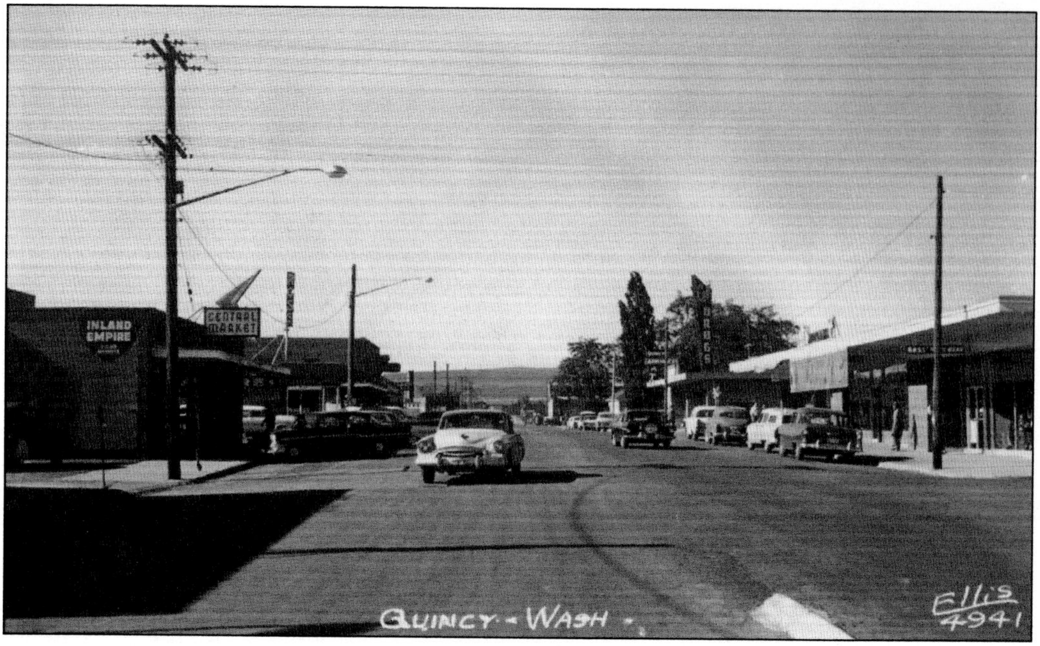

These two images of Quincy and Moses Lake during the 1950s depict the development and location of early Mexican communities. The two street scenes can still be seen today with many of the buildings remaining the same, except for the changing of the names on the front. In comparison to today, the population of Mexicans remained small, but their spirit and drive were strong. Generally communities in NCW were accepting of the movement of Mexicans into the region, but there was also a strong economic need for their presence. (Courtesy Washington State University.)

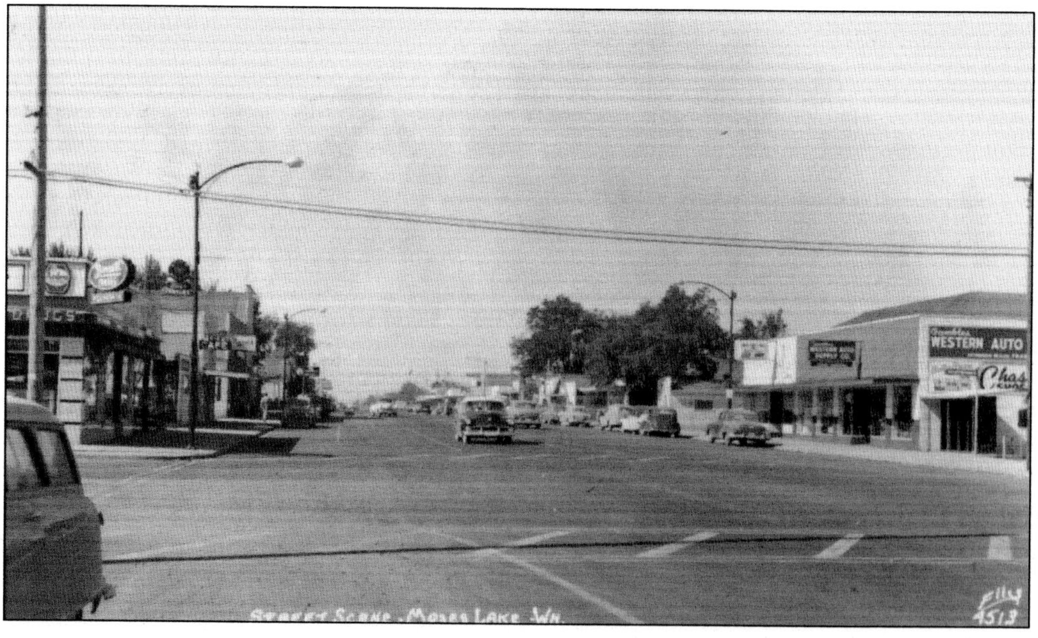

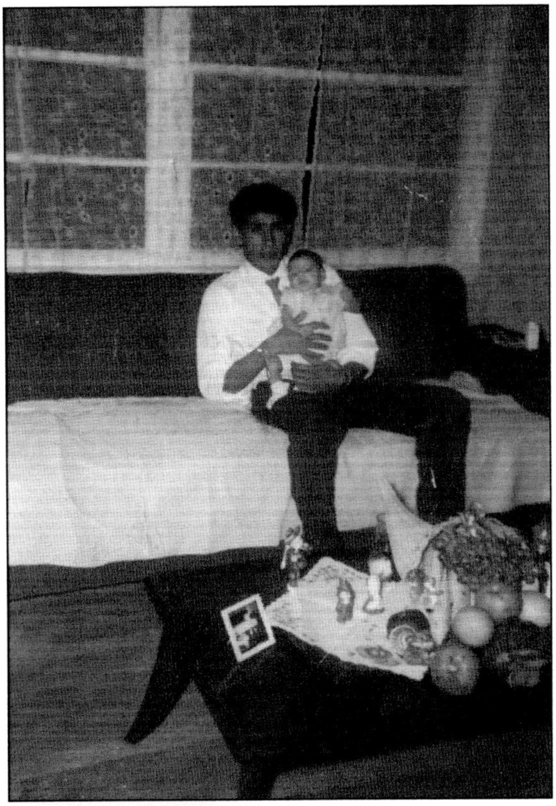

Pictured in 1961 are Cruz "Jerry" Torres and his son Richard Colin (in arms) at right and Rachel (below), Cruz's daughter. Cruz and his sister Gloria migrated in the early 1940s to Toppenish from Arizona, after their parents were unexpectedly killed in 1945. After Gloria and Cruz each married, their families moved to Quincy. Tragically Cruz and his family, including his wife, Sandra, were all killed in a car accident in late 1962. The experience was traumatic for his only living kin, his sister Gloria, but with strong family and community support, she overcame her grief. (Courtesy Jerry Garcia.)

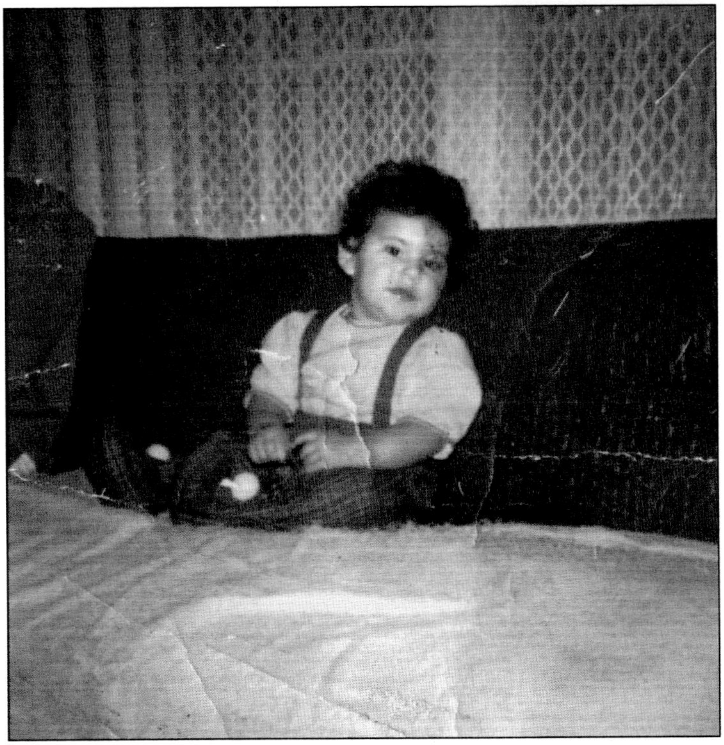

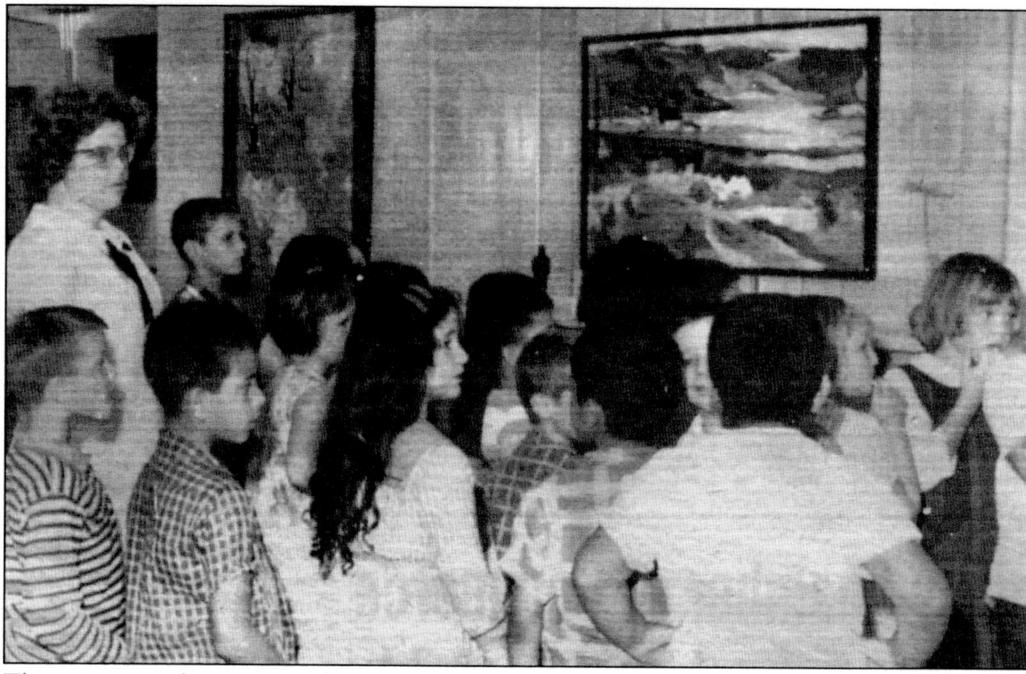

The top image of Mexican and Anglo children was taken in Quincy in 1965 during their annual Quincy Valley Harvest Days celebration. They are attending an art exhibit. More importantly, there is no better way to gage a community than through the lens of education. Integration of Mexican children into the school system has played a vital role in the community's development. The sixth-grade class pictured below provides more evidence of the value Mexican parents placed on education. In the second row third from the left is Rudy Hinojosa, and fourth from the left is R. Robeldo. In the third row at far left is Elvia Garces, and seventh from the left is Sylvia Treviño. (Above, courtesy *Quincy Post-Register*; below, courtesy Garces family.)

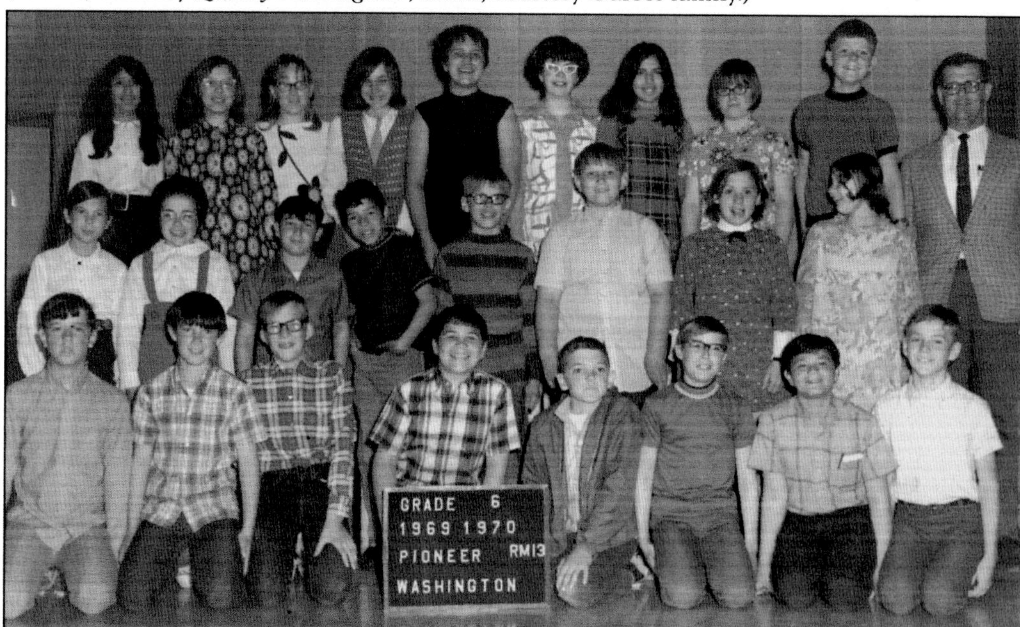

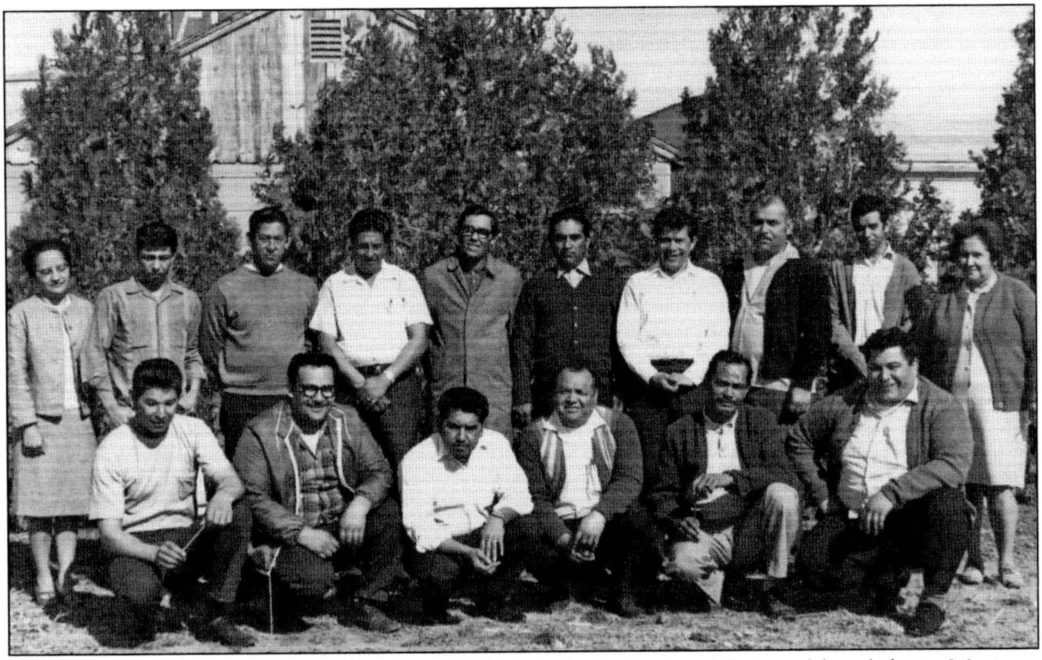

These two photographs taken in the 1960s in Moses Lake (below) and Quincy (above) depict Mexican Americans completing an adult education class. Those identified are (first row) second from the left, Mayo Castro; fifth from the left, Felix Arredondo; and far right, Armando Castro; (second row) far left, Carmen Taylor, longtime advocate of the Mexican community; and sixth from the left, Cecilio Garza. The bottom image in Moses Lake also depicts Mexican Americans in the Columbia Basin completing a Certificate of Educational Competence course at Big Bend Community College in 1968. Pictured in the middle is Andres "Andy" Martinez, who is about to embark on an important civil rights campaign for the Mexican community. (Courtesy Jerry Garcia.)

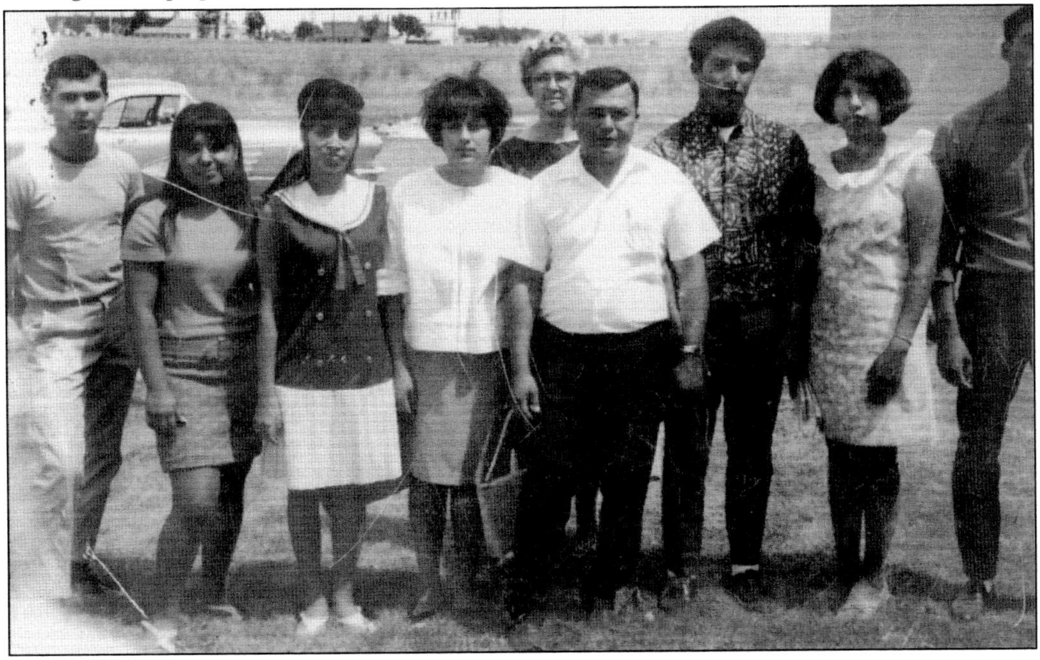

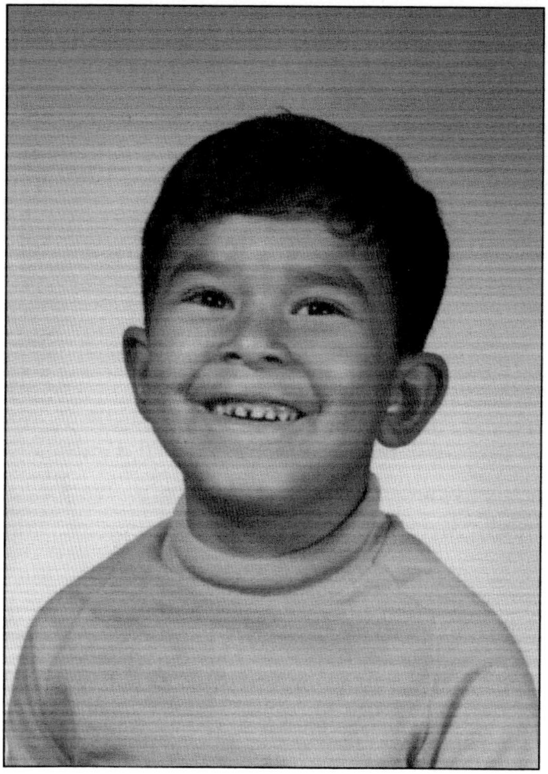

At left is the author at age six and in the first grade. He attended Head Start through grade 12 in Quincy. After being tracked into the military and being commissioned a second lieutenant in the U.S. Army, the author received a B.A. and M.A. from Eastern Washington University and a Ph.D. from Washington State University. Below are two of the author's siblings, Ruben "Mosquito" Garcia Jr. and Yolanda Garcia. Ruben and Yolanda attended Quincy High School and continue to live in Washington. (Courtesy Jerry Garcia.)

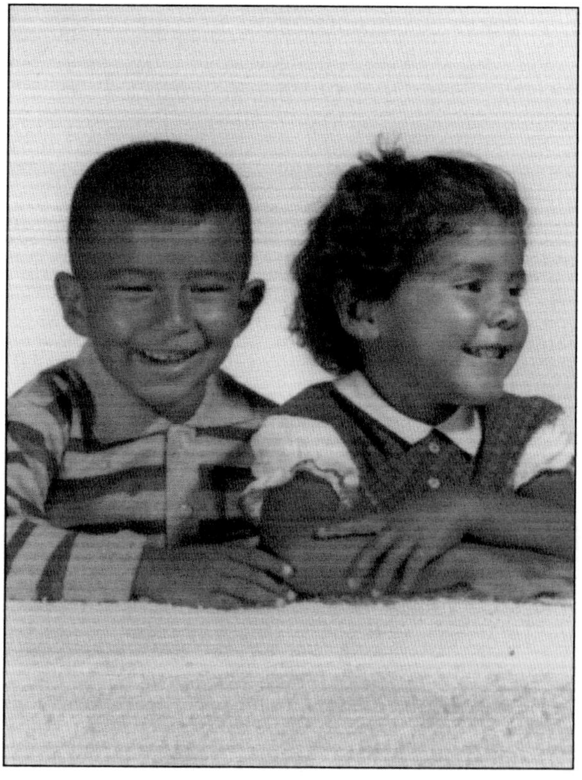

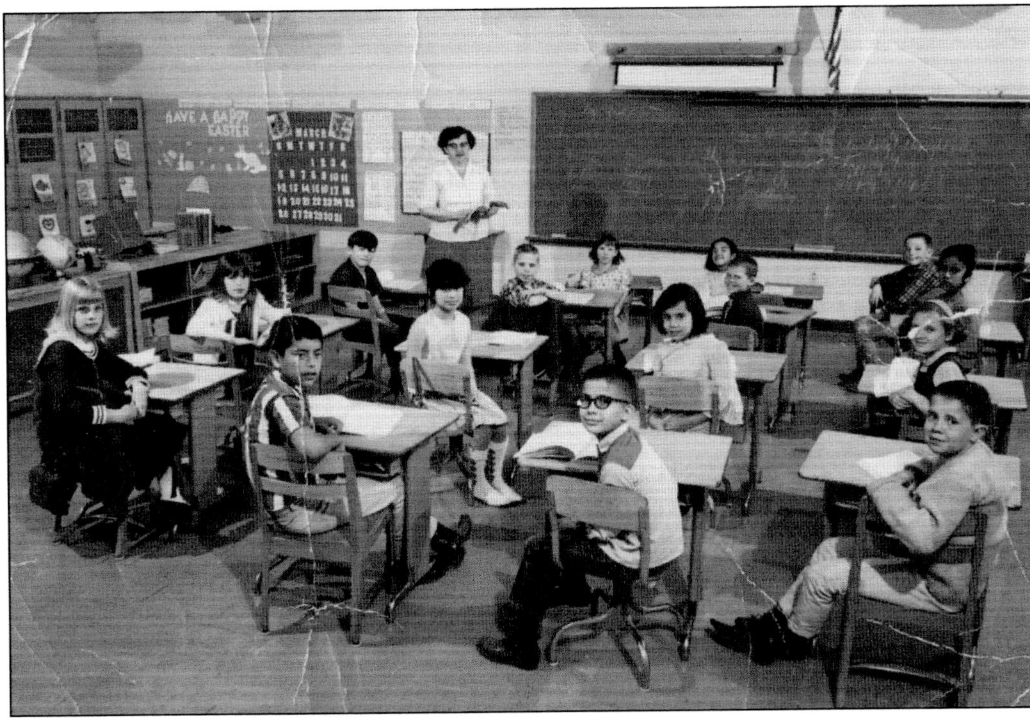

These two photographs were taken in the late 1960s. The top photograph (from the cover) depicts a fourth-grade class with a large contingent of Mexican American schoolchildren. The child seated on the far right row and three seats up from the bottom is Nora Garces. The bottom photograph is an image of a migrant day care center with primarily Mexican American children. The children, ranging in age from four to six, were fed two meals a day and underwent preschool training for up to 12 hours per day while their parents were working as farm laborers. (Courtesy Garces/*Wenatchee World*.)

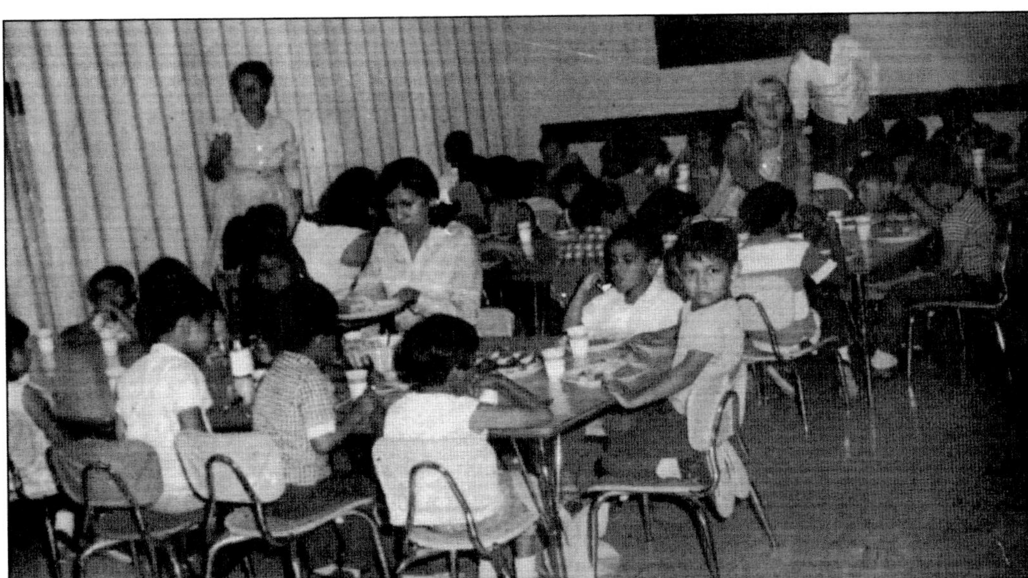

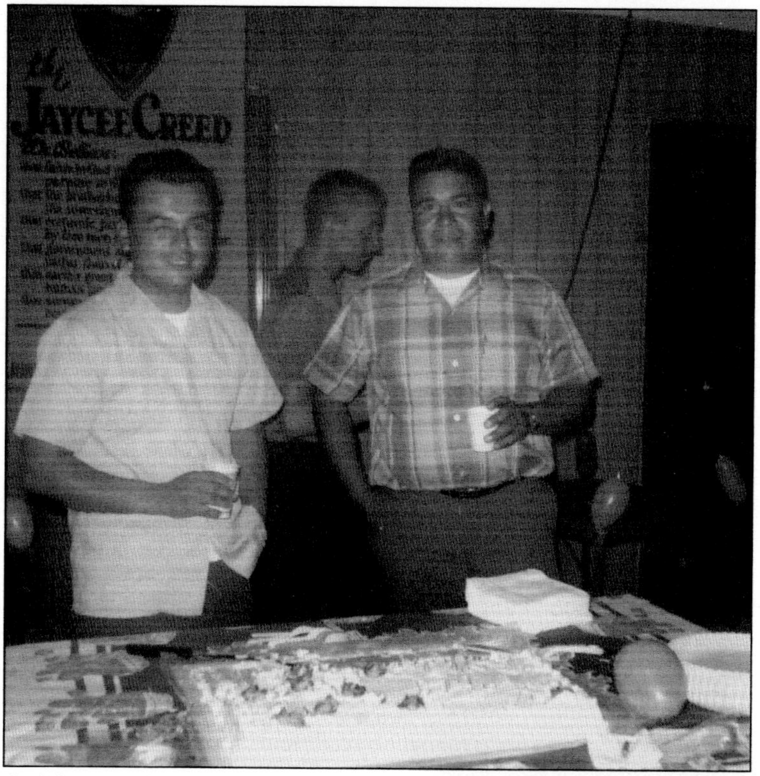

As Mexican Americans began to feel comfortable in their adopted communities, many joined community organizations. These two photographs from the 1960s show these efforts. The top photograph, taken in 1966, is of Andy Martinez (left) and Roy Alvarez, members of the Quincy Jaycees, established in 1920 to provide opportunities for young men to develop personal and leadership skills through service to others. The photograph at right depicts two Mexican Americans constructing a building for the new Grant County Community Action Program, an agency created to fight poverty. Andy Martinez was the program's operations director in the late 1960s. (Courtesy Jerry Garcia.)

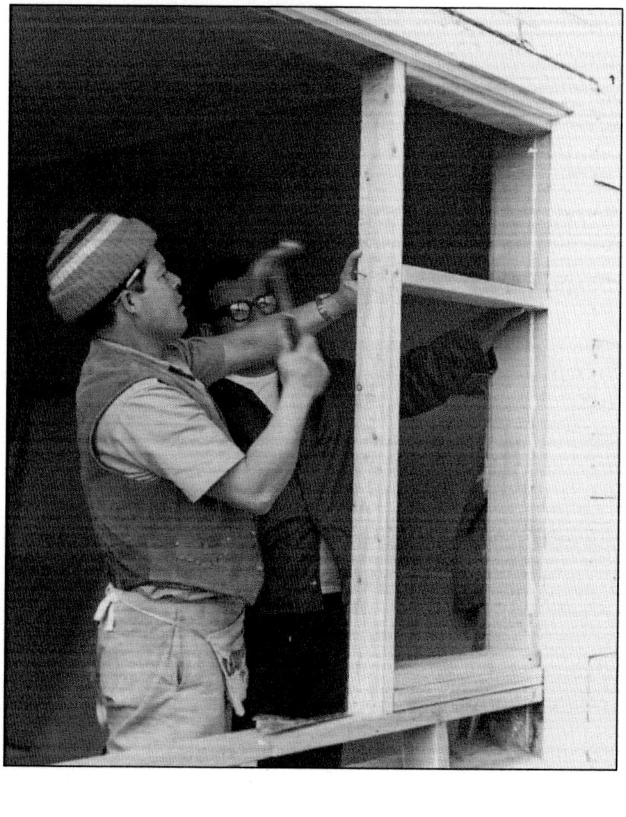

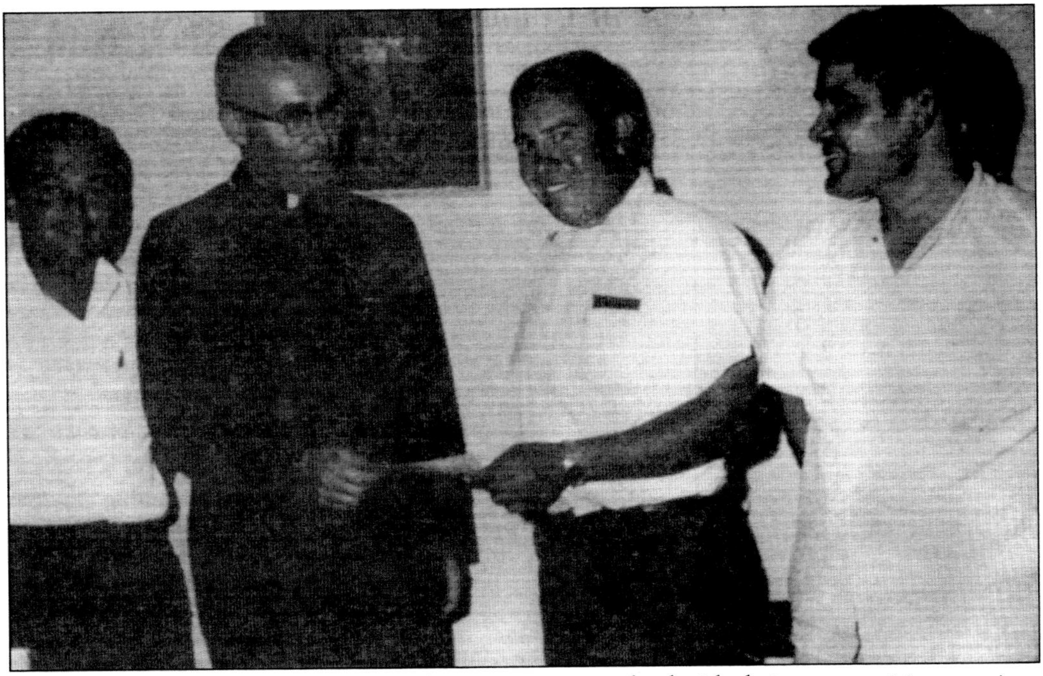

During the 1960s and 1970s, Mexican Americans got involved with their communities at various levels. The top image shows a common organization throughout NCW, the Latin American Club. The 1965 photograph shows Roy Alvarez handing Fr. John Henaghan a $1,400 check, which were the proceeds from the Mexican fiesta. Also pictured are Andy Martinez (far left) and Ray Ambriz (far right). The bottom photograph depicts Chicanas from the Columbia Basin at a leadership institute held at Washington State University in 1970. Many of these Mexican women returned to their communities and led organizations or joined groups to empower themselves or their communities further. (Above, courtesy Jerry Garcia; below, courtesy Washington State University.)

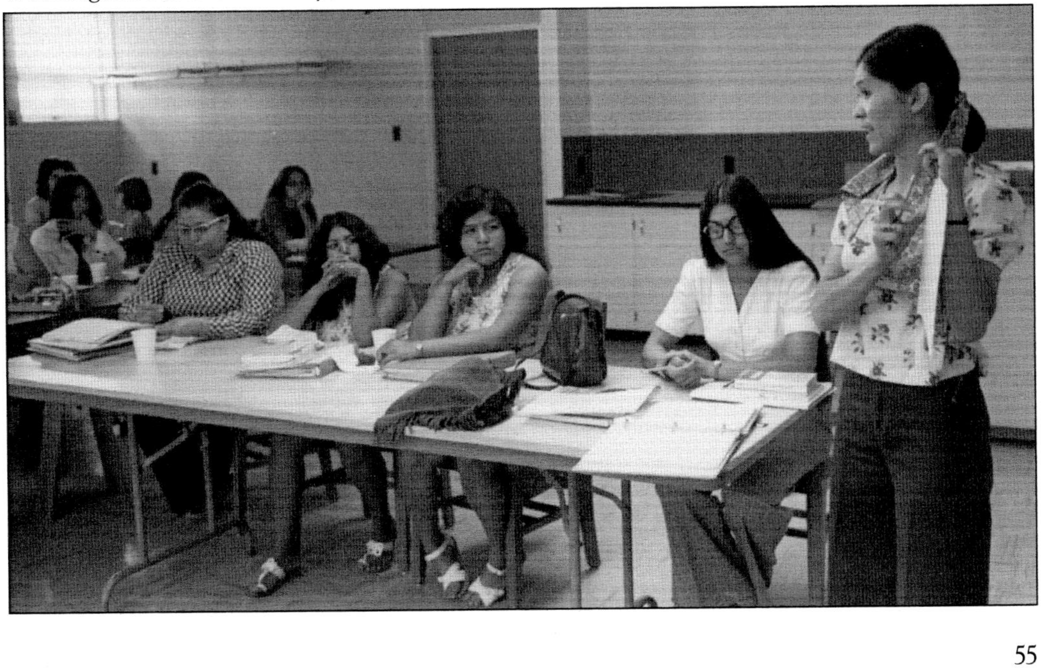

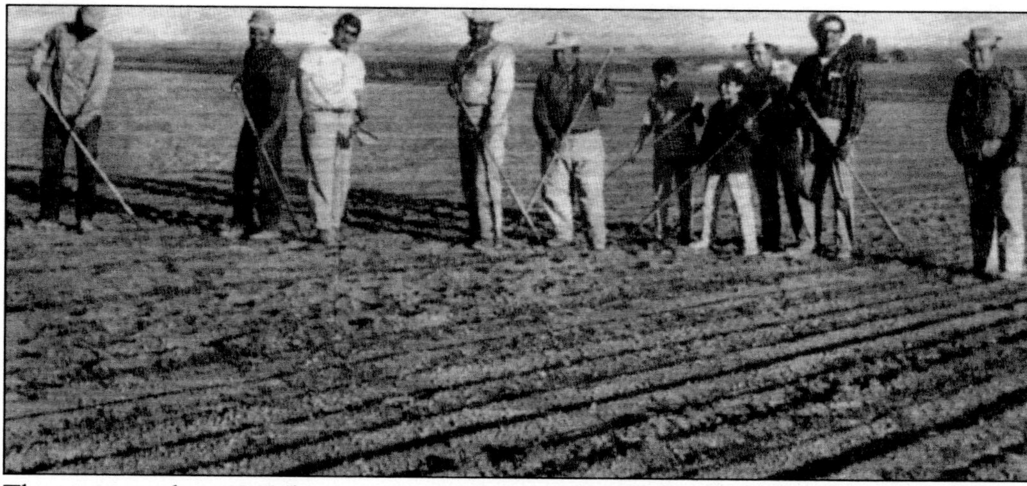

The top image from 1965 shows a group of men in a beet field near Quincy. The men and boys in this photograph weeded this beet field for charity to send four Mexican American children to a Catholic youth camp. From left to right are Ruben Garcia, Andy Martinez, Raymond Ambriz, Alberto Gonzales, Nemecio Rodriguez, two unidentified children, Arnuldo Cantu, Manuel Gonzales, and Roy Alvarez. The bottom photograph, shot in 1970 in Othello, depicts the U.S. flag being raised and saluted at the newly opened migrant day care center. The adults are, from left to right, Luis Garcia, Salvador Ochoa, and Juan Guel. (Above, courtesy Jerry Garcia; below, courtesy *El Mundo*.)

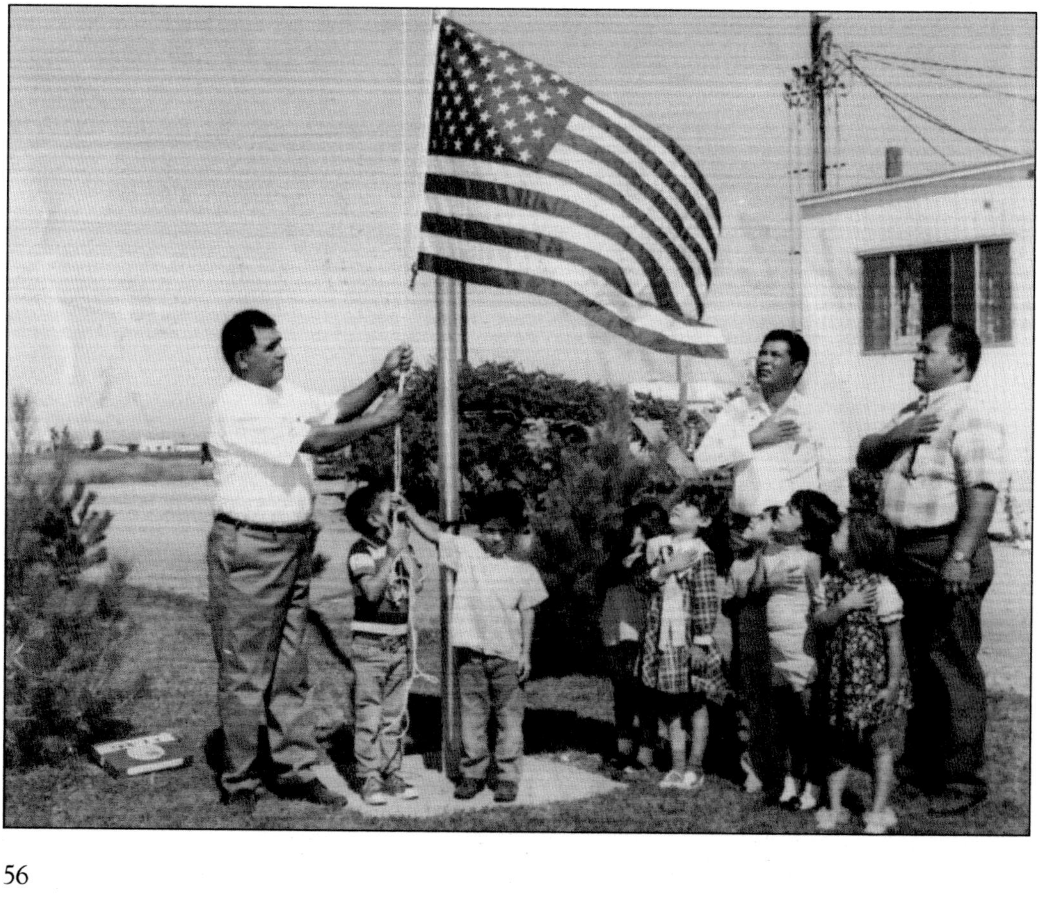

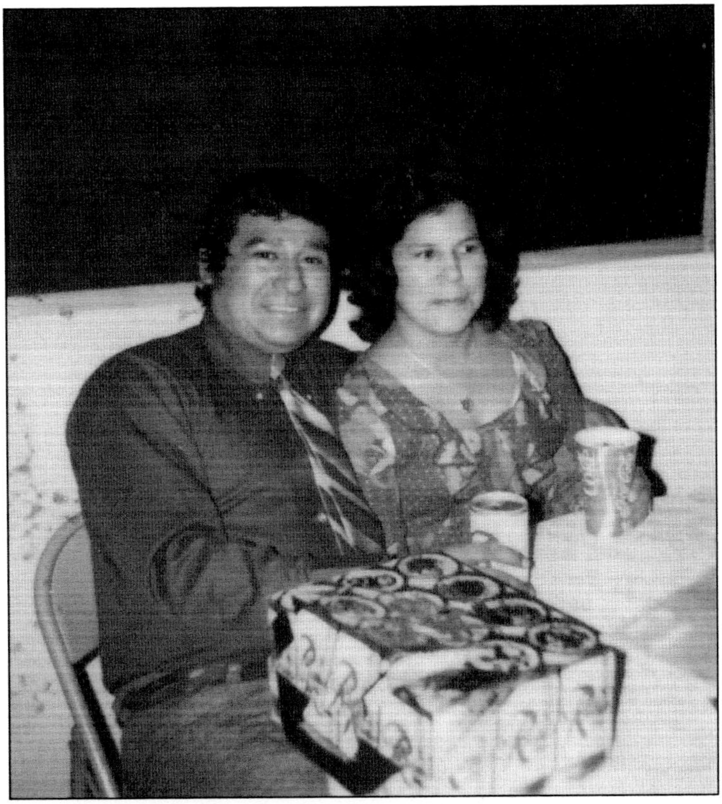

Traditional Mexican *bailes* (dances) are a community affair. These two photographs illustrate that life was not simply about work, but there was a time to relax and come together. The top photograph is of a young couple (Ruben and Gloria Garcia) in the early 1970s enjoying a *baile* and each other's company. The bottom photograph was of a wedding in the late 1990s of Roberto Garcia Jr. and Michelle Lopes. From left to right are Pat Garcia (with camera), Rebecca Reyes, Rene Villegas, Reymundo Garcia (with hat), Antonio Reyes, Gonzalo Reyes Jr. (with his back to the camera), Sammy Treviño, and Tony Velez. (Courtesy Jerry Garcia.)

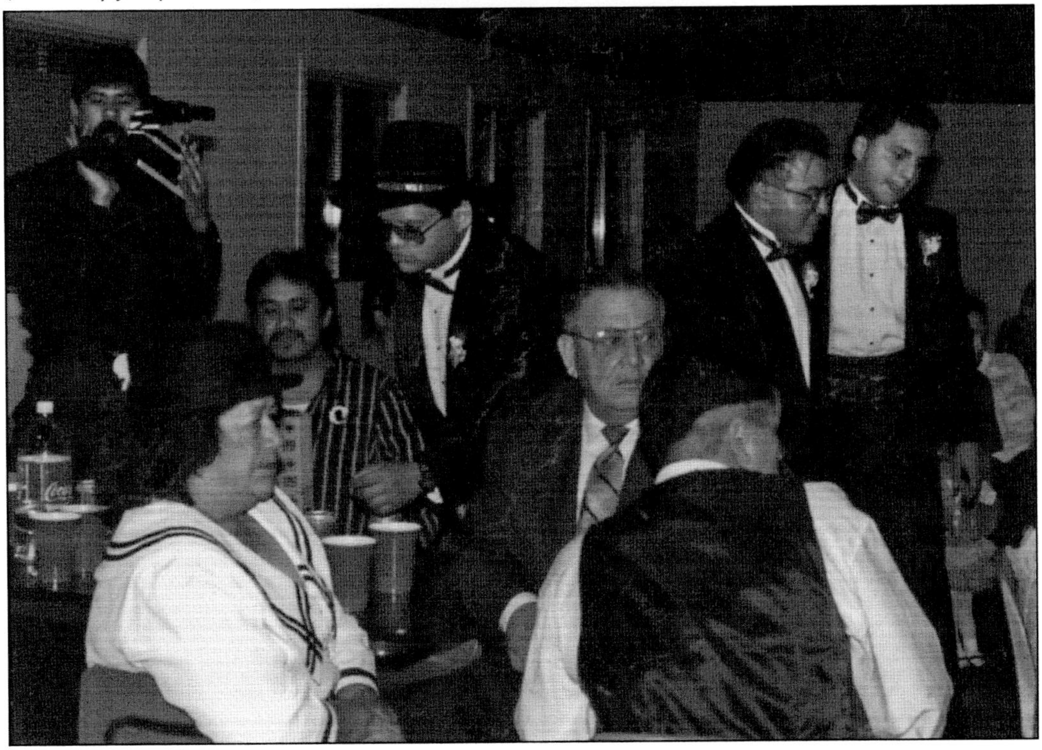

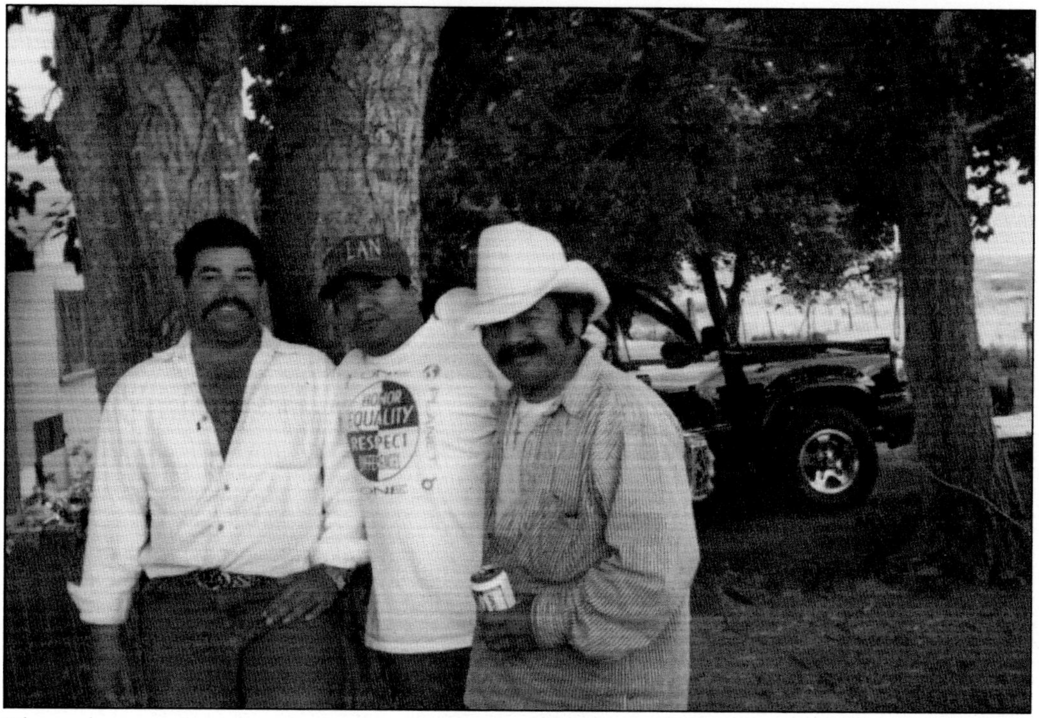

These photographs taken in the late 1990s near Winchester, Washington, depict the gendered space of Mexican males on a leisurely weekend. Although all of these men work in the United States, they choose to spend their non-working hours with their own ethnic group. Many of the men shown in these two photographs are recent arrivals being mentored by long-established Mexican men or elders. The two elders in the bottom photograph, Roberto Garcia (far left) and Ruben Garcia (far right), came from Mexico over 50 years ago. (Courtesy Jerry Garcia.)

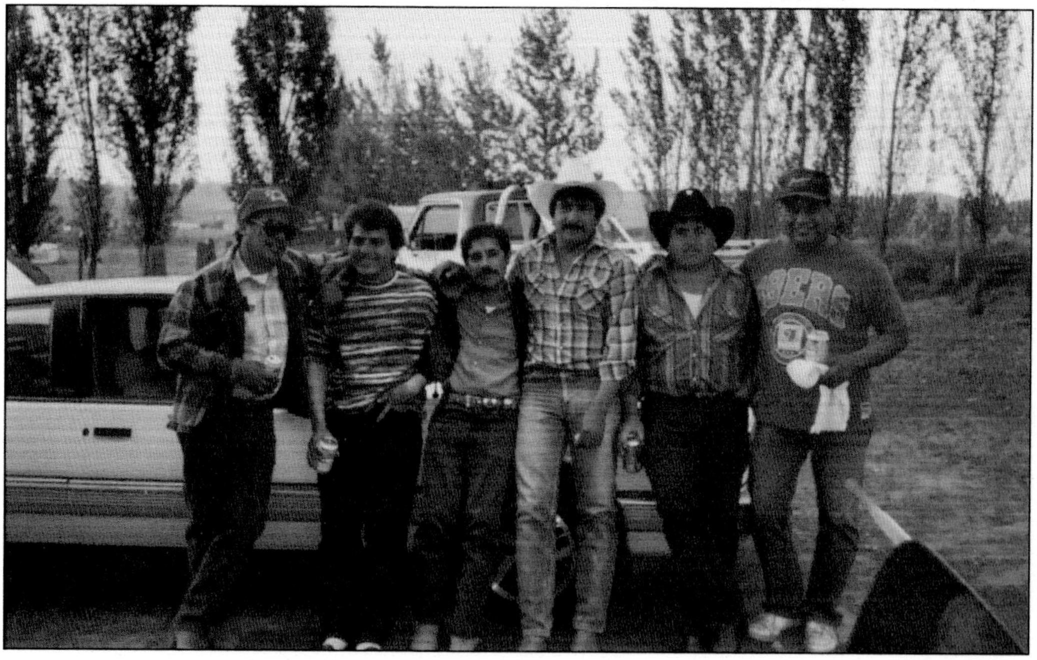

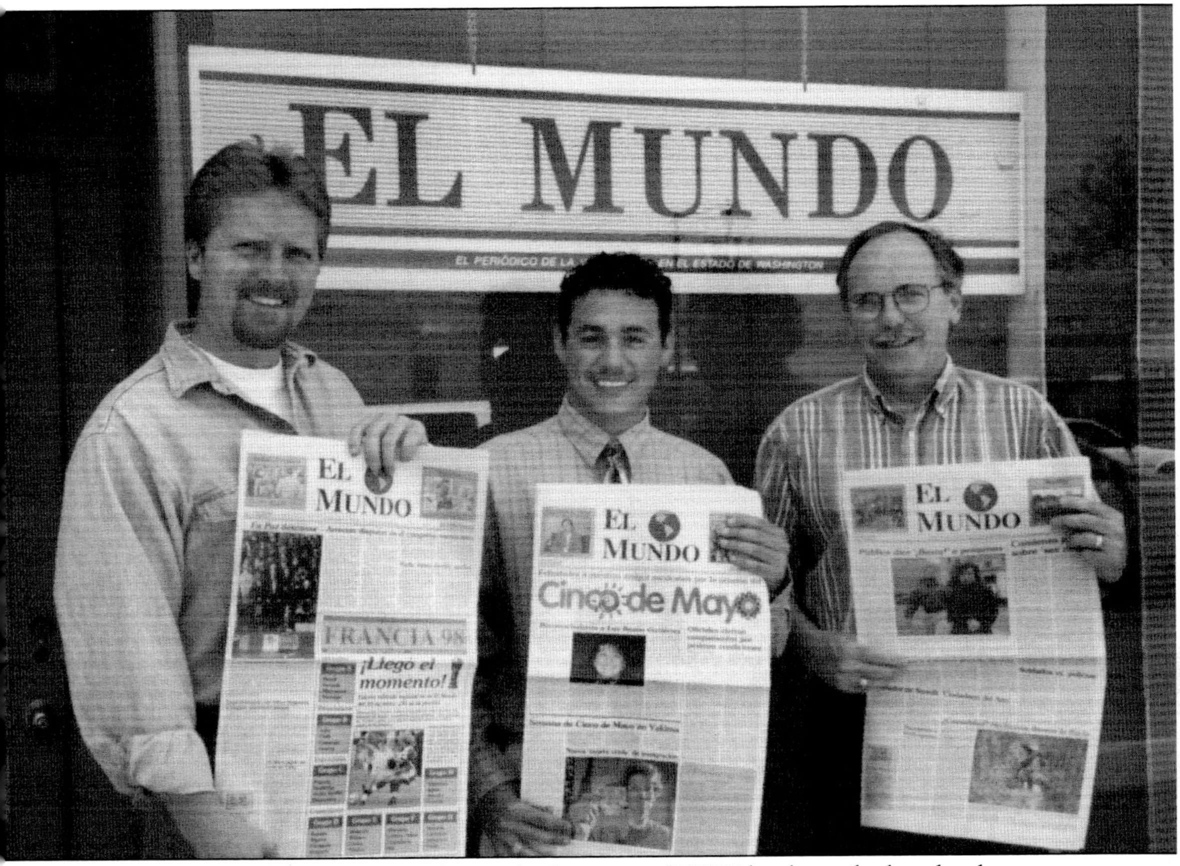

One clear distinction between Wenatchee and other areas of NCW has been the late development of the Mexican community in Wenatchee. Yet in the last 10 to 15 years, Wenatchee's Mexican community has solidified itself in the greater community and is the backbone of the agriculture industry in the region. Because of this importance, Wenatchee is home to the largest Spanish-language newspaper in NCW, *El Mundo*. It was established in 1989 by the *Wenatchee World* but bought by Jim Tiffany in 1995. Jim is pictured on the right in the photograph. For over 30 years, Jim Tiffany has been a strong advocate and friend of the Mexican community. Indeed Jim fought in the trenches during the early years when ethnic Mexicans were arriving in greater numbers and facing stiff resistance. From his humble beginnings in Davenport, Iowa, his work with the North Rural Opportunities program, his role as director of Enterprise for Progess in the Community (EPIC), ownership of *El Mundo*, and now as on the board of trustees for Wenatchee Valley Community College, Señor Tiffany is a trusted ally of the Mexican community in NCW. (Courtesy *El Mundo*.)

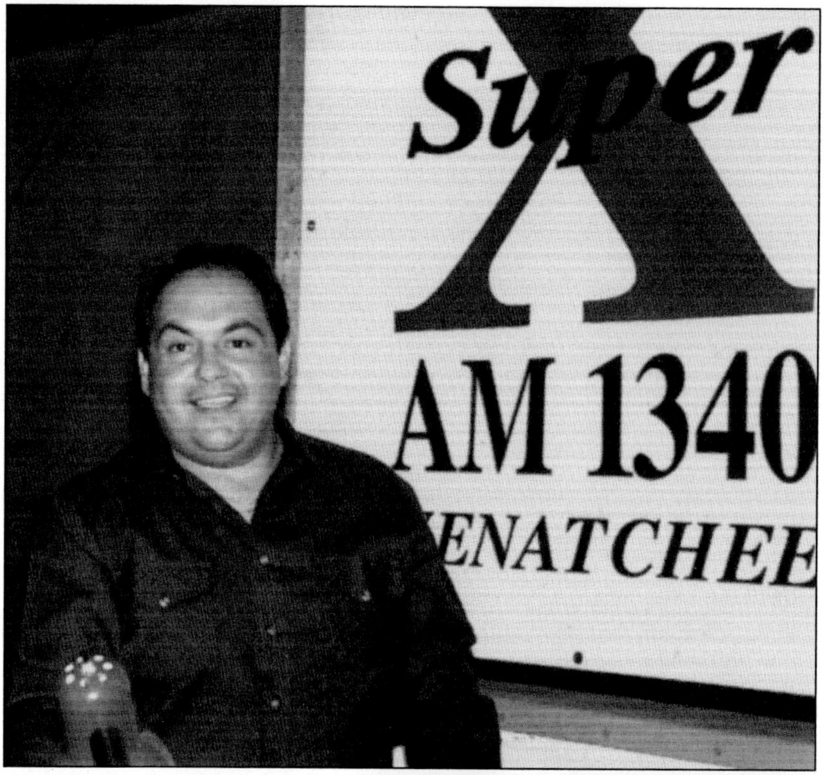

Along with a Spanish newspaper, Spanish-language radio is an important barometer of a community's development. Since the 1960s and 1970s, various Mexican communities have had Spanish radio programs. As a child in the 1970s, the author recalls his mother eagerly awaiting the daily one-hour Spanish-language radio program in Quincy. Wenatchee has experimented with a radio program catering to the Latino community. In 2001, Wenatchee converted FM 92.1 to Spanish-language radio. These two photographs were taken in the early 1990s and are DJs Ralph Ochoa (above) and Juan Torres (at right) for AM 1340, dedicated to the Spanish-speaking audience of the greater Wenatchee area. (Courtesy *El Mundo*.)

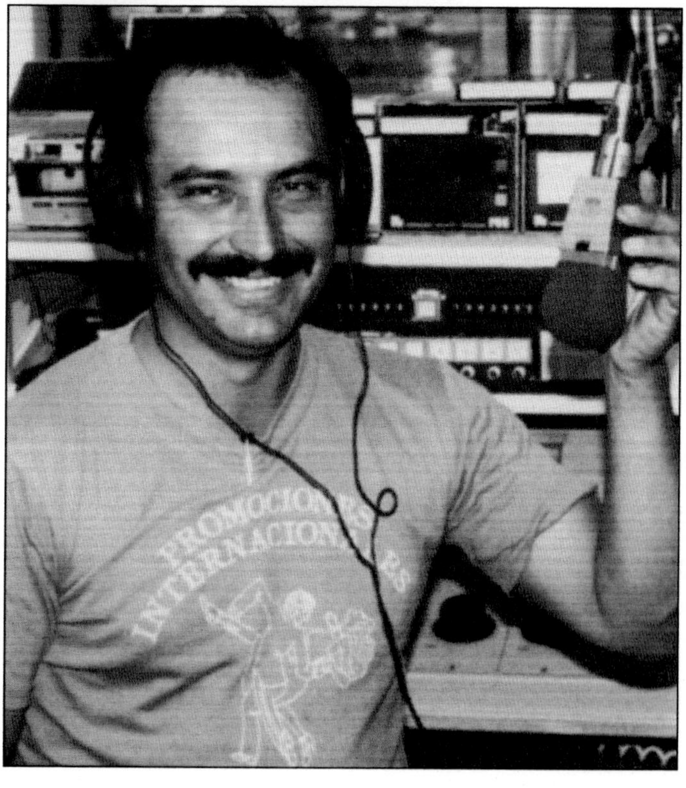

Five

Spiritual and Cultural Life

The religiosity of Mexicans living in the United States is complex. Historically the majority of ethnic Mexicans in the United States practice Catholicism. However, it is evident that the form of Catholicism practiced by many Mexicans is actually a merging of indigenous and European religions that began during the colonial period in what was once known as New Spain. In general, the introduction of Christianity to the Americas had a profound impact on the indigenous population. Yet, through a process of cultural amalgamation, a large portion of the Mexican population embraced Catholicism by the beginning of the 19th century.

This process was facilitated by the appearance of La Virgen de Guadalupe, the patroness of Mexico. In Mexican Catholicism, La Virgen represents religiosity, unity, and faith. However, when ethnic Mexicans reached the NCW, their faith was often relegated to the basements of parishes or images of La Virgen were not allowed. Thus, the early pioneers faced discrimination within the Catholic Church that played out into the community. Prof. Gilberto Garcia has written extensively on the Catholic Church in the Pacific Northwest and indicates that "by the 1950s a small Mexican population in Eastern Washington posed a threat to predominately white institutions," including the church. In some cases, like in Othello, Washington, the white and Mexicans parishioners split, with Mexicans forming their own religious center called El Centro Guadalupano.

The photographs that follow depict the spirituality of the Mexican community in NCW.

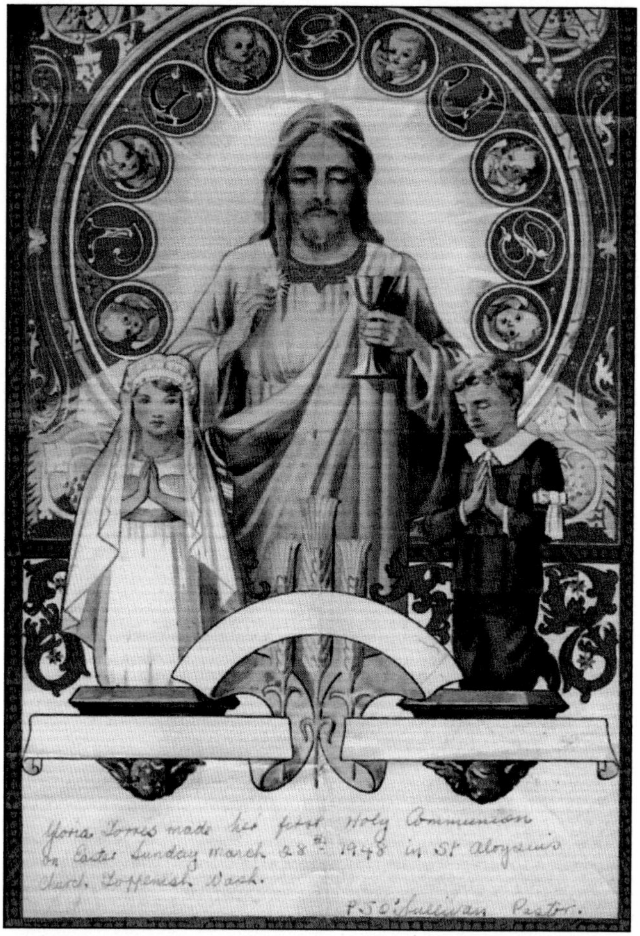

Regardless of their origin, ethnic Mexicans bring their spirituality with them and proudly display it whenever possible. Mexicans remain overwhelmingly Catholic, and after being baptized, the next important step within this denomination is the first Holy Communion. The picture at left is the 1948 certificate Gloria Torres received after making her first Holy Communion. The bottom image depicts Mexican children at St. Pius X Church in 1963 after their Holy Communion in Quincy. Of the 49 children baptized, 30 were Mexican American children. (Courtesy Jerry Garcia.)

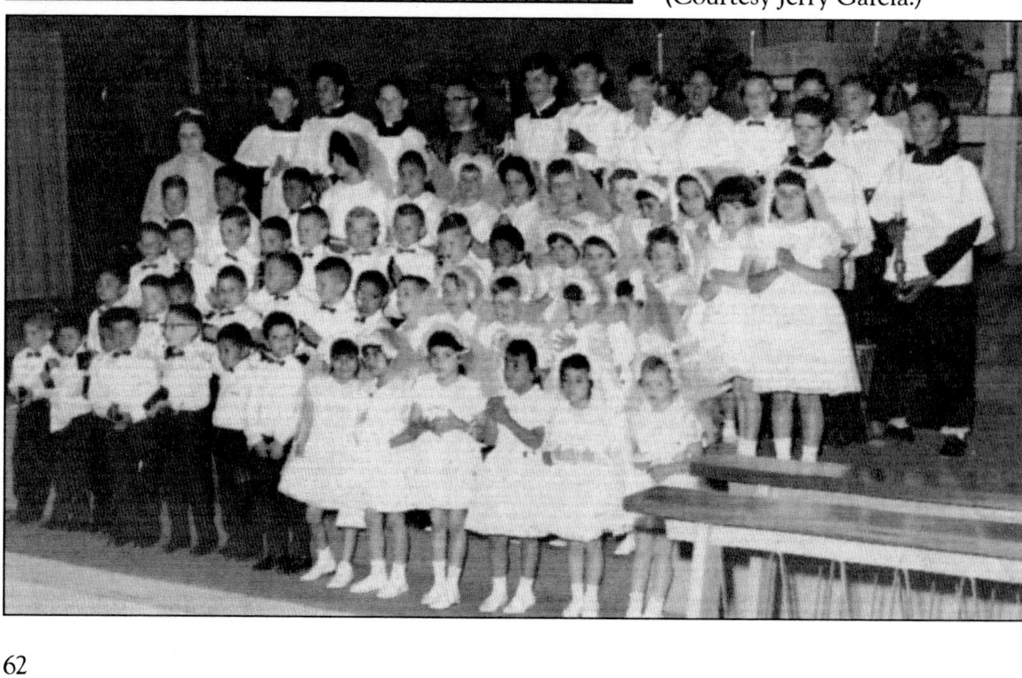

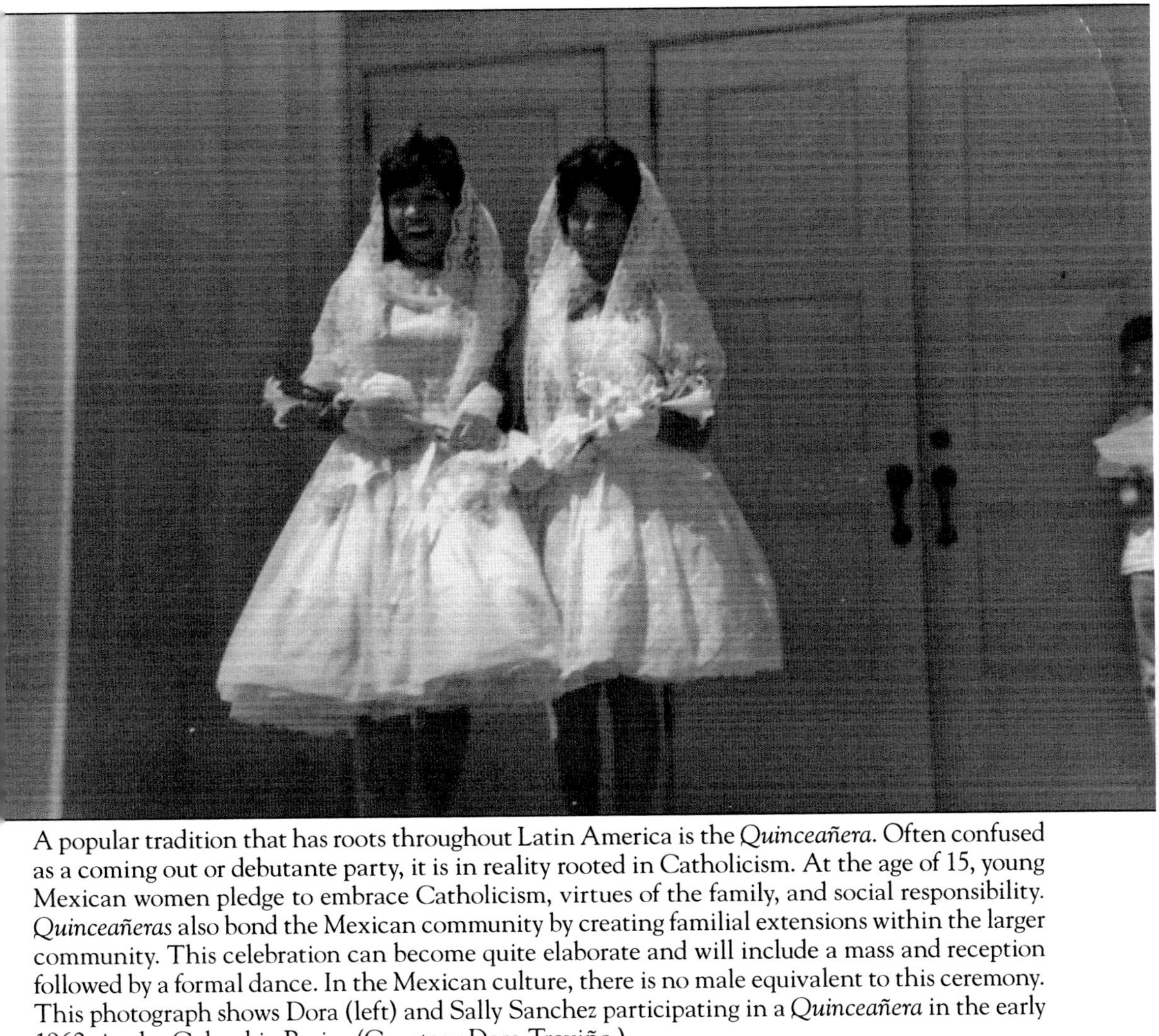

A popular tradition that has roots throughout Latin America is the *Quinceañera*. Often confused as a coming out or debutante party, it is in reality rooted in Catholicism. At the age of 15, young Mexican women pledge to embrace Catholicism, virtues of the family, and social responsibility. *Quinceañeras* also bond the Mexican community by creating familial extensions within the larger community. This celebration can become quite elaborate and will include a mass and reception followed by a formal dance. In the Mexican culture, there is no male equivalent to this ceremony. This photograph shows Dora (left) and Sally Sanchez participating in a *Quinceañera* in the early 1960s in the Columbia Basin. (Courtesy Dora Treviño.)

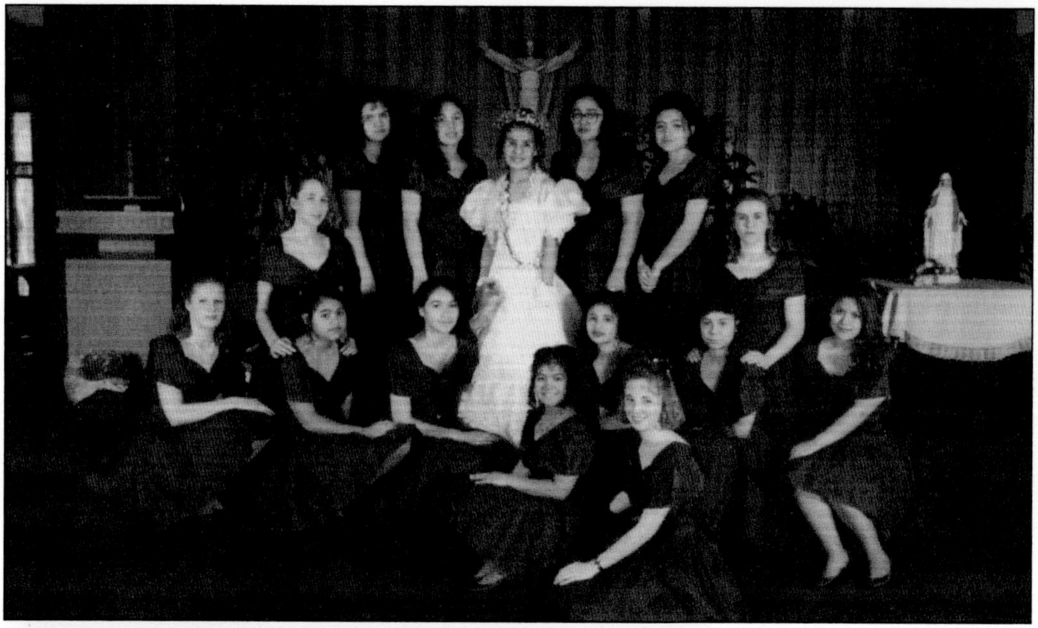

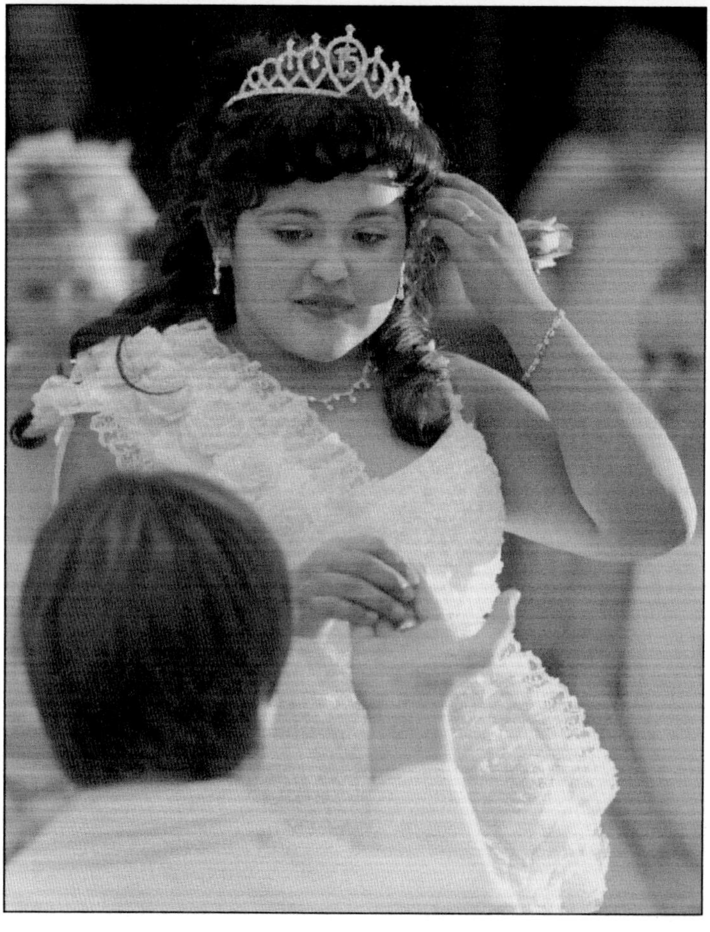

These two photographs depict contemporary *Quinceañeras* that were celebrated in Quincy and Wenatchee. The top photograph shows Shanna Villegas on her 15th birthday with her female court. To the untrained eye, this photograph resembles a wedding. Note the imagery of the Catholic Church, which signifies the religious importance of the ceremony, and the incorporation of Anglo girls. The image at left is of Ariana Elias, who is accepting a rose from her escort, Tyler Thibault, after a traditional Mexican waltz during her *Quinceañera* in East Wenatchee in 2003. (Above, courtesy Jerry Garcia; below, courtesy *Wenatchee World*.)

By the 1960s, Mexican culture was proudly displayed throughout many communities in NCW. The photograph at right is of Yolanda Garcia's fifth birthday party in 1965. She is pictured posing by her piñata. The bottom photograph, taken in 1968 in Quincy, depicts Mexican American singers celebrating at the annual Mexican fiesta. The *Wenatchee World* covered the event and wrote, "The music was provided by the Mexican people, who play an important role in making the Quincy Valley productive." (Above, courtesy Jerry Garcia; below, courtesy *Wenatchee World*.)

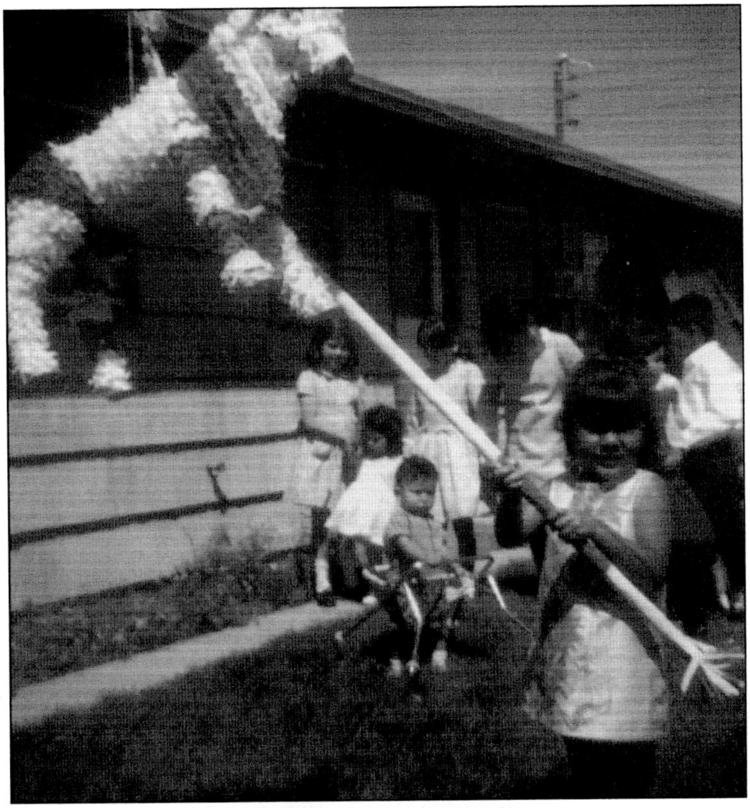

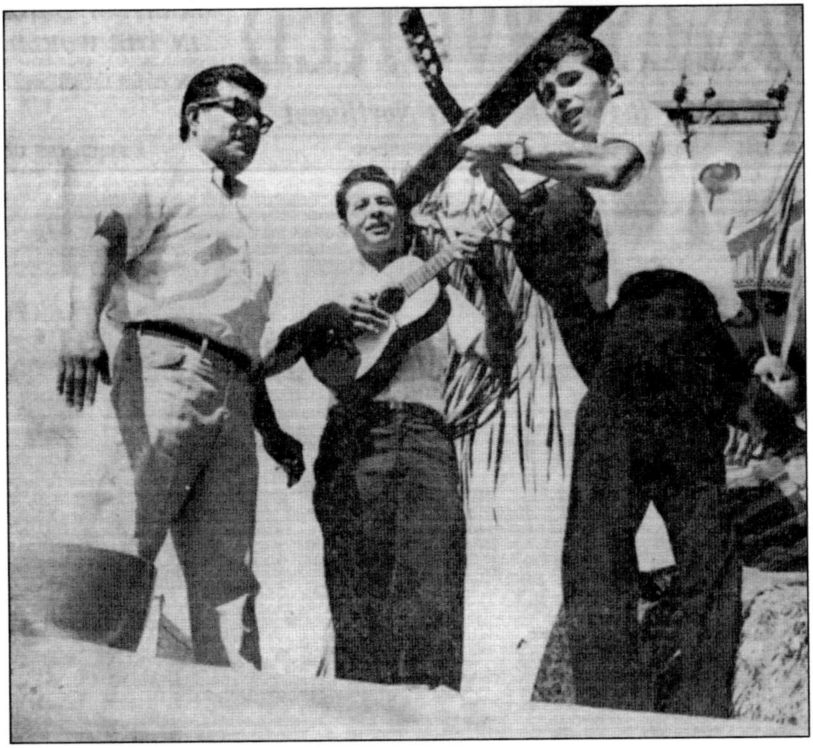

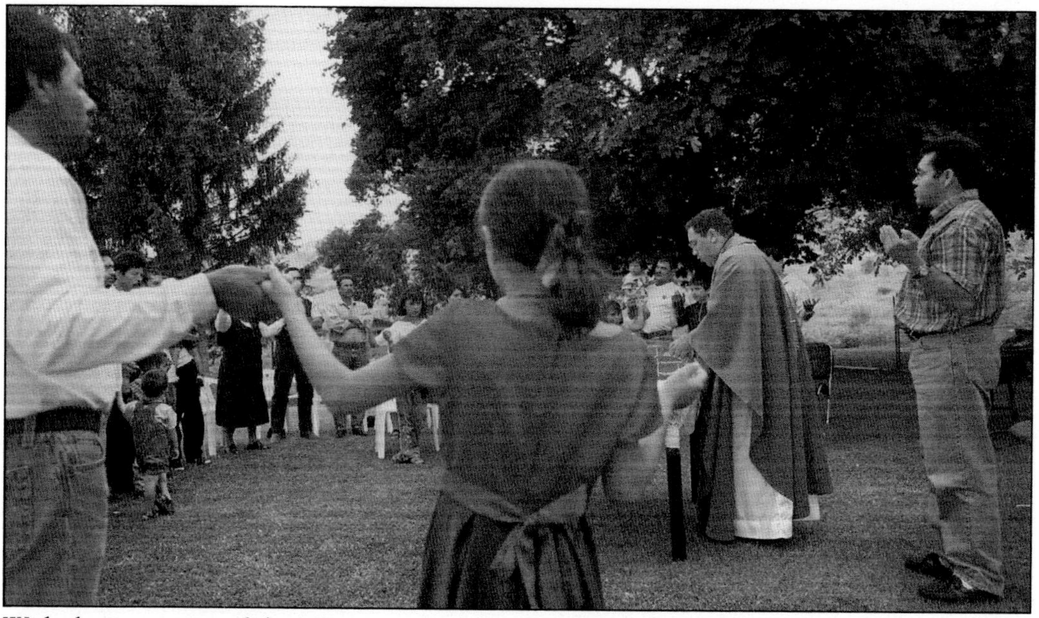

With the expansion of the Mexican population in NCW, the Catholic Church has expanded. Historically some conflicts have emerged regarding the increase of Mexicans within the church, but by and large, most communities have been able to overcome these differences. The top image, taken in 2000, is of seminary student Alejandro Trejo (far right) from Mexico, assisting Padre Ricardo with a Catholic mass for a group of Mexican families in the yard of a home north of Entiat. The bottom photograph, taken in 2002, is of Bishop Gilberto Valbuena from Colima, Mexico, speaking to several hundred Latino parishioners from the Wenatchee Valley at the Holy Apostles Catholic Church in East Wenatchee. (Courtesy *Wenatchee World*.)

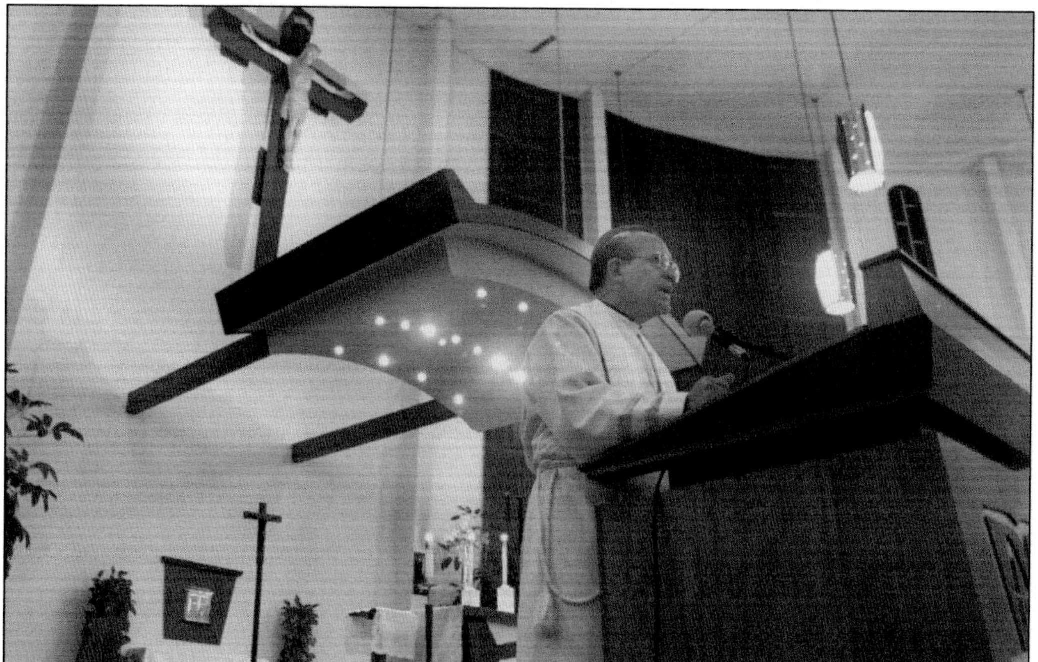

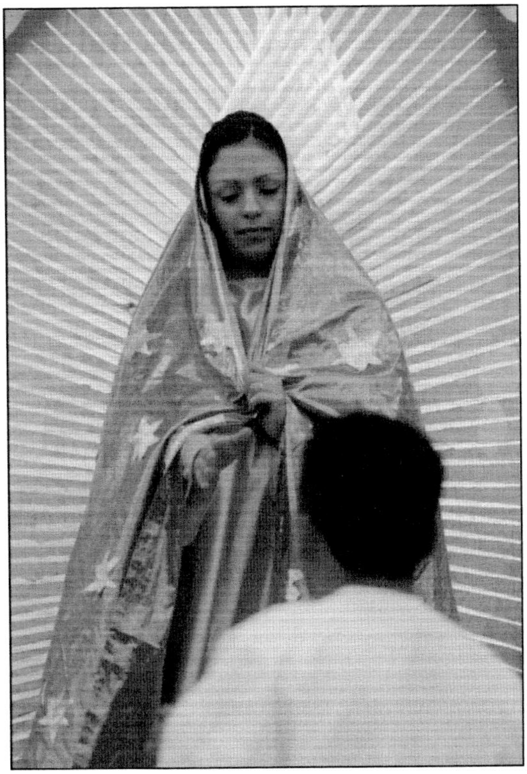

La Virgen de Guadalupe represents Mexican Catholicism, and her image is venerated by most Mexicans. The patroness of Mexico symbolizes a connection to the Indian past and she unifies those in discord and brings peace to those who believe in her. Her image represents Catholicism for ethnic Mexicans. The two images on this page show her importance to the Mexican community in NCW. The image at right is of Elida Blanco, Wenatchee, portraying La Virgen de Guadalupe as she blesses Juan Diego, played by Mario Hernandez of East Wenatchee, as they reenact her appearance on December 12, 1531. The bottom photograph depicts a traditional image of La Virgen on top of a float during the Apple Blossom Parade. (Courtesy *Wenatchee World*.)

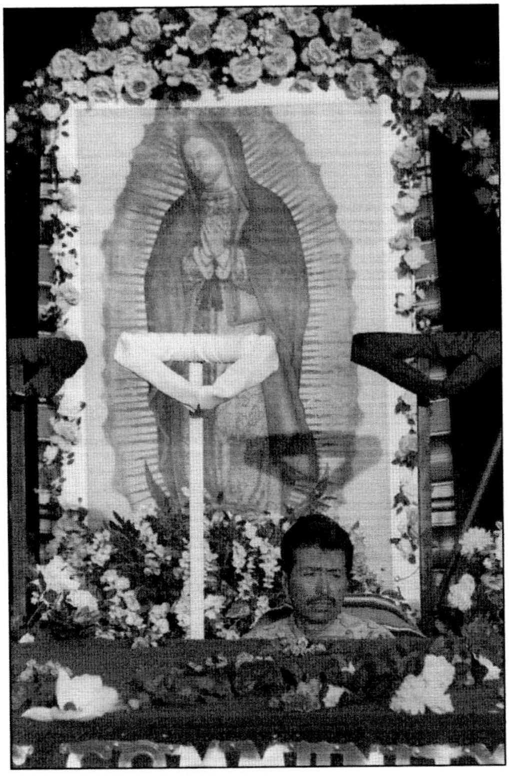

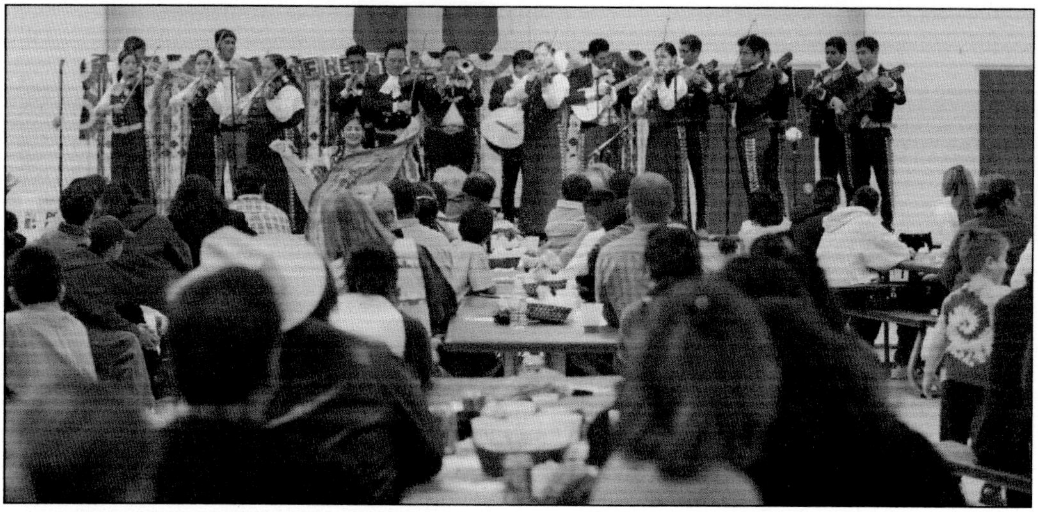

Mariachi music as a genre originated in Europe and was brought to Mexico during the French invasion and occupation of the country in the 1860s. However, since then, Mexicans have given it a uniquely distinct sound and flavor from various regions of Mexico. Today it remains one of the most popular Mexican sounds inside and outside of Mexico. A very unique program was started at Wenatchee High School in the 1980s that allowed students to learn and perform mariachi music. Since that period, Wenatchee High School's Mariachi Huenachi has become an award-winning band. The two photographs are of this band performing and accepting awards for their performances. (Courtesy *Wenatchee World*.)

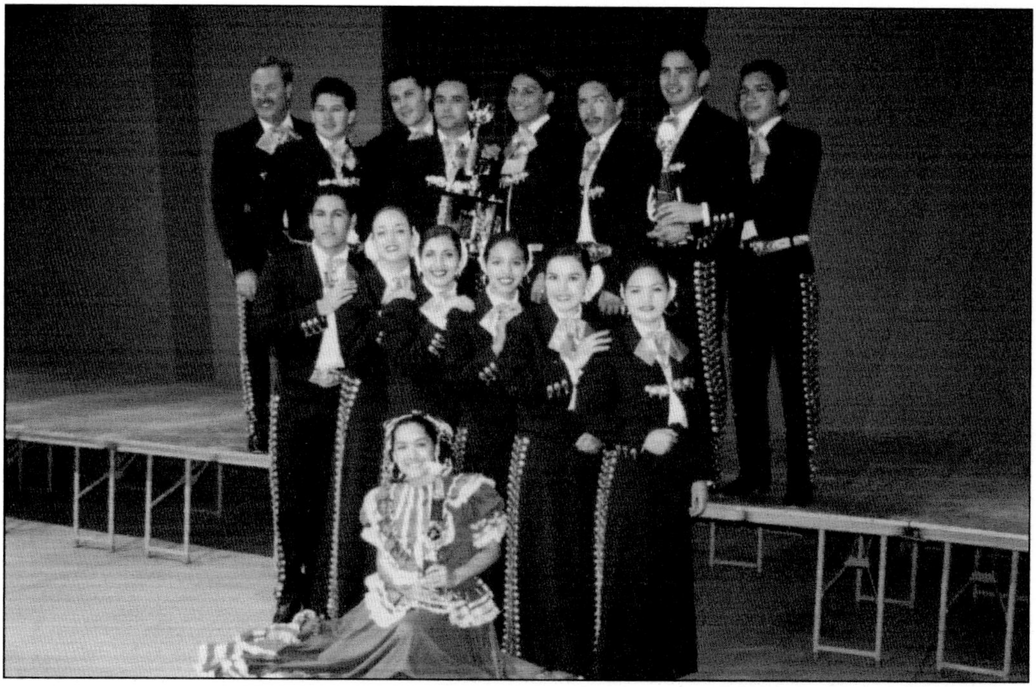

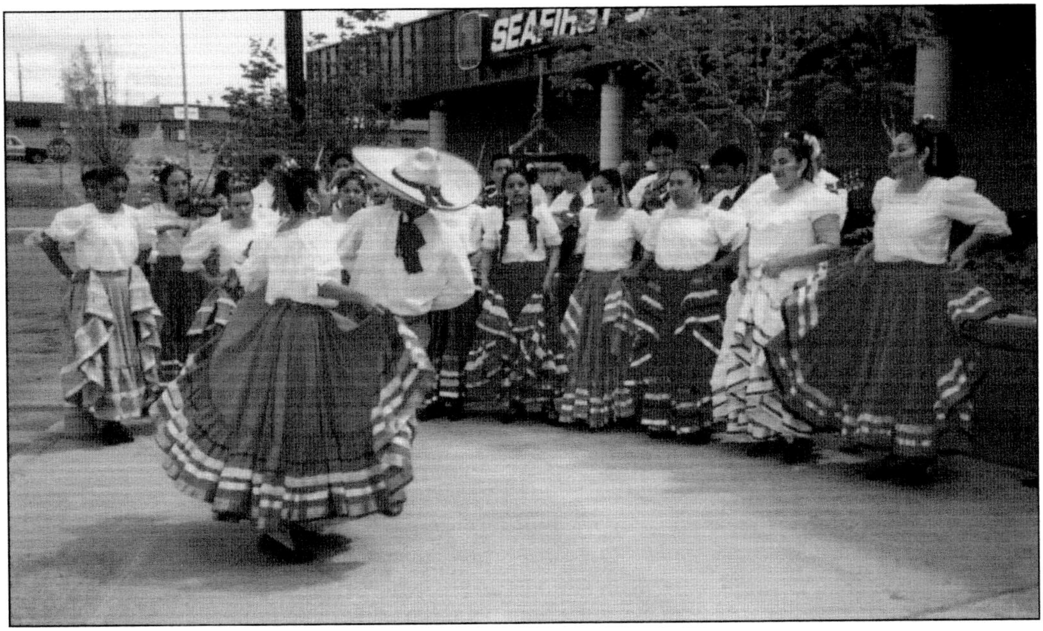

Ballet folklorico, like mariachi music, has many influences and many styles depending on the region of Mexico. For Mexicans in NCW, the practice of this genre reinforces the cultural continuity of the community. The reemergence of Aztec dancing during the cultural renaissance of the 1960s also reaffirmed the indigenous culture for Mexicans living in the United States. The two photographs on this page were taken during the Washington State Apple Blossom Festival. The top image is of ballet folklorico, and the bottom image is of Aztec dancers. (Courtesy *Wenatchee World.*)

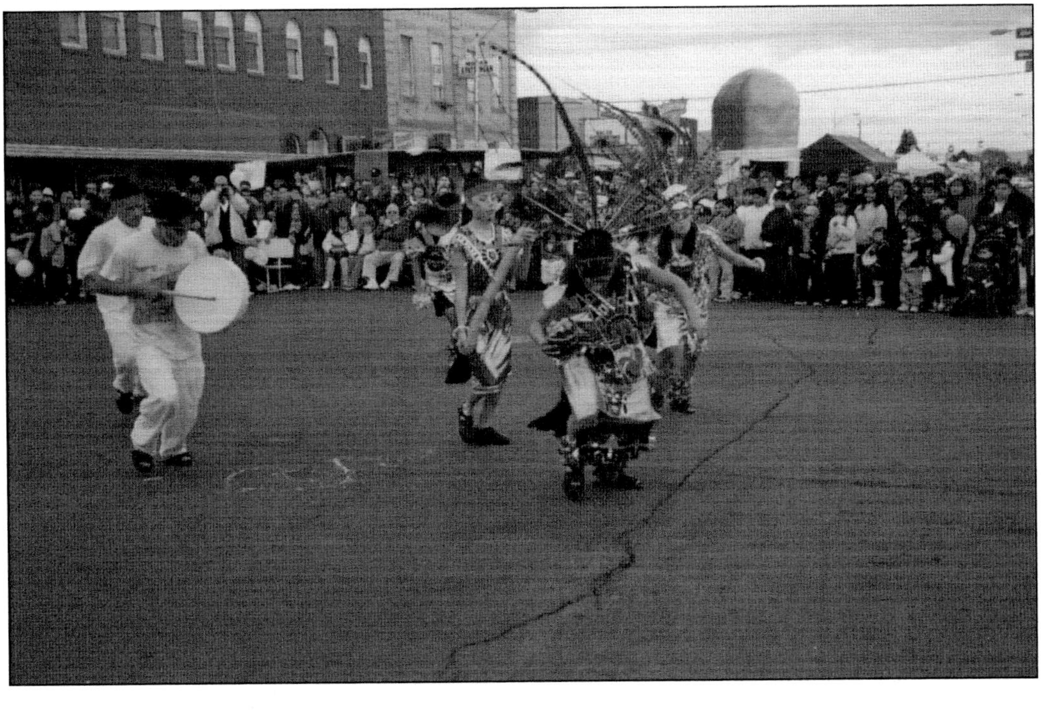

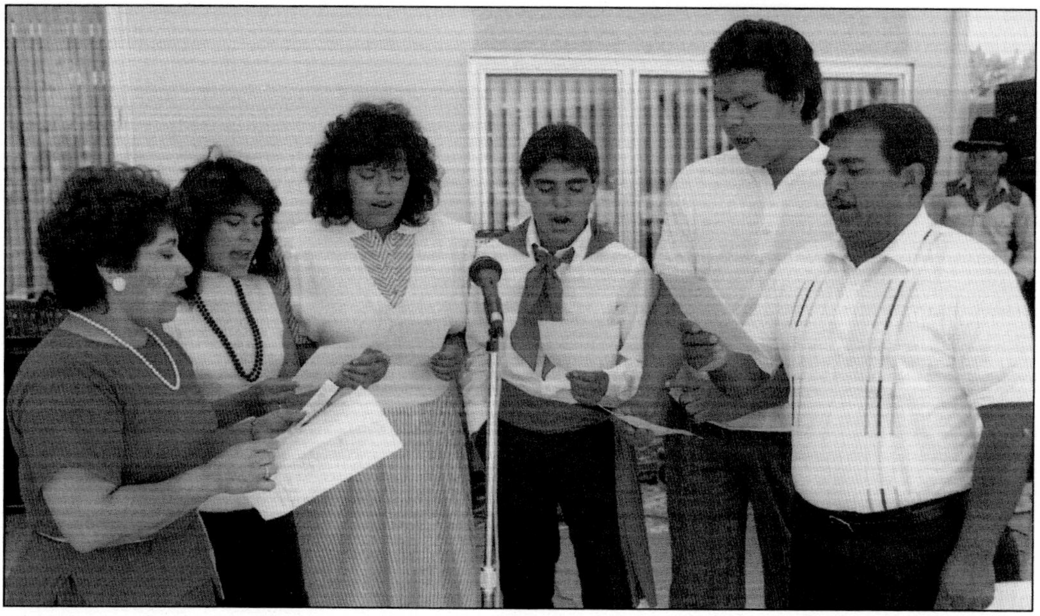

The Hernandez family of Quincy has been strong supporters of music and has been performing in the community since the 1960s. This family regularly sings at the Catholic church in Quincy, and as seen in this image taken in the late 1980s in Wenatchee, they also perform at community functions and gatherings. Pictured from left to right are Esperanza Hernandez, Isabel Hernandez, unidentified, Jack Hernandez, unidentified, and Alex Hernandez.

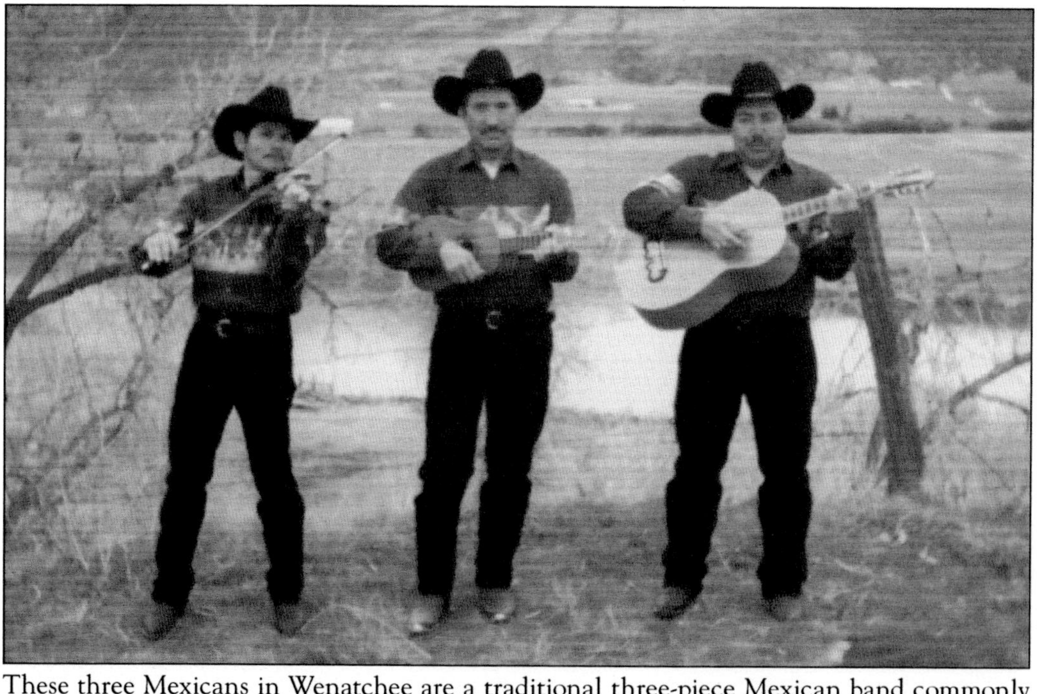

These three Mexicans in Wenatchee are a traditional three-piece Mexican band commonly referred to as a *conjunto*. This genre is traditionally from the northern regions of Mexico and Texas. The instruments shown in this picture are the violin, Spanish guitar, and bajo sexton. Often the accordion is used with this ensemble. (Courtesy *Wenatchee World*.)

Six

SOCIAL ACTIVISM

As one author put it, "Mexicans were born in fire and blood." For Mexican Americans, the struggle for social equality and justice intensified with the invasion and conquest by the United States of Mexico's northern territories. By the early 20th century, most Mexicans living in the United States had been relegated to second-class status. Yet one of the hallmarks of the Mexican American experience in the United States has been its resiliency in the face of oppression.

By the late 1960s, many Chicanos found their economic, social, and political position well below their Anglo counterparts in the state of Washington. As a result, many became socially active within their communities. Oftentimes it was in support of national causes such as Cesar Chavez's grape boycott. Chicanos in the region also formed chapters of the Brown Berets, a group that espoused Chicano nationalism. Student activism was very strong at the university and high school levels. In North Central Washington, individuals and groups emerged in an attempt to change the status quo. For example, in 1967, the Latin American Association in Quincy changed to the Progressive League of United Mexican Americans (PLUMA) to reflect an ideological shift that was occurring within the Chicano movement. In 1973, protests erupted at Quincy High School when 40 Chicano students walked out of school. Their demands were better treatment and an end to discrimination within the school. The United Farm Workers entered Grant County and organized workers in such places as Mattawa. In Wenatchee, during the late 1990s, the teamsters attempted to unionize Stemilt workers. The photographs that follow provide excellent examples of the social activism that has empowered the Mexican community.

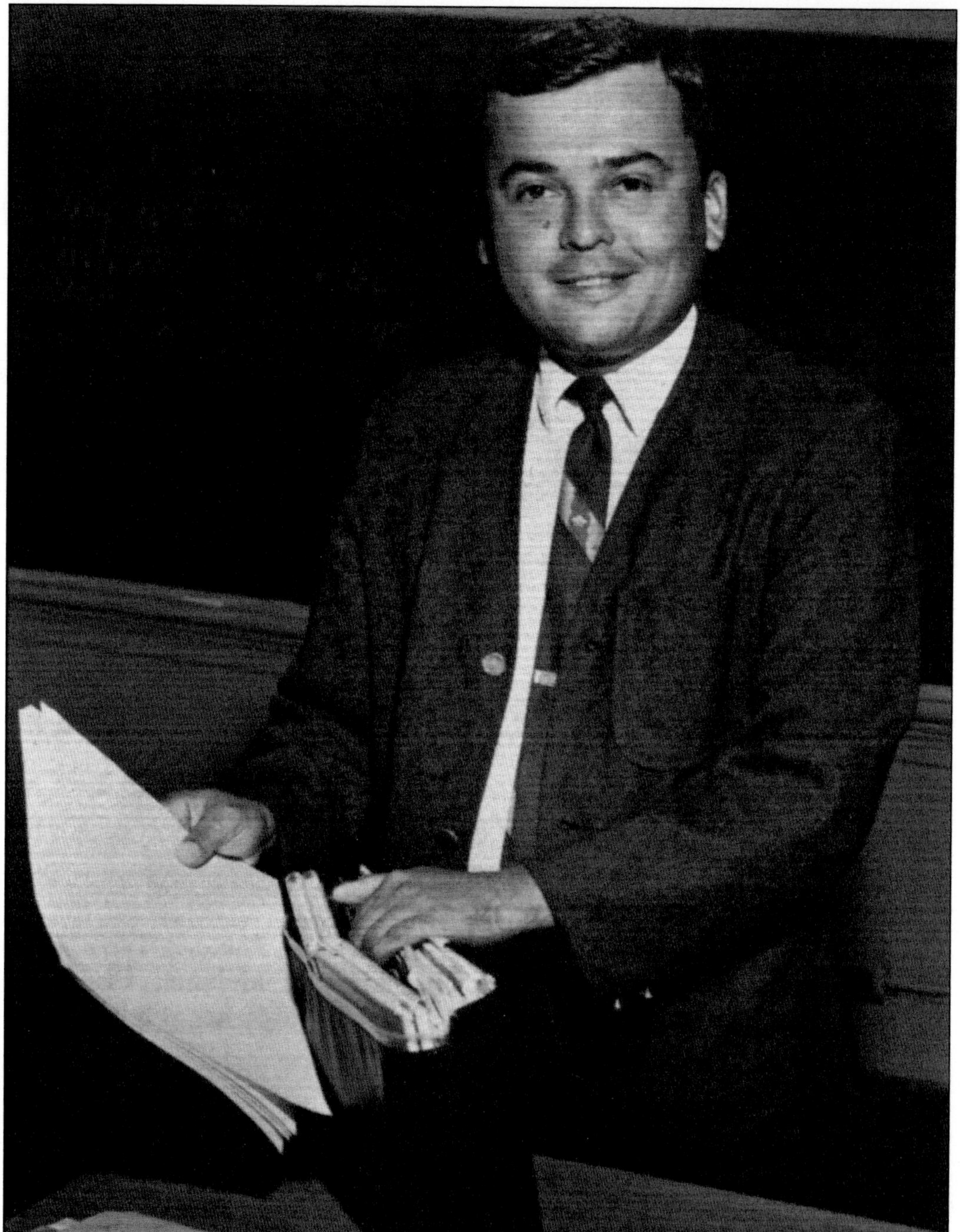

This 1970 photograph of Andres "Andy" Martinez was featured in the book *I Am One of These* by Kay Koschnick. From the 1960s through the 1980s, Andres Martinez developed grassroots organizations to address the needs of migrant laborers throughout NCW. As a member of the Grant County Community Action Program, Andy actively pursued the needs of low-income families. He was instrumental in attempting to integrate Mexican communities throughout the region. (Courtesy Jerry Garcia.)

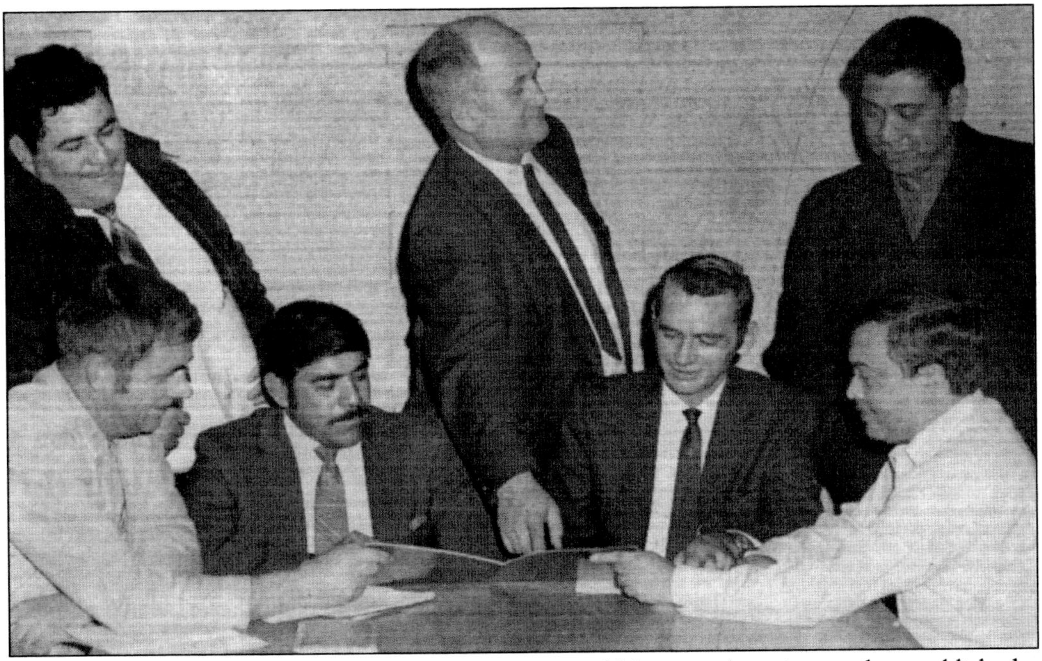

In this photograph from the early 1970s are a group of Mexican Americans who established a corporation, Quincy United Enterprises, to build institutional furniture. The venture was to raise capital, build a facility, and train and employ ex-migrant workers. Pictured from left to right are (first row, seated) Bill Smith, Hank Agripino, Henry Fonda, and Andy Martinez; (second row, standing) Armando Castro, Peter Boyle, and Narciso Medrano. In the bottom picture, a group of Chicanos attend an adult basic education course at the home of activist and teacher Carmen Taylor of Quincy. (Courtesy *Wenatchee World*.)

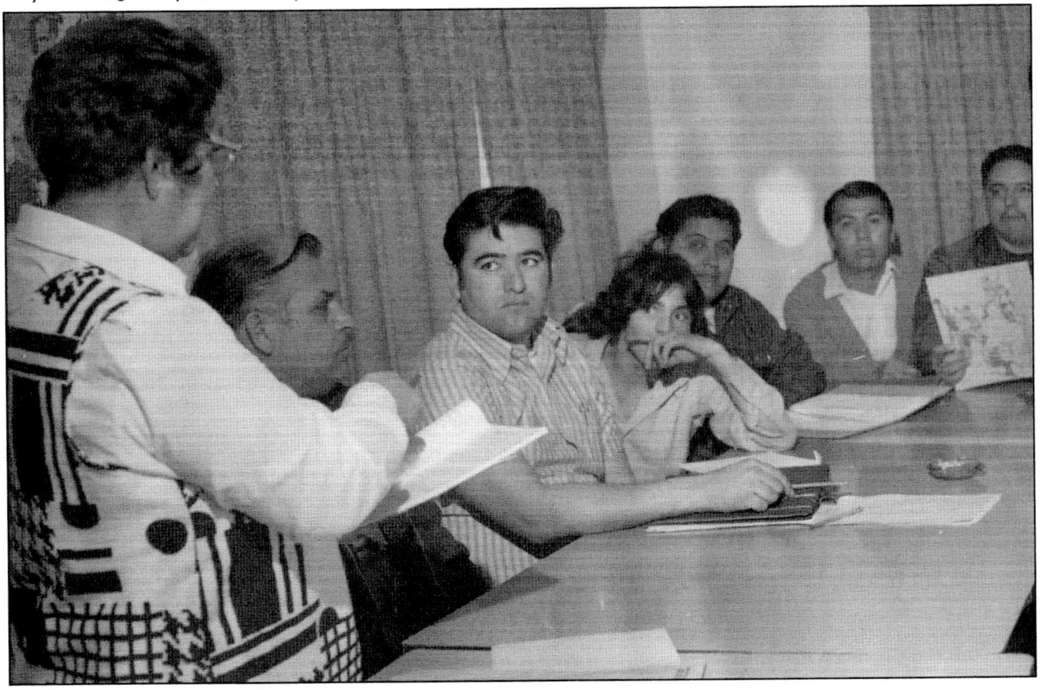

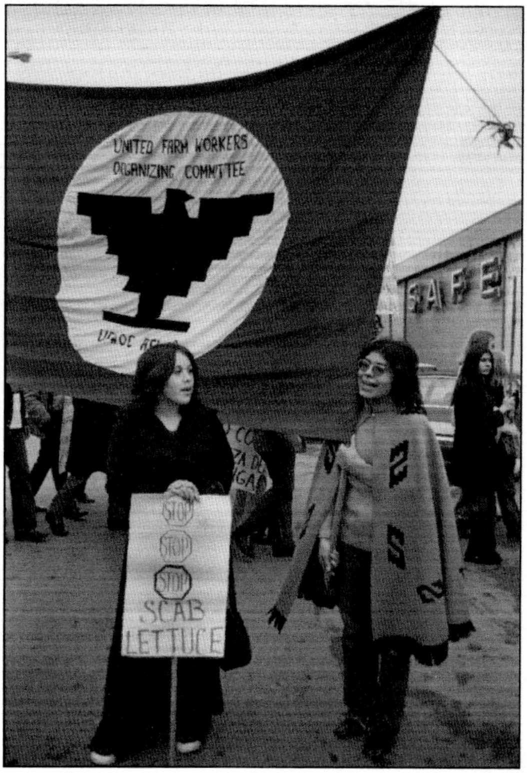

The early social activism of NCW was impacted by the farm labor organizing occurring in neighboring regions, counties, and communities. By the time the United Farm Workers brought their boycott of California lettuce to Washington, Mexican American labor organizers were in the formative years of organizing the state's farm labor. In these two photographs, Chicanas are picketing Safeway stores. Groups of Chicanos from NCW also picketed local Safeway stores in Ephrata and Moses Lake. (Courtesy Washington State University.)

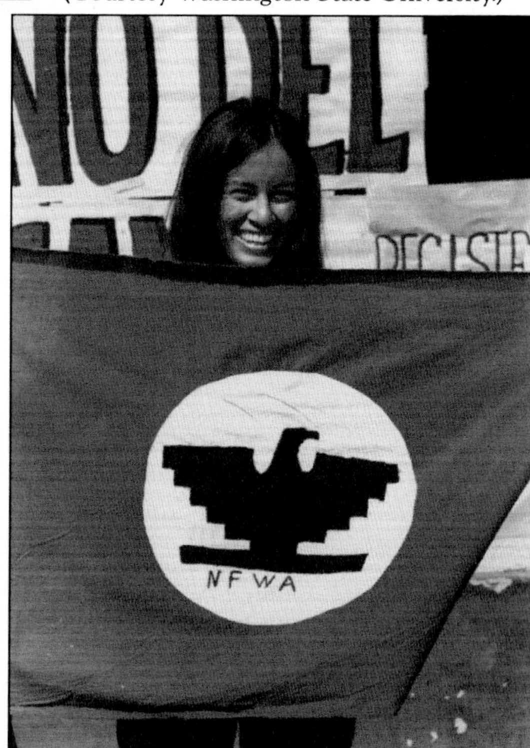

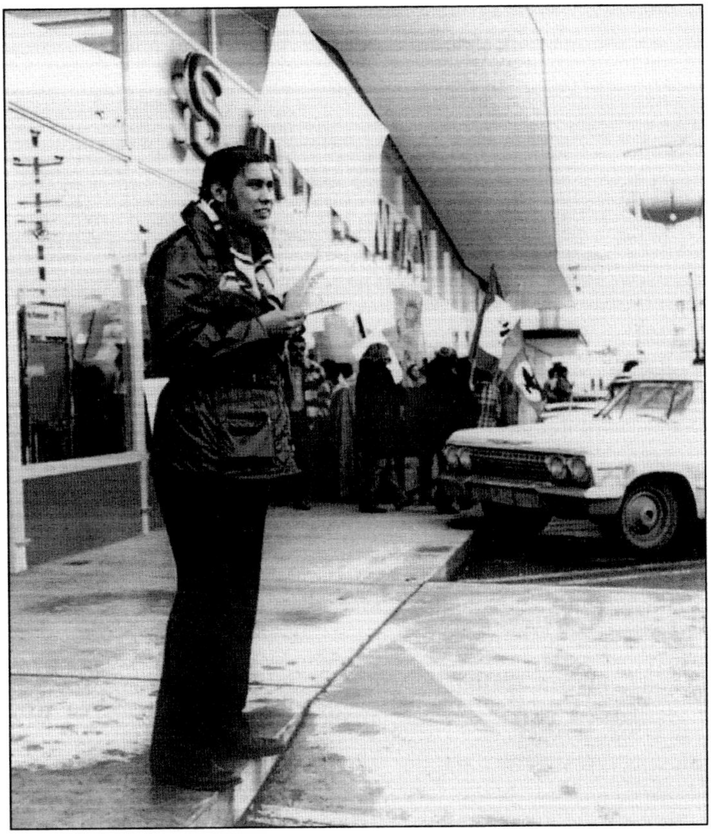

An impact of the Chicano movement of the 1960s and 1970s on the state of Washington was the development of community leaders and activists. Pictured in the top image is Ricardo Garcia from the Yakima Valley, whose activism would expand throughout the region. Here he is seen participating in the picket of Safeway stores. Ricardo's activism reached NCW by the development and expansion of his radio station and network emanating from Granger, Washington. The four women in the bottom photograph are laborers on strike at a local hops farm. These ladies are proof of the activism emerging from the Mexican American community. (Courtesy Washington State University.)

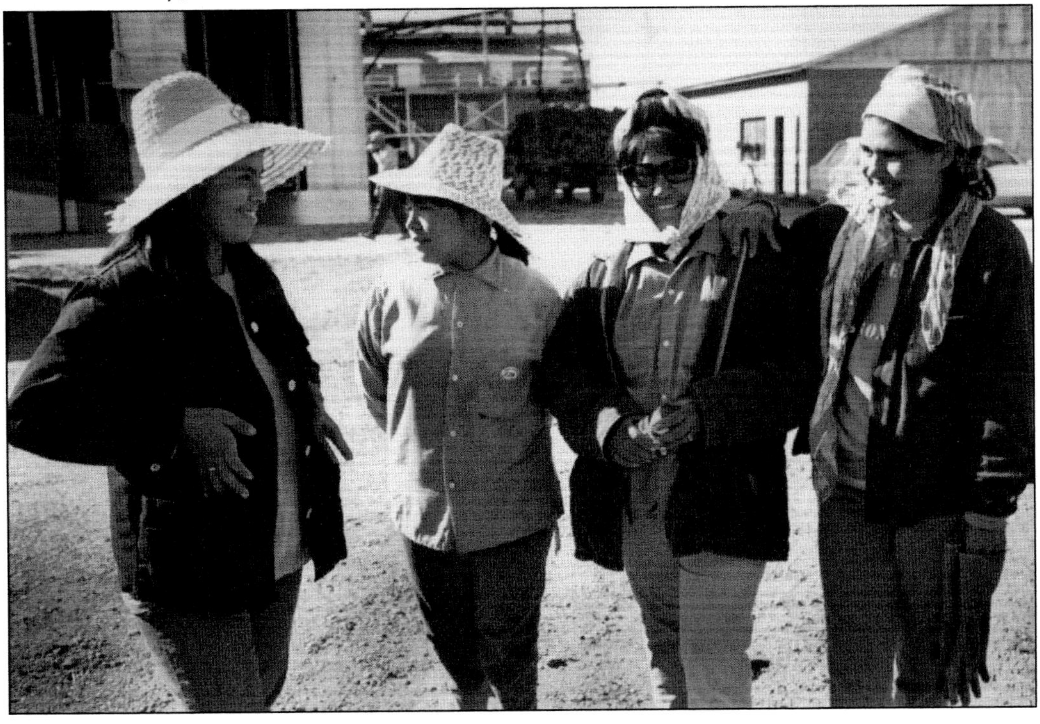

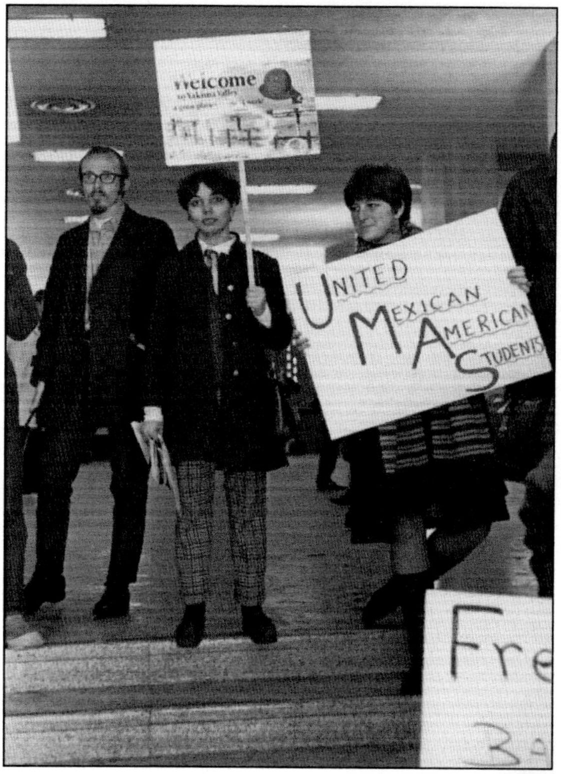

By the late 1960s and early 1970s, Chicanas and Chicanos began attending various institutions of higher education in Washington. Many of these students were from such places as Quincy, Moses Lake, Othello, and Warden. As they entered such schools as the University of Washington, they joined social and political organizations that empowered them and their communities. In these two photographs taken in the late 1960s at the University of Washington, Chicanas are shown holding signs addressing the concerns of the farm worker. These Chicanas will eventually become the leaders of their communities and advocates for strong social change throughout the state. (Courtesy Washington State University.)

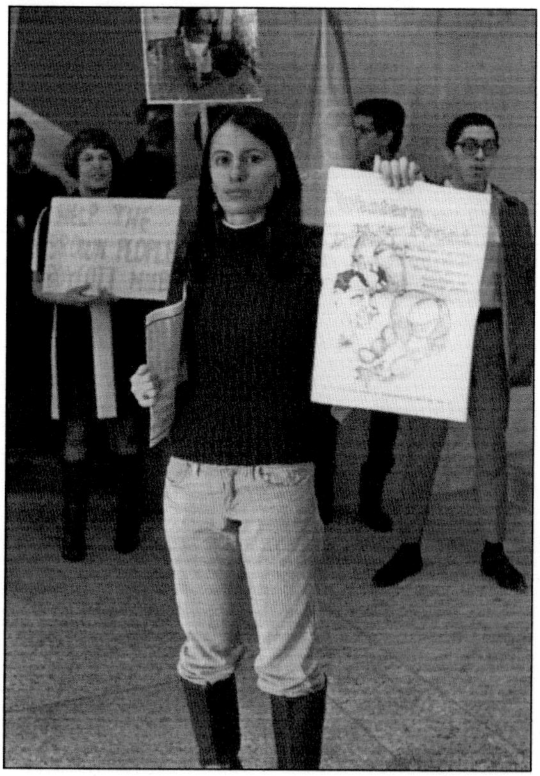

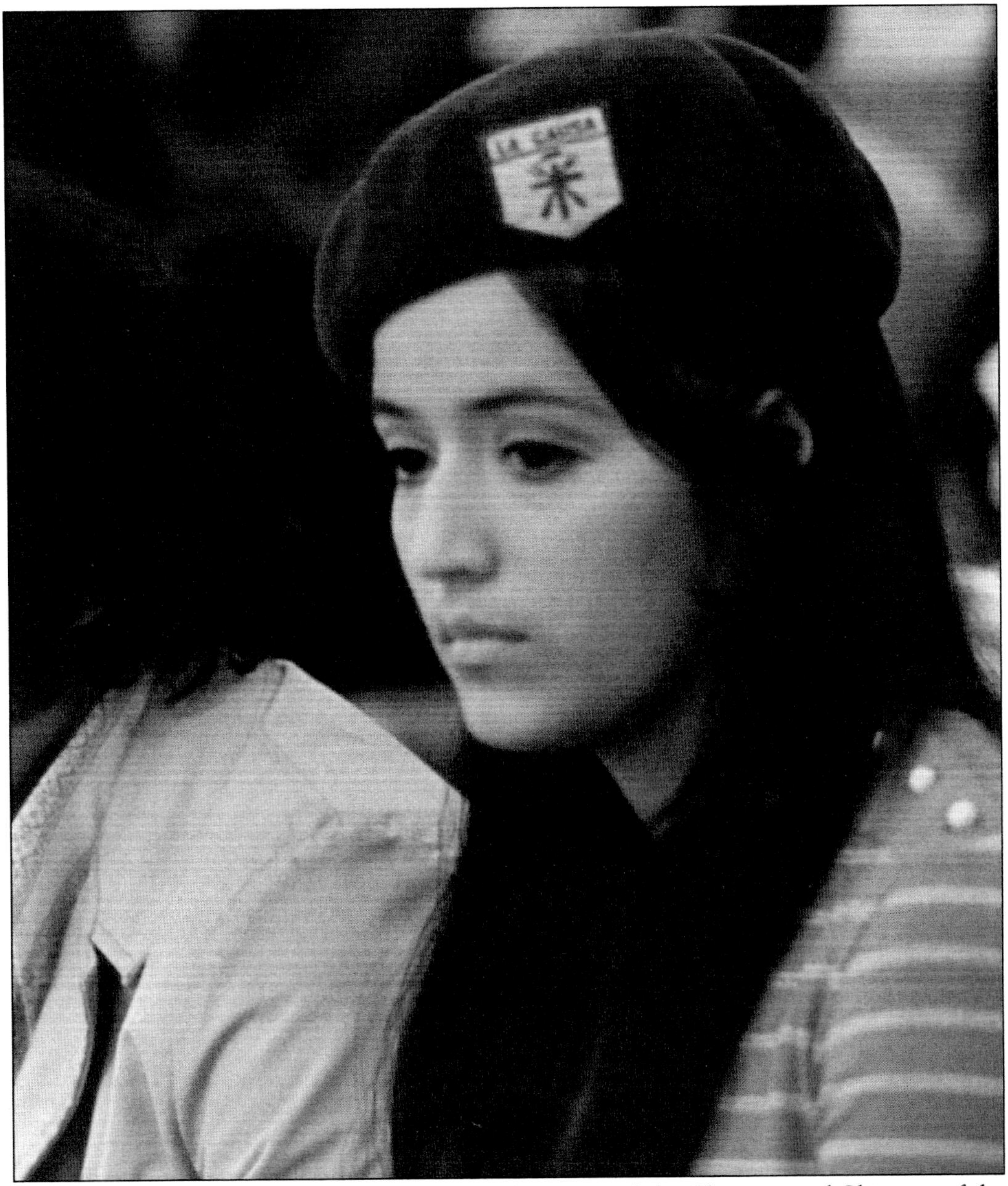

The 1960s represented a sharp departure from the past, and the Chicanas and Chicanos of the 1960s were determined to change their treatment by any means necessary. Washington had one the strongest movements throughout the United States, and many of the photographs depicted in this section illustrate the contributions of Chicanas and Chicanos to the overall Chicano movement and its impact on NCW. One of the strongest groups to advocate real change was the Brown Berets of Washington. The organization stood for direct action but was misunderstood by the Anglo community, who saw them as a militant organization. Areas of the Columbia Basin, such as the Tri-Cities, had a contingent of Brown Berets. The presence of Brown Berets in NCW helped bring change to various communities. Brown Berets participated socially and politically at many levels. In this photograph from the early 1970s is a Brown Beret attending a legislative session in Olympia, Washington. (Courtesy Washington State University.)

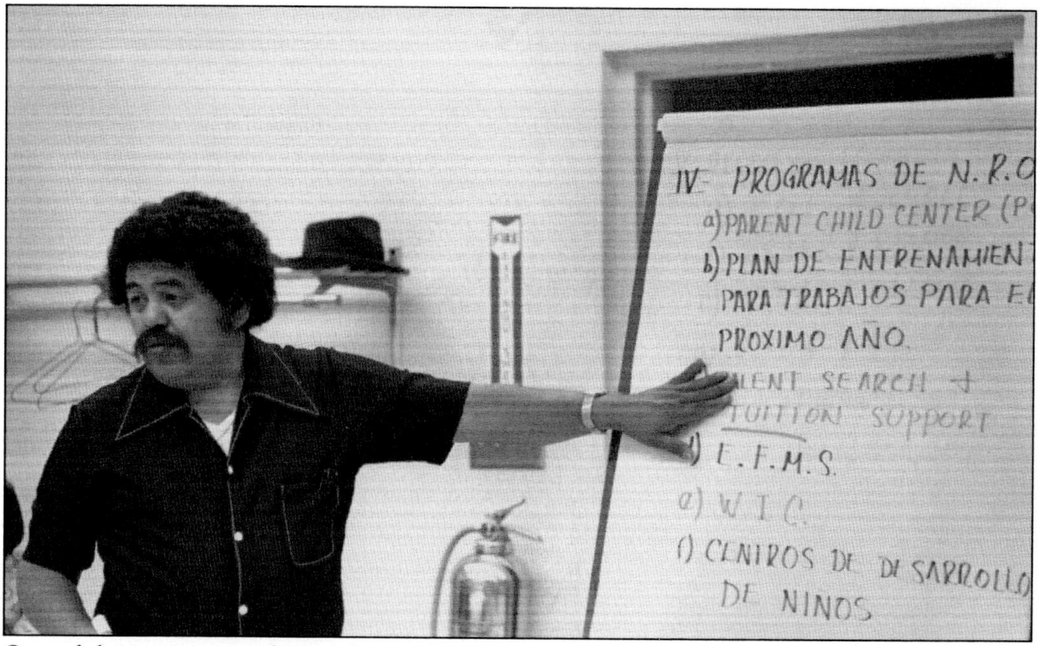

One of the strongest and most far-reaching social grassroots organizations was the Northwest Rural Opportunities. Established in the late 1960s as part of the war on poverty, the NRO had offices throughout NCW. The primary objective of this organization was to provide services to the migrant community and offer leadership workshops for self-empowerment. Because of its impact and leadership, which included Andy Martinez from Quincy and his brother Sam, from the Yakima Valley, the NRO also acquired a strong political orientation and voice for the Mexican American community. These two photographs show NRO officials and workers attending a workshop on the organizations needs and objectives. (Courtesy Washington State University.)

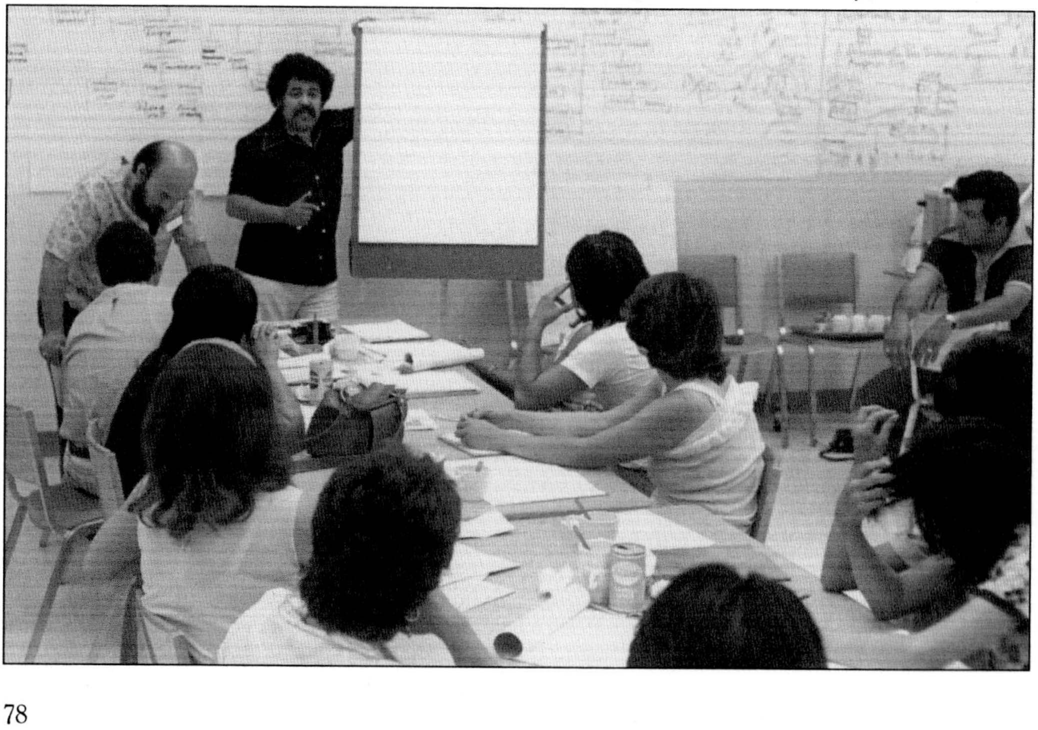

As organizations and groups expanded throughout NCW, individuals from local communities began to voice their concerns regarding the direction and needs of the community. Many meetings were held throughout the region to try to determine the needs, and often groups and individuals had to have intense discussions to settle on commonalities and objectives. These two photographs are of the same meeting being sponsored by the NRO in Quincy, Washington. Pictured at right and making an important point is Alicia Saenz and at the bottom are representatives of the NRO, Sam Martinez (left) and Manuel Guerrero. (Courtesy Washington State University.)

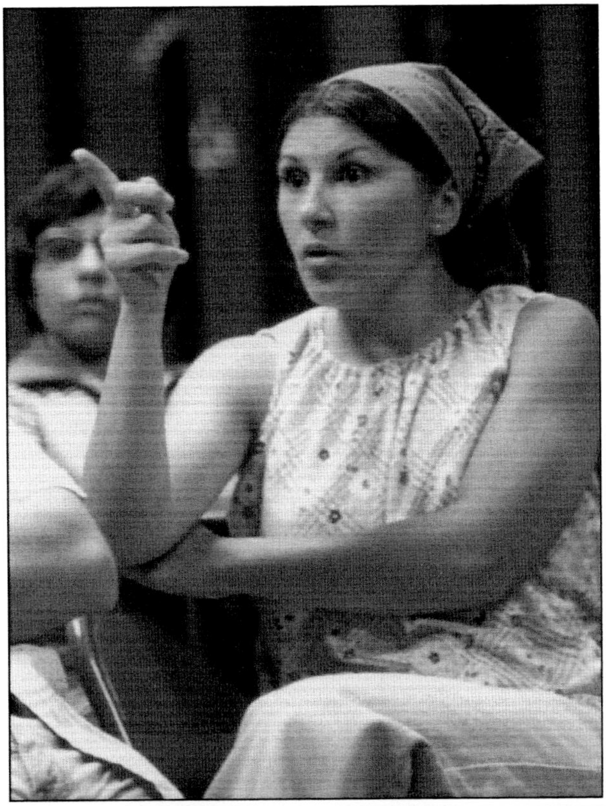

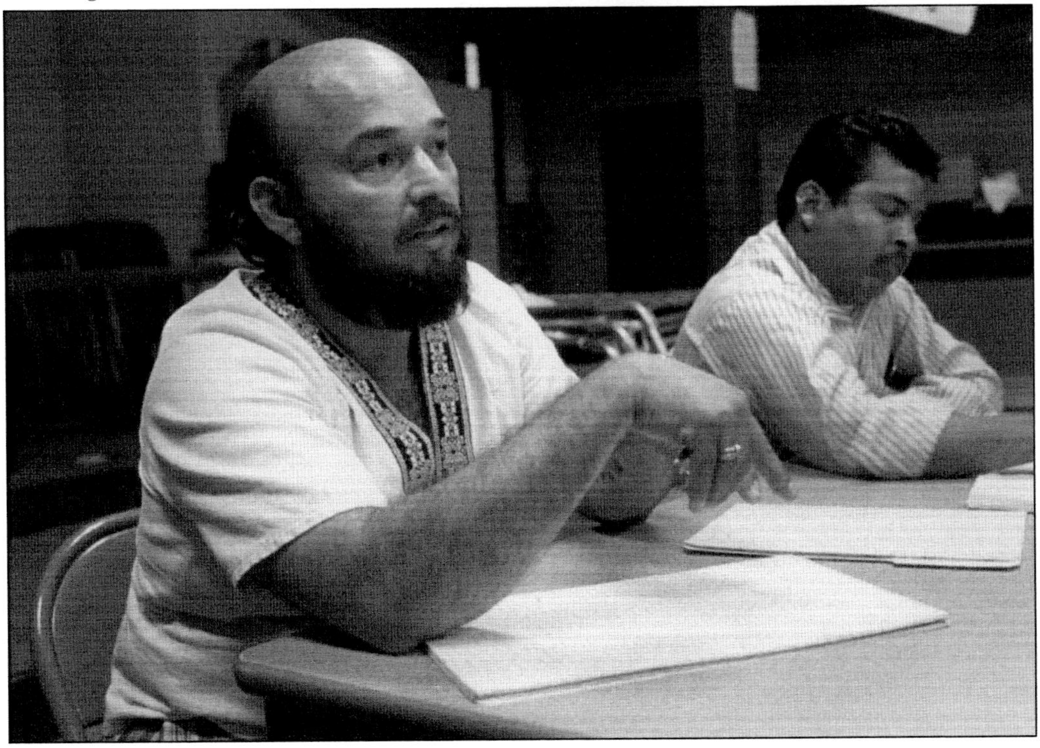

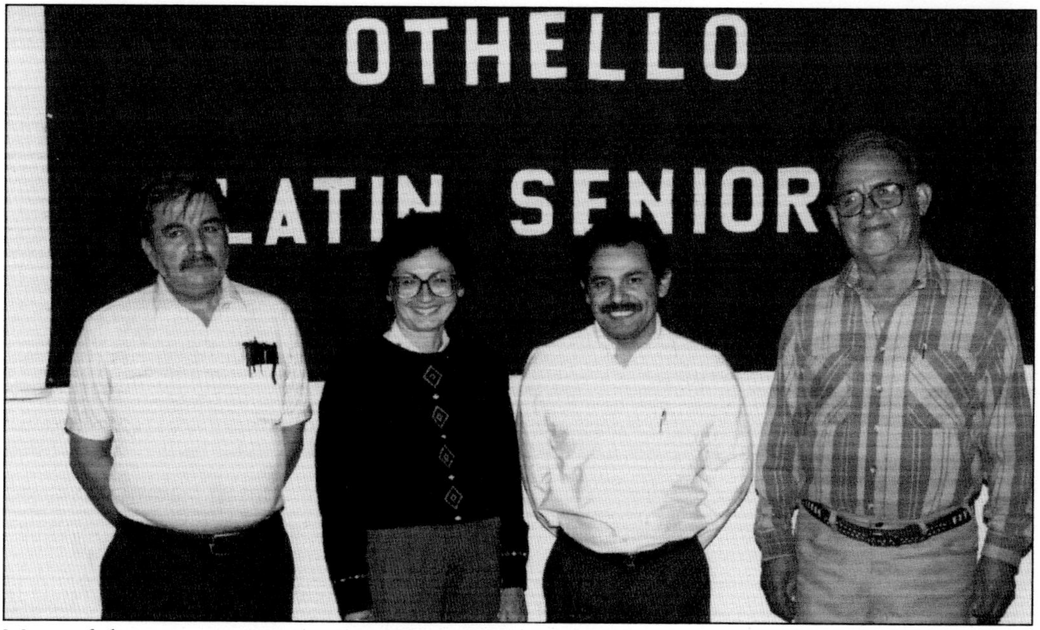

Many of the organizations developed throughout NCW during its formative years were able to sustain themselves through the turbulent years of the late 1960s and 1970s. One such organization was the Othello Latin Seniors, who have a long history in the community. In the top photograph is some of the leadership of Othello's Latino Seniors organization. At the far left is Art Borunda and far right is Luis Garcia. The two individuals in the middle are unidentified. One of the greatest concerns has been the need for affordable housing or, in some cases, simply housing, for farm laborers. In the second photograph, taken in the late 1990s, two children sleep and wait in a makeshift camp while their parents are working near Quincy. (Above, courtesy *El Mundo*; below, courtesy Jerry Garcia.)

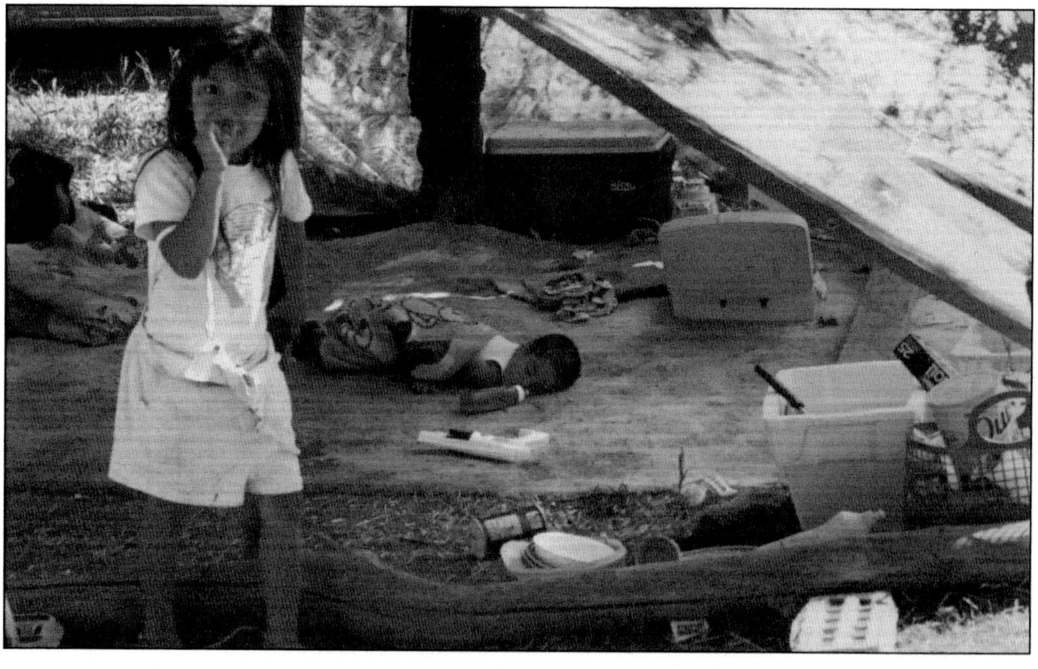

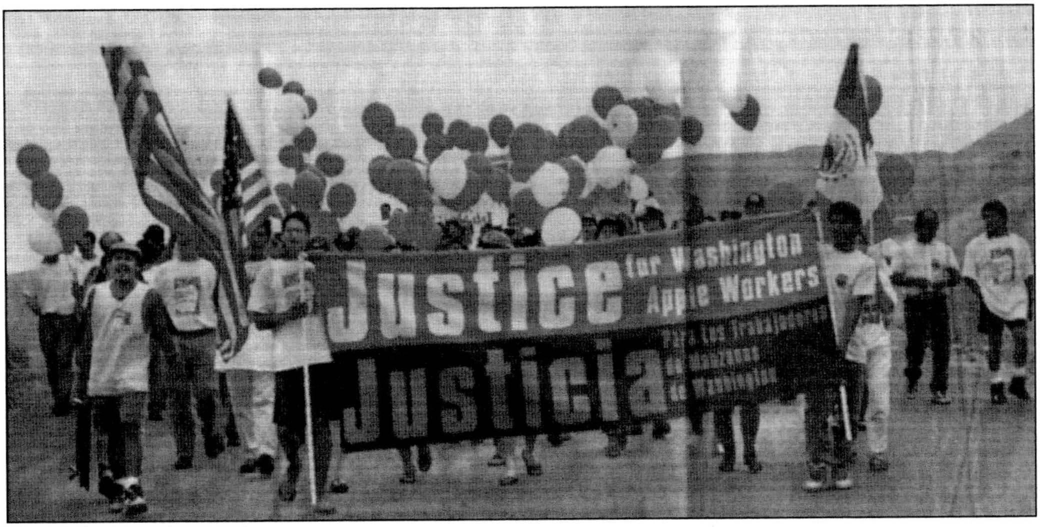

By the late 1990s, NCW was experiencing a new wave of social activism. This was spurred by an increase in the Mexican population, maltreatment and conditions in the agriculture industry, and a new awareness of social responsibility. Although labor organizing has been present in Washington for over 100 years, it has been only in the late 20th century that unions have attempted organizing agriculture laborers. More surprising was the attempt by the teamsters to organize the laborers in the apple industry in Wenatchee. This campaign lasted for several years in Wenatchee with the community being divided on the issue. These two images depict the activism on part of supporters for the unionization of Stemilt workers in Wenatchee. (Above, courtesy Jerry Garcia; below, courtesy *Wenatchee World*.)

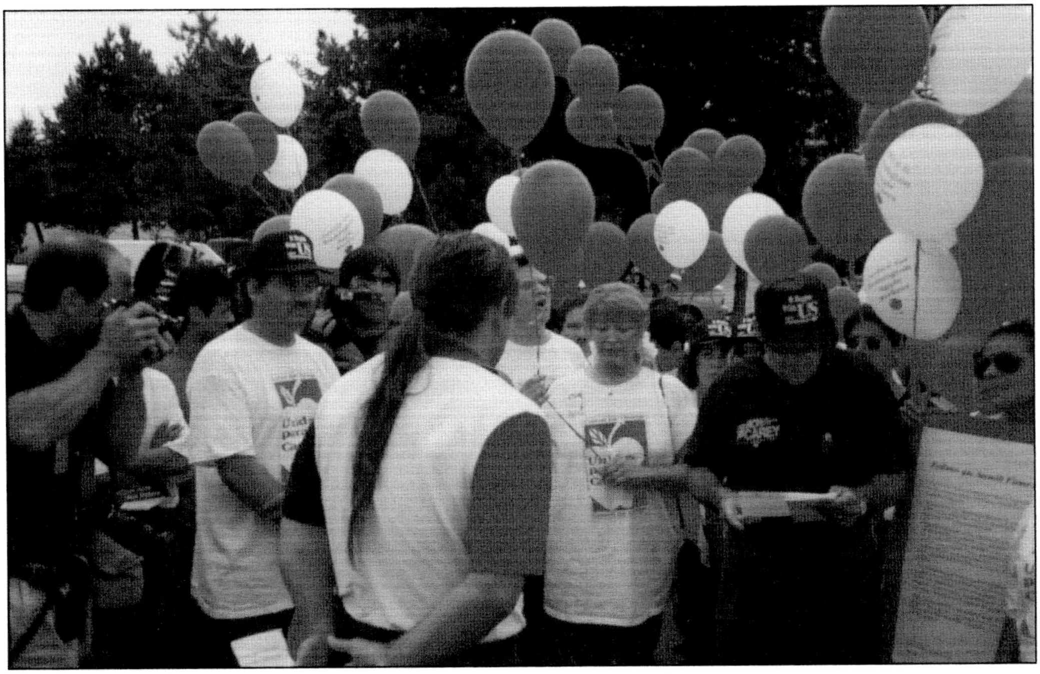

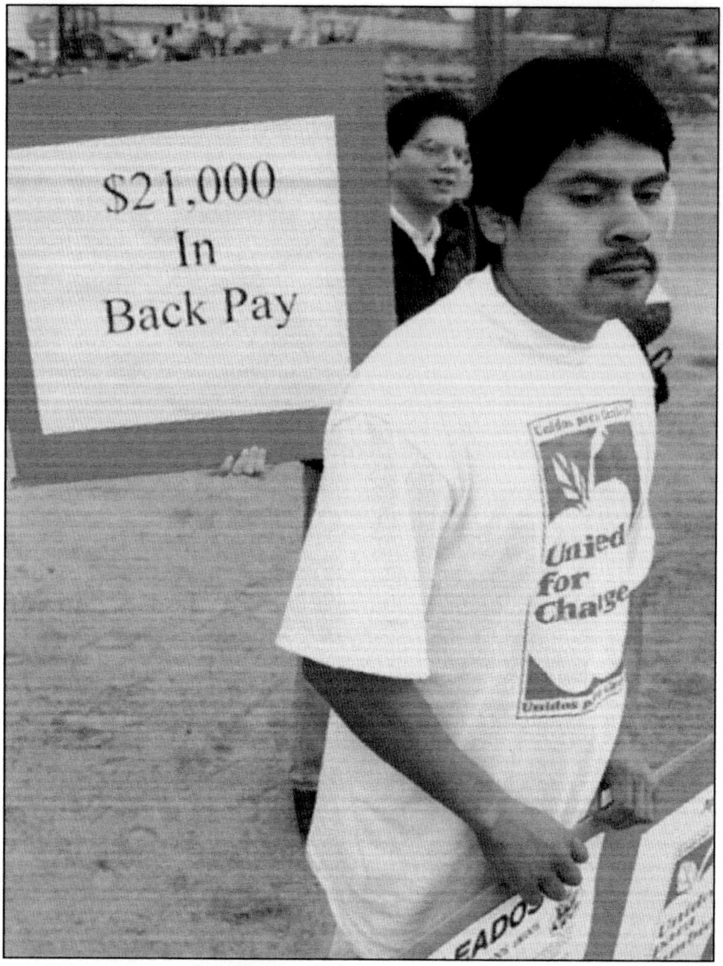

The attempt by workers at Stemilt Growers in Wenatchee was probably instigated when the company unfairly fired a number of Mexicans workers for their activism. Some workers also felt that a union could benefit them economically and support such efforts. However, it should be noted not all workers supported these efforts for unionization. Furthermore, it was inevitable that immigration became an issue that was tied to the apple industry and union efforts. The photograph at left shows workers picketing Stemilt Growers and asking for back pay for some of its workers. The bottom image is of the same union campaign, but clearly other issues such as immigration had come to the forefront as well. (Courtesy *Wenatchee World*.)

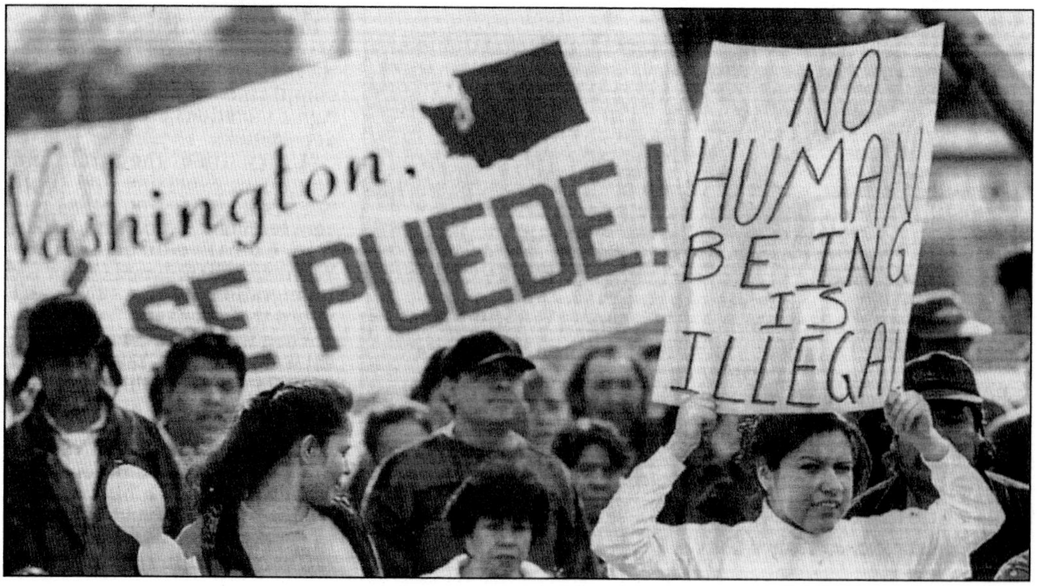

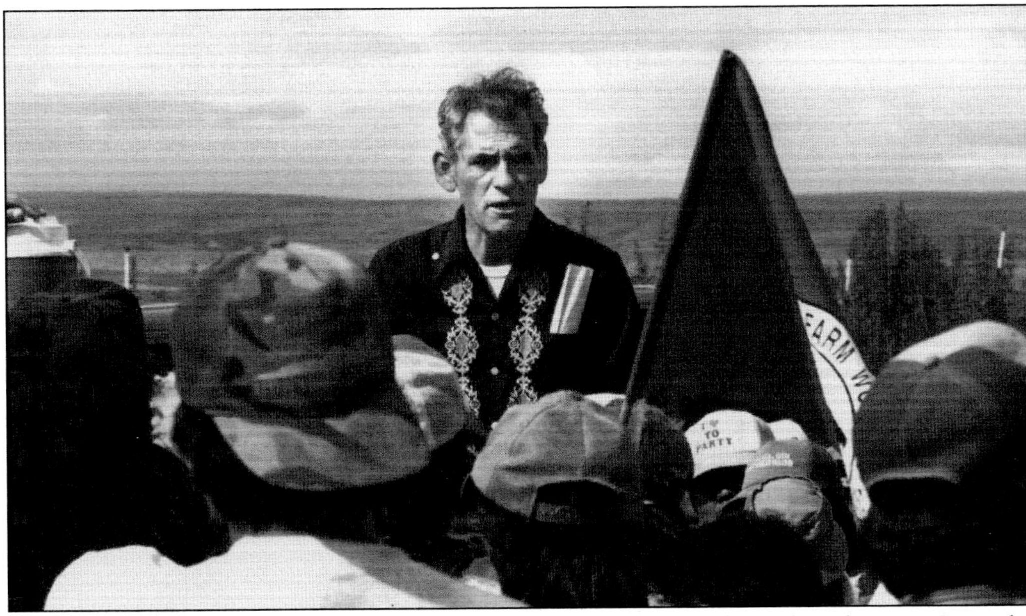

With a long history of farm laborers in NCW, the United Farm Workers of Washington State also made attempts to unionize farm laborers in the region and were successful. The top photograph shows Tomas Villanueva, president of the United Farm Workers of Washington State, talking to a group of workers in the Wenatchee area. The bottom photograph shows another Farm Worker organizer talking to farm laborers in the Wenatchee Valley. The political economy of the agriculture industry of NCW makes the labor force a prime target for unions as well as allies to the growers, who advocate for their immigration status in order to benefit from their labor. In the final analysis, agriculture laborers in NCW are in a difficult and unusual position. (Courtesy *Wenatchee World*.)

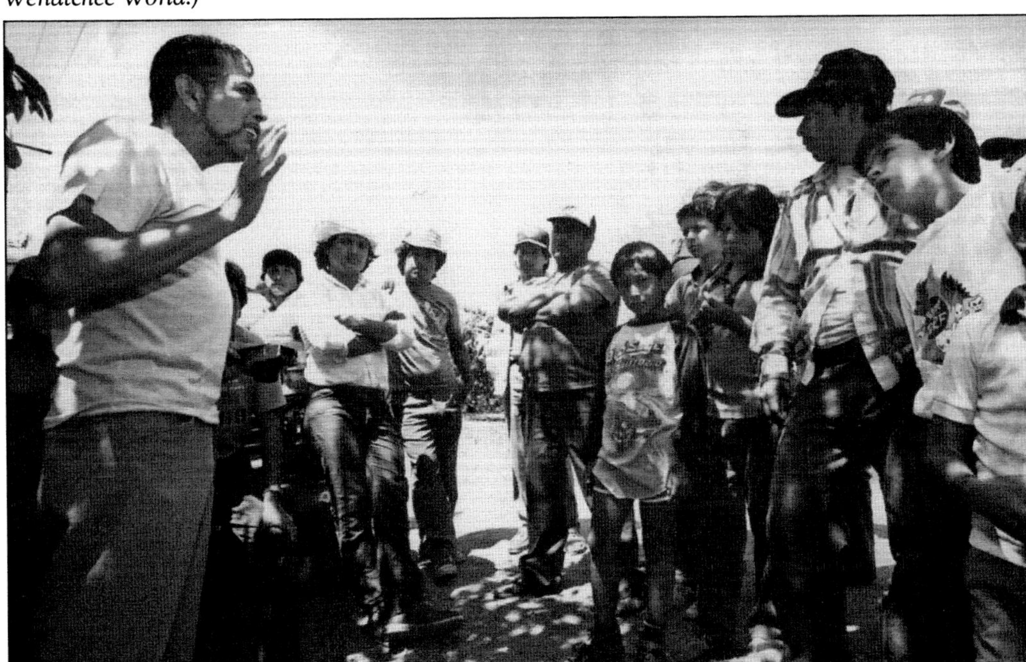

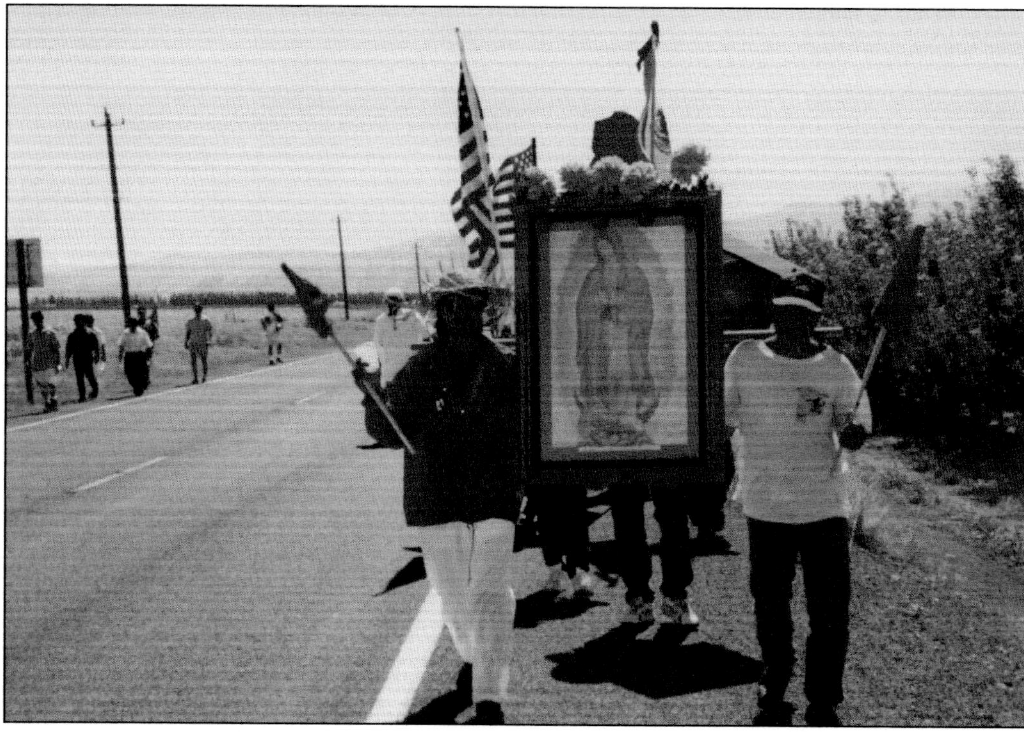

The United Farm Workers (UFW) in the late 1990s also helped organize Mexican laborers in Mattawa, Washington, located in Grant County. One of the many historical strategies dating back to Cesar Chavez's historic march on Sacramento is the pilgrimage. In these two photographs, Mexican laborers and their supporters march on Highway 243 in order to gain support. Besides the banners of Washington State, the UFW eagle, and the U.S. and state flags, two important images also appear. La Virgen de Guadalupe and the image of Cesar Chavez are prominently displayed. La Virgen brings unity, strength, and honor to the march, while Chavez's image provides inspiration and is a reminder of his sacrifice to the farm laborer. (Courtesy Jerry Garcia.)

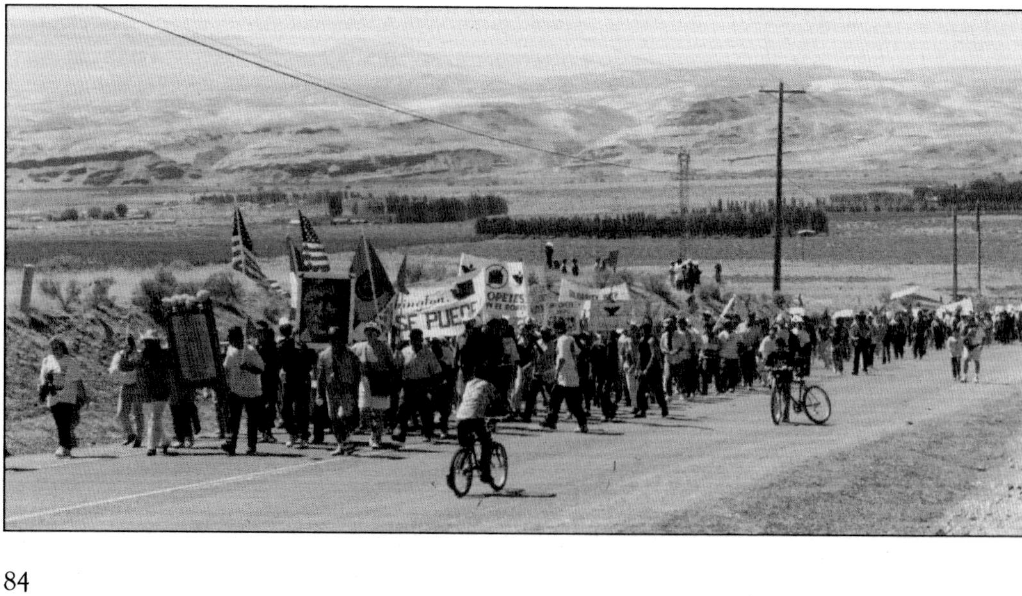

Seven

POLITICAL ACTIVISM

Politics in North Central Washington (NCW) has primarily been an Anglo affair until the very recent past. By and large, the political landscape has been in the control of a predominately Republican constituency and the landowning elite of the region. The Mexican population of the region, historically, has lacked a critical mass to challenge Anglo hegemony, but this is not to say that Mexicans have not been involved in politics. Elected officials of Mexican ancestry have been few, yet throughout their history in NCW, Mexican Americans have been involved in politics at the local, regional, and national levels. The emergence of political activism in the 1960s galvanized Mexican Americans throughout the country, including NCW.

The first signs of a changing political landscape and mentality in NCW emerged with organizations that had previously been socially oriented, such as the Latin American Associations, began to reorient towards political empowerment. Thus, the emergence of the Progressive League of United Mexican Americans in the late 1960s began to replace less active organizations. Other individuals, organizations, and agencies also appear to lend a political voice to the Mexican American population. Throughout NCW, community action programs appeared in the 1960s and 1970s. The Northwest Rural Opportunities Program (NRO) developed out of similar circumstances. Although a federally and state funded program, this organization developed chapters throughout the NCW and was primarily administered by Mexican Americans. Its main objectives were to provide social and health services to the migrant community, but its nature provided a political voice for its constituency. During this era, many Mexican communities throughout NCW held voter registration drives in an attempt to mobilize the community for political participation and empowerment.

By the 1970s, many communities in NCW had a Mexican population of at least 10 percent. Some communities saw a lack of political representation as a community issue and appointed Mexican Americans to city councils. Quincy and Othello are excellent examples. The photographs in this section illustrate the political activism of the Mexican community.

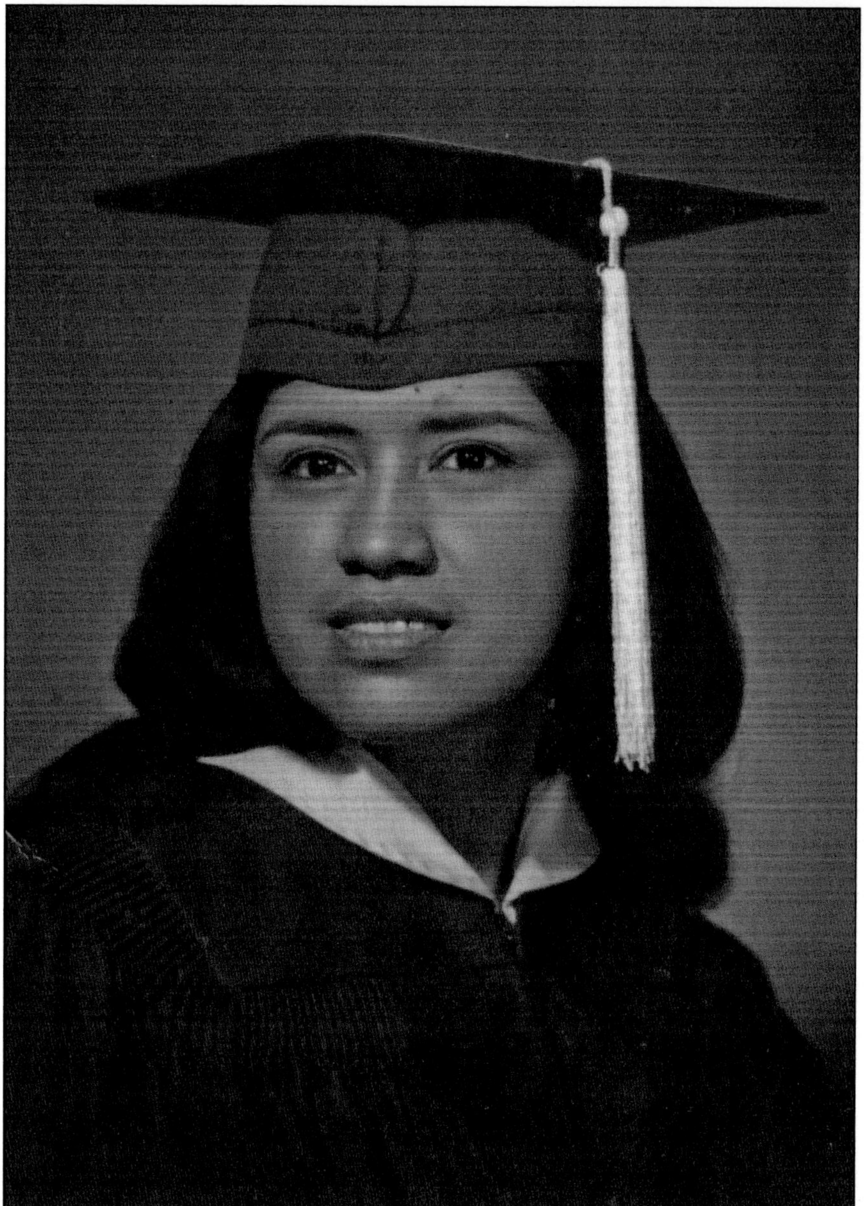

Born in Texas but raised in NCW, Dora Sanchez Treviño is an eyewitness to the expansion and development of the Mexican community in the region. As a minority in the Columbia Basin, she experienced isolation and marginalization. She worked the fields and packing sheds and witnessed the mistreatment of the labor force. As a woman, she has also felt the effects of gender bias in and out of her own ethnic group. Dora also recognized that an education was the ticket out of the fields and to greater empowerment. Over the past 30 years, she has worked as a teacher's aide and as an employee for a government agency. She is an excellent lens to see this evolution. From her story, there is a glimpse at the race relations in NCW, the traditional patriarchal structure of her Mexican upbringing, her involvement with various social and political organizations, and her involvement with state politics. The photograph is Dora's high school graduation picture from 1963. (Courtesy Dora Treviño.)

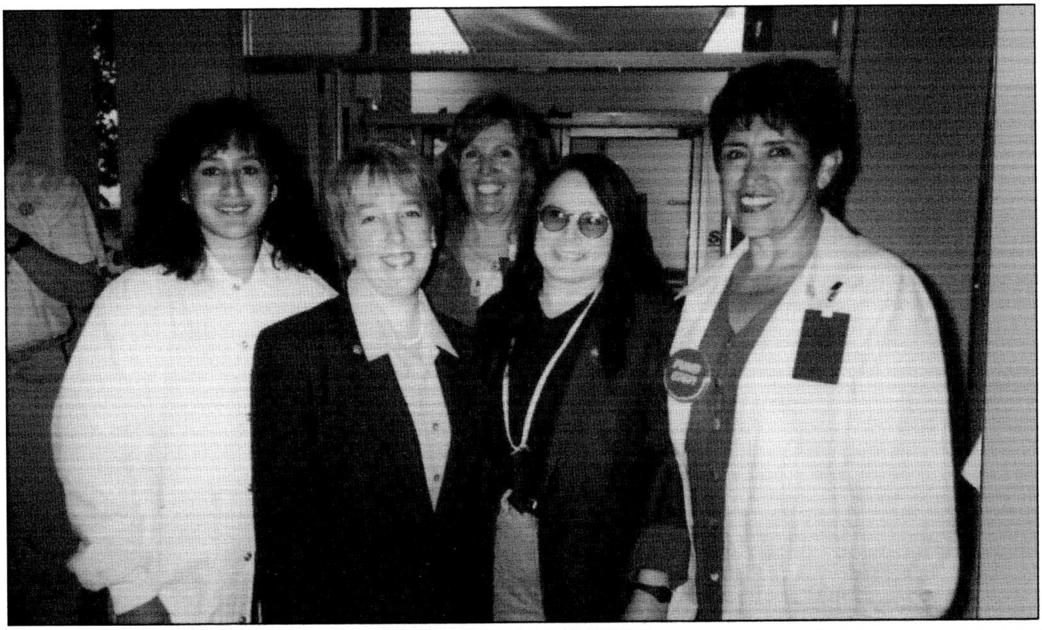

These images portray Dora and other Chicanas from NCW involved at the highest levels of state and national politics. Dora, pictured on the far right in both photographs, has been involved with the Washington State Democratic Party since the 1970s and has advocated for the Latino community as a whole regarding educational issues and basic services; she has recently been involved with addressing the issue of youth violence in the community. In the top photograph from left to right are Veronica Gottchalk, U.S. Sen. Patty Murray, Cheri Garrett, Chevy Zarate, and Dora Sanchez Treviño in Spokane in 1998. At right are, from left to right, Cheri Garrett, Washington state governor Gary Locke, and Dora Sanchez Treviño at the Washington State Democratic Convention in 1998. (Courtesy Dora Treviño.)

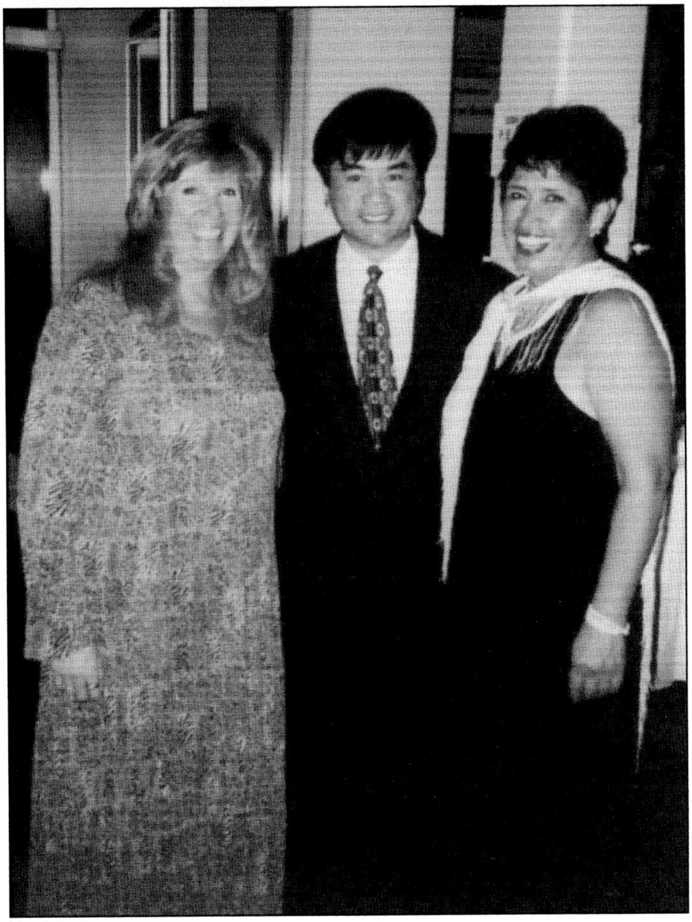

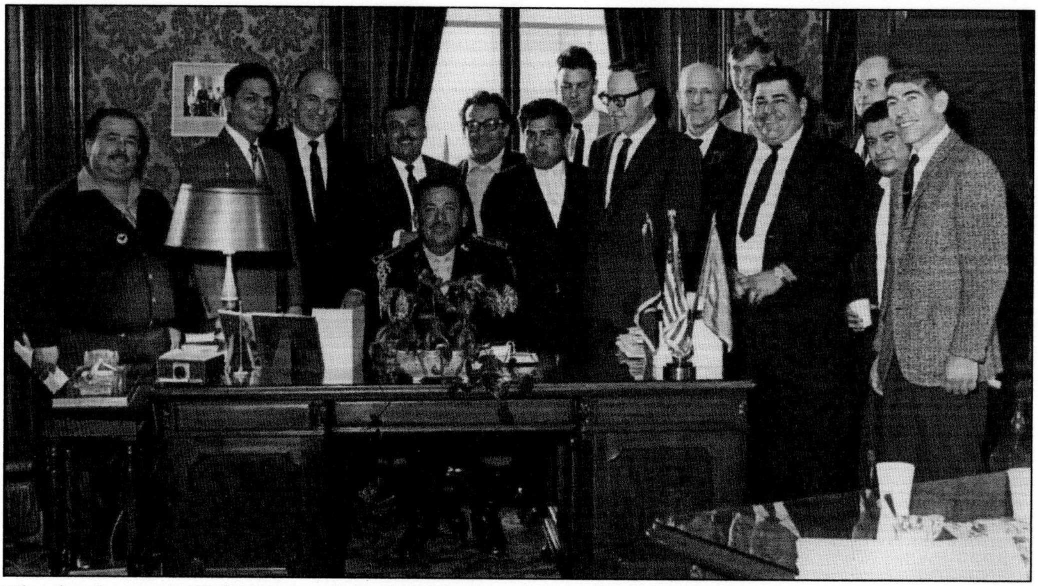

The development of PLUMA is directly related to the emergence of progressive politics in the region. The early organizations were important regarding their impact on such communities as Quincy, Othello, and Moses Lake. However, as Chicanos became more involved in their communities, their political orientation became more about empowerment, rather than accommodation. PLUMA represents this change for the region, and in these photographs, they are shown visiting the state legislature in Olympia, Washington. The top photograph is PLUMA with Mexico's military attaché seated in the chair. The bottom photograph is part of the group in the rotunda of the capital. Other known members in both pictures are Armando Castro, Manuel Guerrero, Andy Martinez, Mayo Castro, Refugio Martinez, and Roberto Treviño. Although these pictures are exclusively of male members, women were also part of PLUMA. Female members included Dora Sanchez Treviño, Jovita Valdez, and May Gonzales. (Courtesy Jerry Garcia.)

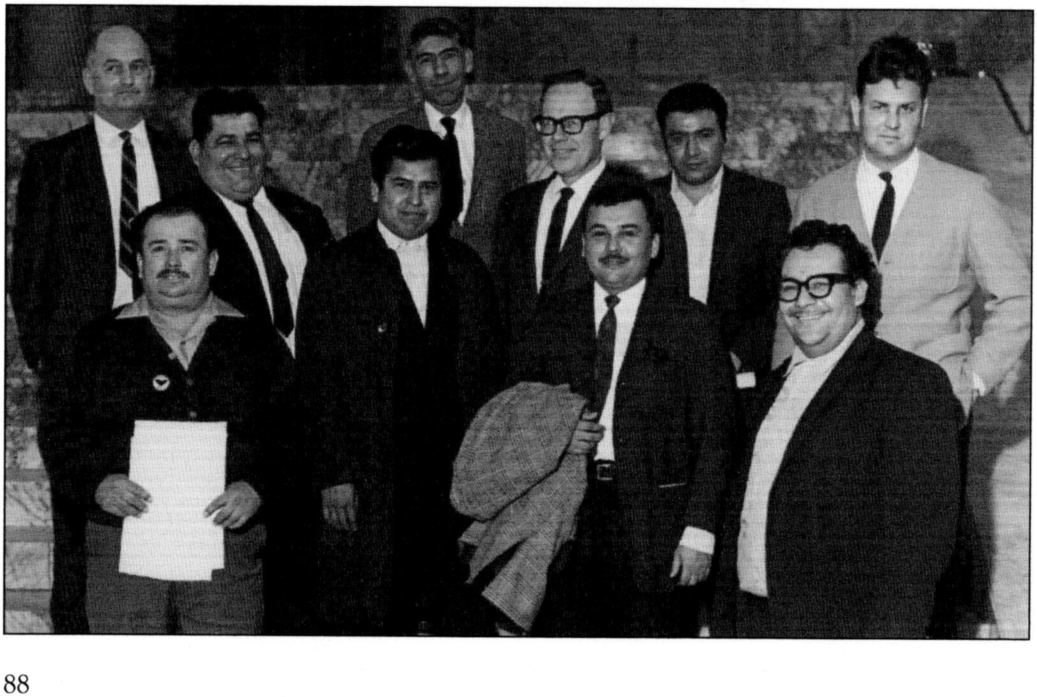

By the early 1970s, Andy Martinez had been impacted and changed by the *El Movimiento* or Chicano movement. Similar to other Chicanos and Chicanas of the period, he saw limited progress working within the mainstream political structure. Andy followed Democratic Party politics and immersed himself in the war on poverty programs in the 1960s. Yet Andy realized that Chicanos had to take control of their destiny and not rely on others for change. In 1972, Andy became a member of La Raza Unida Party, a third-party ticket for Chicanos in the United States. He was also selected as Washington state's delegate to the national convention held in El Paso, Texas, in 1972. The top photograph shows Andy (right) with Rodolfo "Corky" Gonzales, the founder of the Crusade for Justice and one of the leaders of the new party. The bottom photograph depicts Andy (left) with Reies Lopes Tijerina, the founder of the Alianza from New Mexico. Both photographs were taken in 1972 at the national convention. (Courtesy Jerry Garcia.)

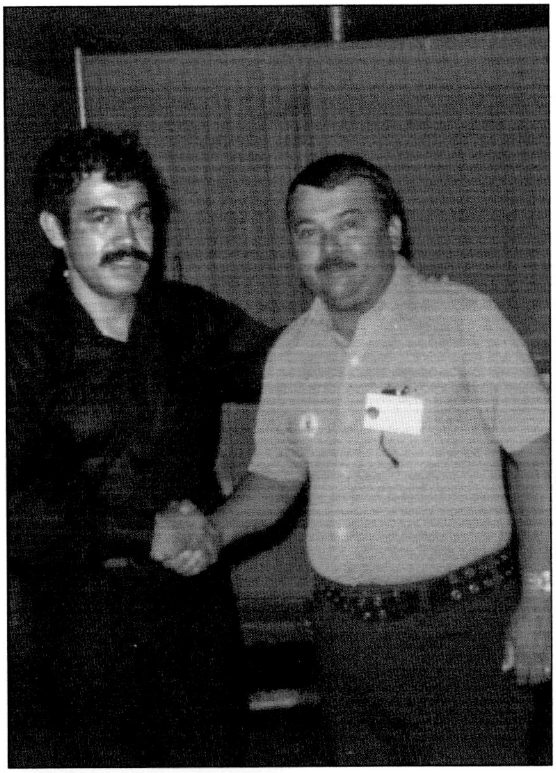

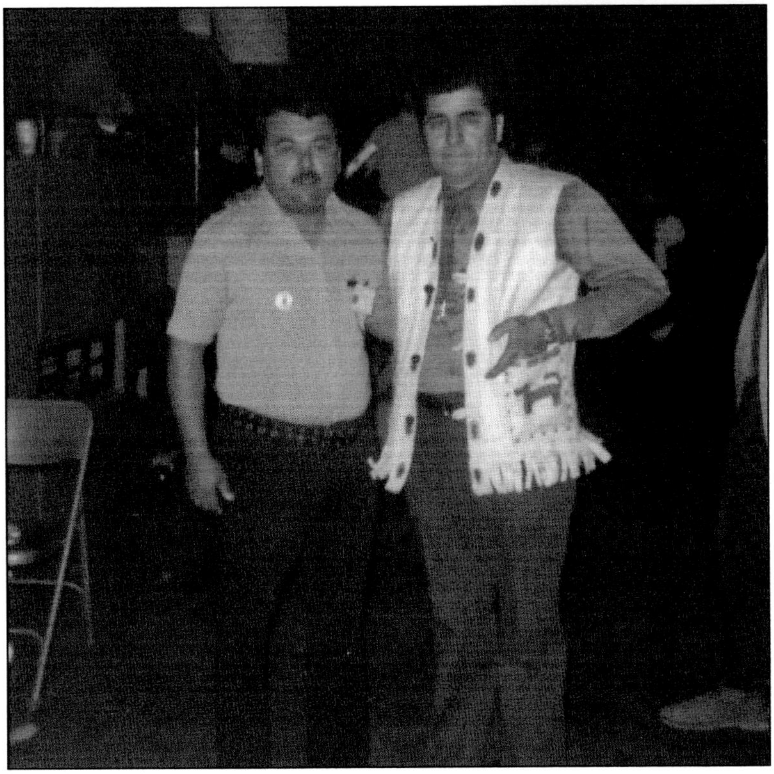

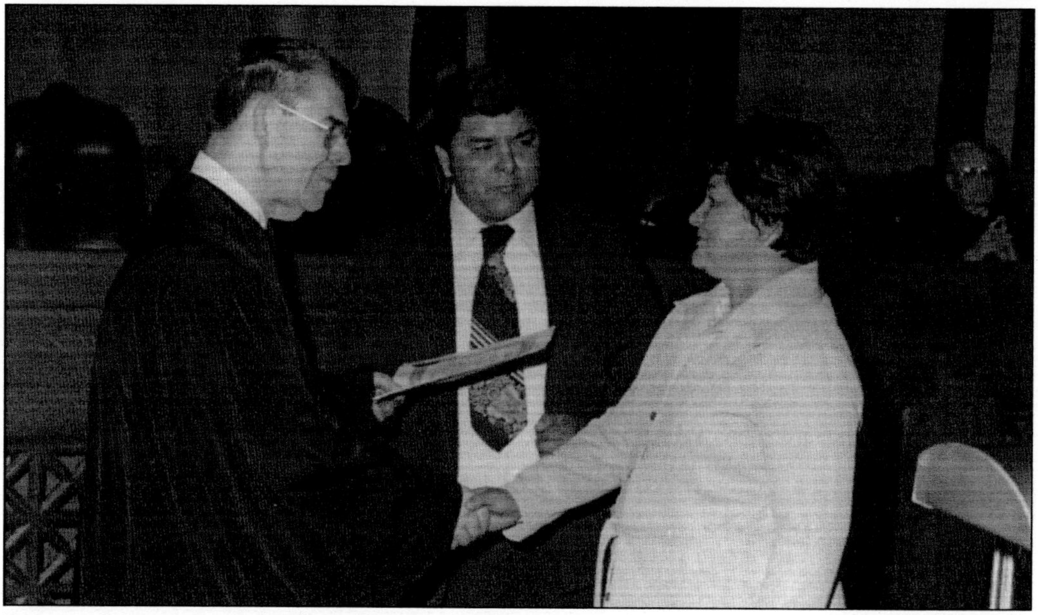

Prior to the existence of today's Washington State Commission on Hispanic Affairs, there was the Washington Mexican American Federation (MAF). Established in the Yakima Valley in 1968, it had as its main concerns the issues facing the Mexican American worker. Unlike western Washington, the eastern side of the state has been dominated by individuals of Mexican ancestry, which explains the focus on Mexican issues within the MAF. The initial organization of the MAF was divided into five areas: Puget Sound, Moses Lake, Tri-Cities, Bellingham-Lynden, and the Yakima Valley. In 1971, through an executive order of the governor, MAF became the Washington State Commission on Hispanic Affairs. These two photographs depict some of the early commissioners being sworn in at Olympia in the 1970s. The mandate for today's commission is to improve public policy development and the delivery of government services to the Hispanic community in Washington. (Courtesy Washington State Archives.)

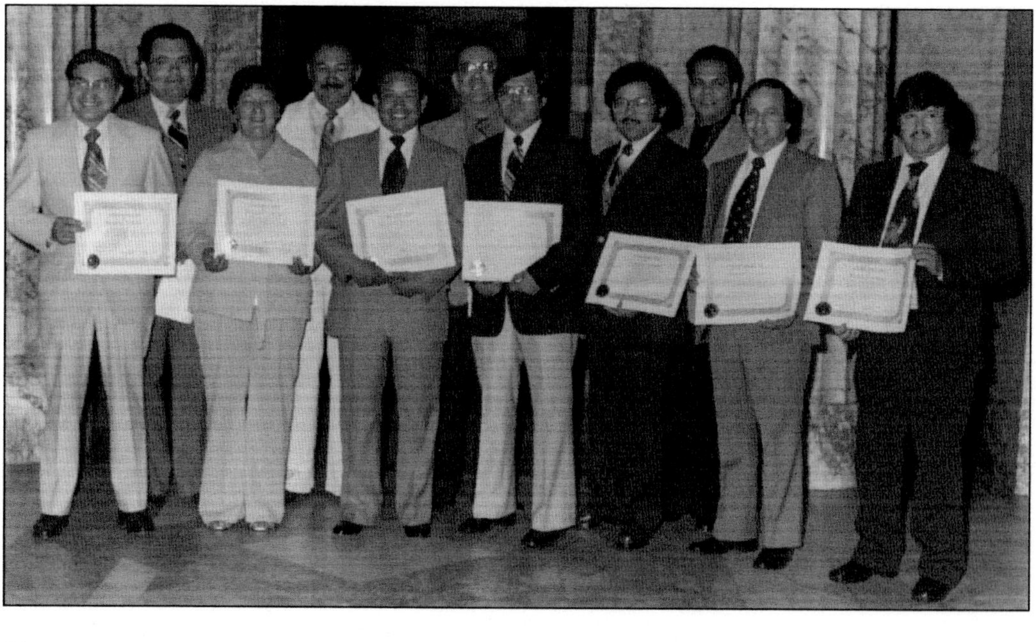

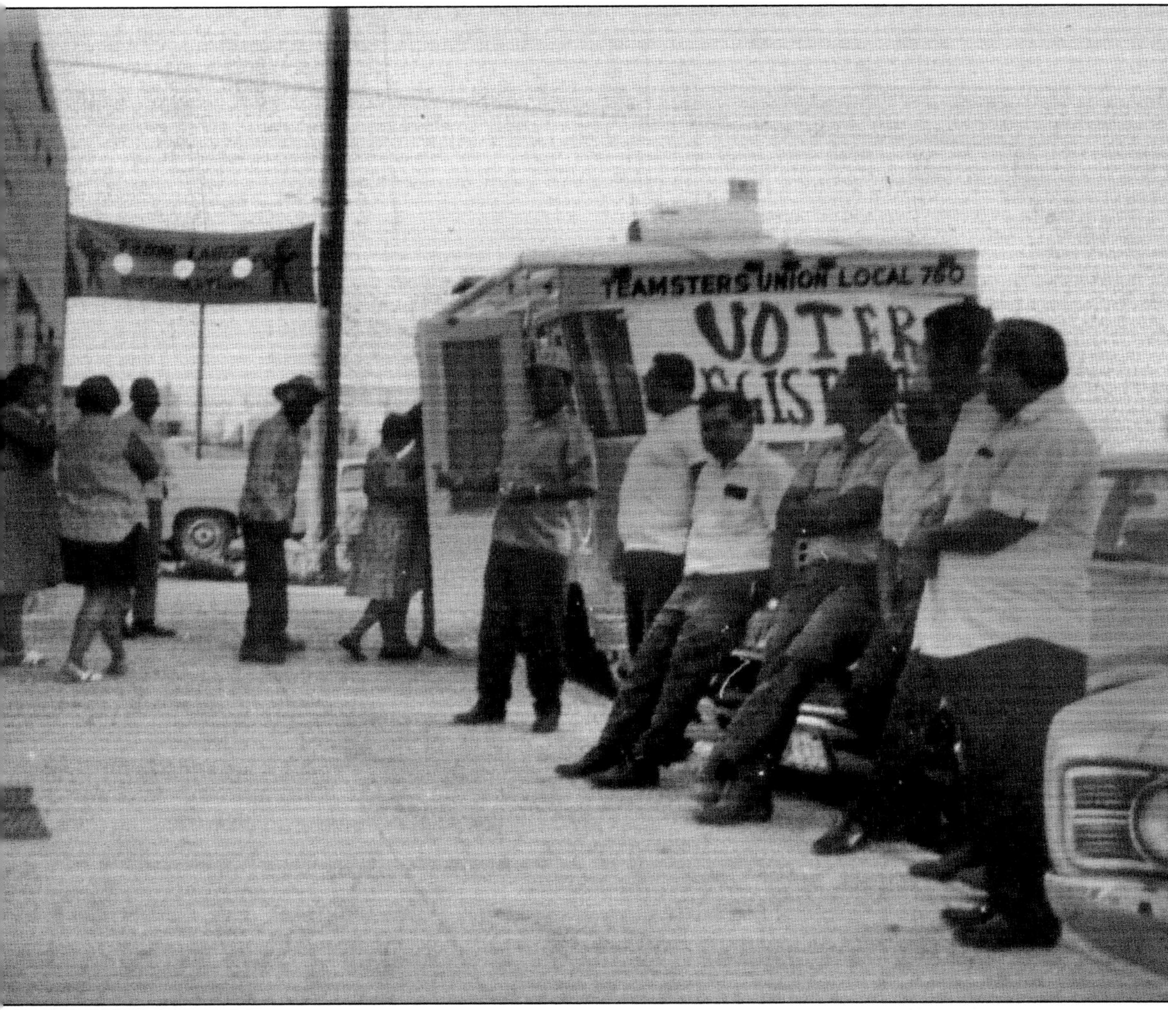

Various organizations organized voter registration drives throughout the Columbia Basin. PLUMA understood that political change would only occur if Mexican Americans were registered to vote. However, during the 1960s, strong efforts were made to register Chicanos with the hope of political empowerment. Many of the individuals from NCW agreed that Mexicans Americans lacked support from local and regional representatives. Furthermore, with communities with a substantial Mexican population, it was unheard of to have a Mexican American on the city council or local school board. Without a voice and representation, Mexican Americans would remain second-class citizens. This photograph taken in 1970 depicts a voter registration drive in Moses Lake. (Courtesy Jerry Garcia.)

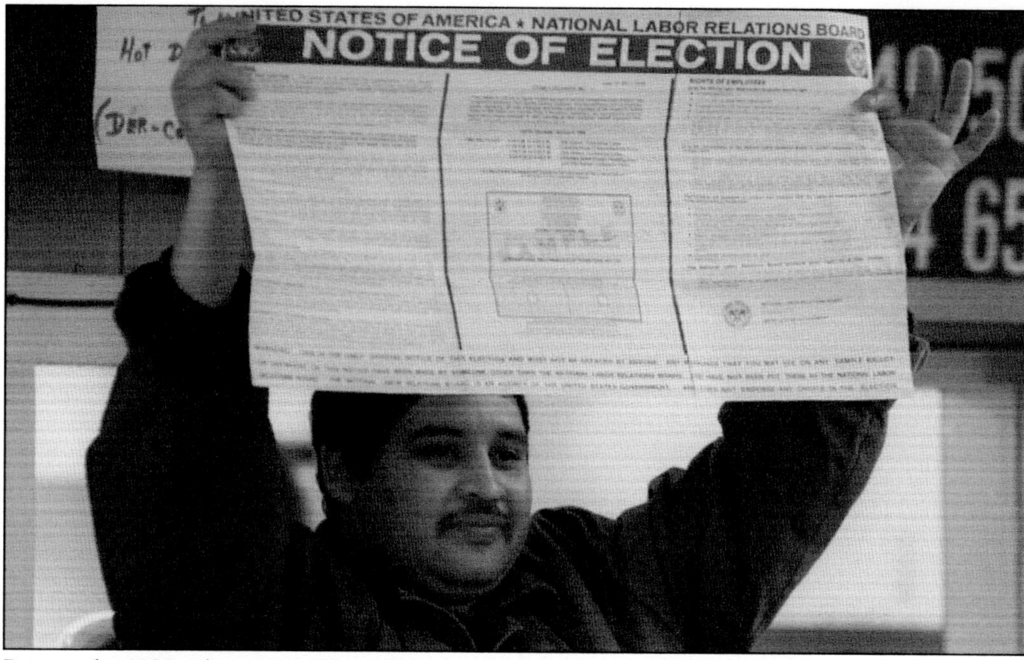

Prior to the 1990s, the greater Wenatchee area had not been known as a bastion for labor organizing or agitation. This had mostly to do with the transient nature of most of the agriculture labor that came to the region. However, all that changed by the late 20th century. The teamsters union attempted to unionize workers at Stemilt Growers. These two photographs depict some of the organizers and workers at Stemilt Growers. The top image, taken in 1998, is of Roberto Guerrero displaying a sample ballot to Stemilt workers at a rally before the vote. The bottom image is of Stemilt worker Asuncion Santiago at a union meeting in 1997. (Courtesy *Wenatchee World*.)

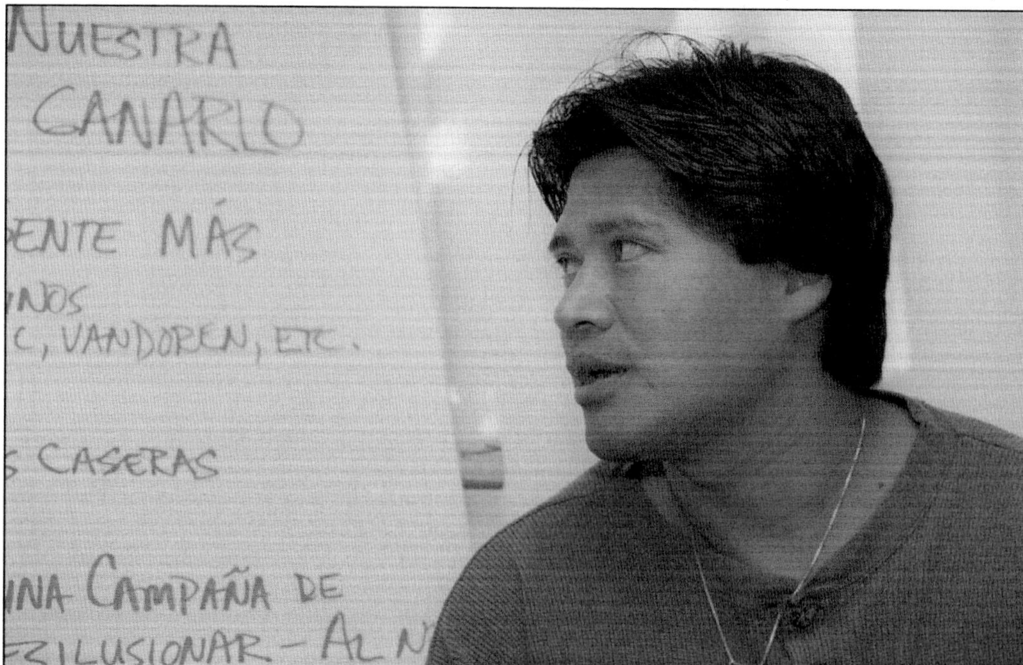

Eight

The Warrior Spirit

On February 18, 1966, Reynaldo R. Cavazos, a Quincy native, became the first Vietnam War death for North Central Washington. He was killed in a helicopter crash while on a rescue mission in Vietnam. Six days before his death, he wrote in one of his letters to his sister Diane, "I guess its God's will that I be one of those men he has picked to fight for our country and our people, and I am very proud to be one!"

The Mexican American pioneers of NCW and their descendants served their country during times of need. Refugio Garces, whose family migrated from Texas to the Columbia Basin, is a decorated World War II veteran. The Garces family is an excellent example of the military tradition within Mexican families. When Refugio's grandson, Ricky Garces, joined the military, he became the third generation to follow the same path. Ricky was eventually deployed to Iraq in 2004. Ricky's father, Baldemar Garces, served seven months in Vietnam, returning to NCW in 1973.

Ramiro Hinojosa, whose family first came to the Columbia Basin in 1956, was drafted and served in Vietnam from January 1969 to January 1971. Ramiro was assigned to Alpha Company, 4th Engineers. As an army engineer, he and others were responsible for disarming booby traps, clearing bunkers, and creating landing zones for helicopters. For saving the life of a fellow soldier, Ramiro was awarded the Bronze Star, but he also received the Vietnam Gallantry Cross with Palm Device, National Defense Medal, Vietnam Service Medal, and Good Conduct Medal.

The U.S. military has had divergent roles within the Mexican American community. On the one hand and as just mentioned, Mexican Americans have served with honor throughout every American campaign since the Civil War. The military for many Mexicans has provided an outlet from poverty and opportunities for higher education. In spite of this tradition, Mexican Americans, because of high rates of poverty, often found themselves disproportionately represented in conflicts. Nonetheless, the following pictures depict the Mexican American heroes from World War II to the present.

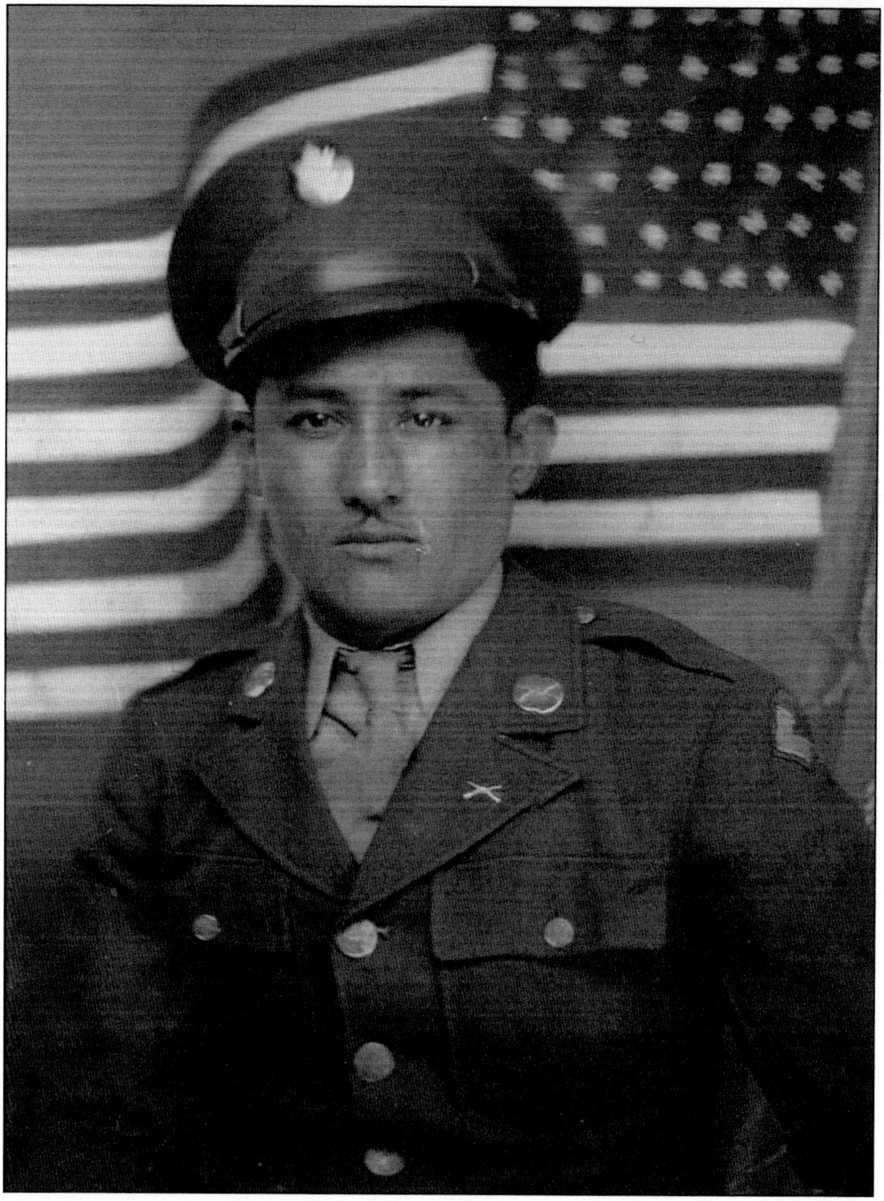

One of the many heroes of World War II who fought for freedom and showed the world what it meant to have the warrior spirit was Refugio Garces. He was born and raised in Texas, served in the Pacific theater of war with the Company F, 381st Infantry Battalion, from October 1942, and was honorably discharged in January 1946. While in the Pacific, Refugio fought in the Philippines and Okinawa and was wounded in action. His campaign medals include two Bronze Stars and Bronze Arrowhead, Philippines' Liberation Ribbon with two Bronze Stars, Purple Heart, Combat Infantry Badge, and Good Conduct Medal. Refugio Garces also embodied the spirit of the "Greatest Generation." In public, Garces said little about his participation in the war, but his family was well aware of his sacrifices. Señor Garces carried forth the Mexican American legacy of defending the United States, even during a period when many Mexican Americans were denied their civil rights. He passed this legacy on to his children and grandchildren. (Courtesy Alicia Garces.)

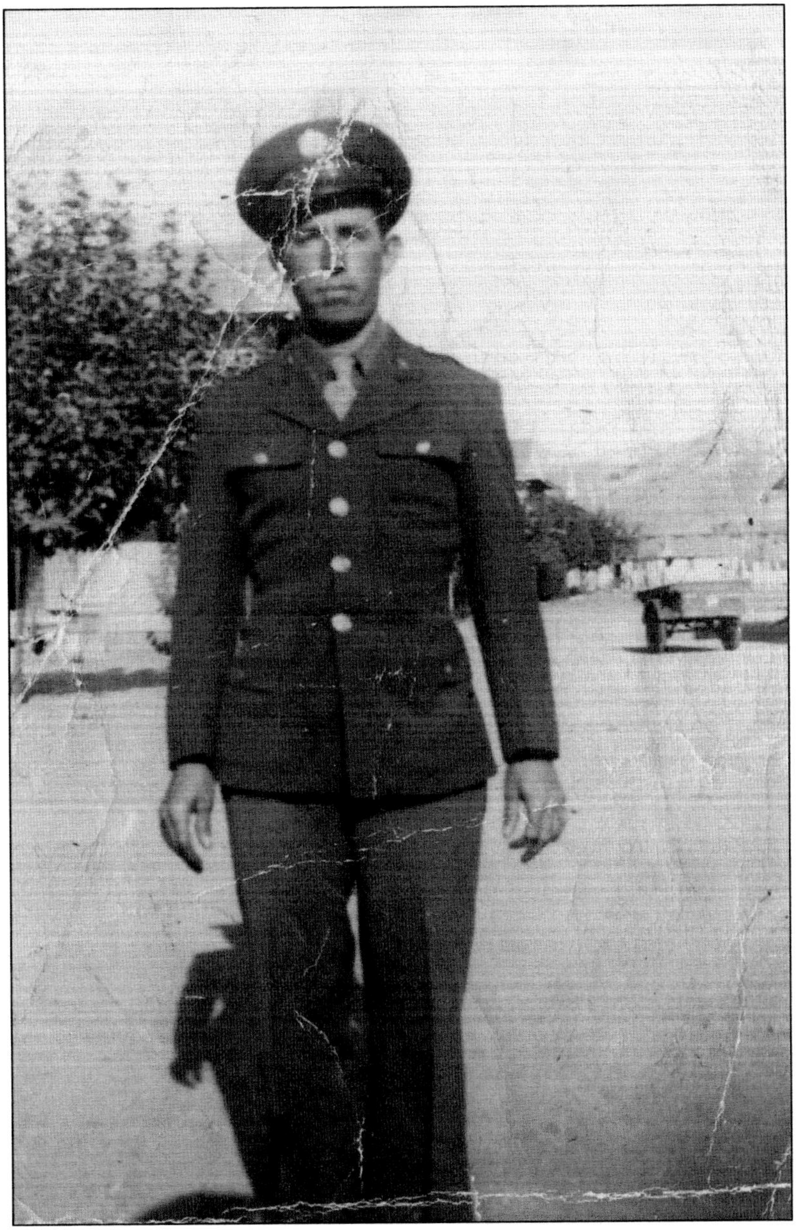

It is estimated that nearly 500,000 Mexican Americans participated in World War II. Mexican Americans from throughout the United States enlisted or were drafted into all branches of the armed services. Approximately 250,000 Mexican American servicemen were casualties of World War II. Furthermore, Mexican American soldiers had the highest percentage of Medal of Honor winners of any minority group, 12 during World War II and 39 altogether. After World War II, Gen. Douglas MacArthur described the 158th Regimental Combat Team, comprised mostly of Mexican Americans and Native Americans from Arizona and known as the "Bushmasters," as "the greatest fighting combat team ever deployed for battle." Pictured in this photograph is Señor Jesus Hinojosa, also Texas-born, who served in the European theater of war. Part of his family migrated to Washington in the 1950s and 1960s and eventually settled in the Columbia Basin. (Courtesy Hinojosa family.)

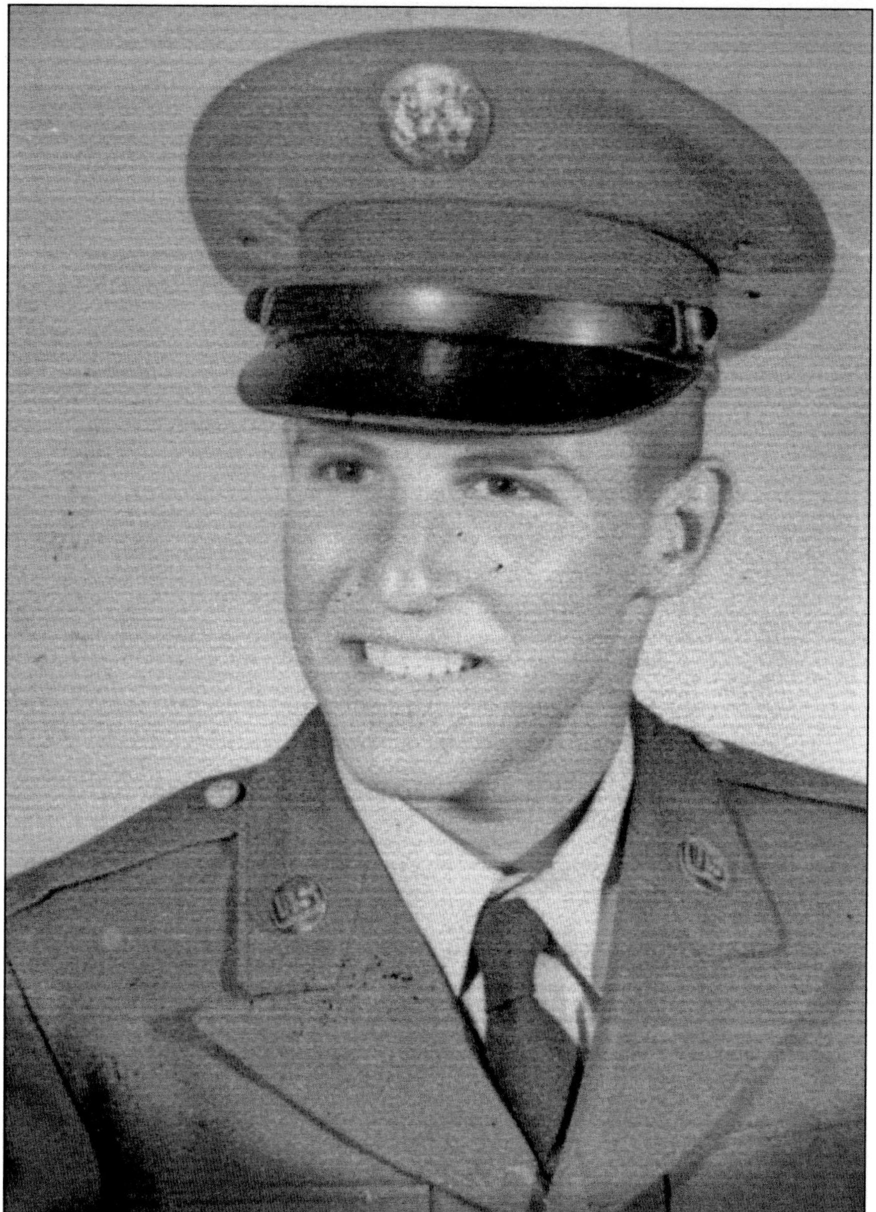

In 1966, the life expectancy in the United States was 70.2 years; the global population was barely 3.4 billion; the Baltimore Orioles swept the Los Angeles Dodgers in the World Series; the first episode of *Star Trek* was shown ("Man Trap"); and the *Sound of Music* won the Oscar for best picture. This year also represents the escalation and Americanization of the Vietnam War, sometimes called the Vietnam conflict. In 1966, the first year of Operation Rolling Thunder comes to an end. And Pres. Lyndon Johnson authorizes the use of 429,000 American soldiers. With a national draft and escalating numbers of U.S. personnel, it was inevitable that the Vietnam War impact the Columbia Basin. In February 1966, NCW experienced its first war casualty—PFC Reynaldo R. Cavazos. Reynaldo was killed in action while on a rescue mission in Vietnam. Reynaldo was raised in Quincy and was just 17 when he enlisted. He died at the age of 19. This is Reynaldo's official military photograph. (Courtesy Jaramillo family.)

Baldemar Garces (right) follows a tradition of military service. His father, Refugio Garces, fought in World War II. Before being drafted, Baldemar Garces has vivid memories of growing up in Texas and being on the migrant trail with his family. Eventually he came to NCW with his family in the 1960s. Baldemar was drafted in 1971 and served seven months in Vietnam. Ramiro Hinojosa (below) was drafted into the Vietnam War in 1969. Ramiro was trained as a combat engineer and assigned to Alpha Company, 4th Engineers. His specialization after arriving in Vietnam was disarming booby traps, clearing out bunkers, and creating landing zones for helicopters. By the end of his tour, he served with 15 different companies. Below is Ramiro at Fire Base Oasis. (Right, courtesy Garces family; below, courtesy Hinojosa family.)

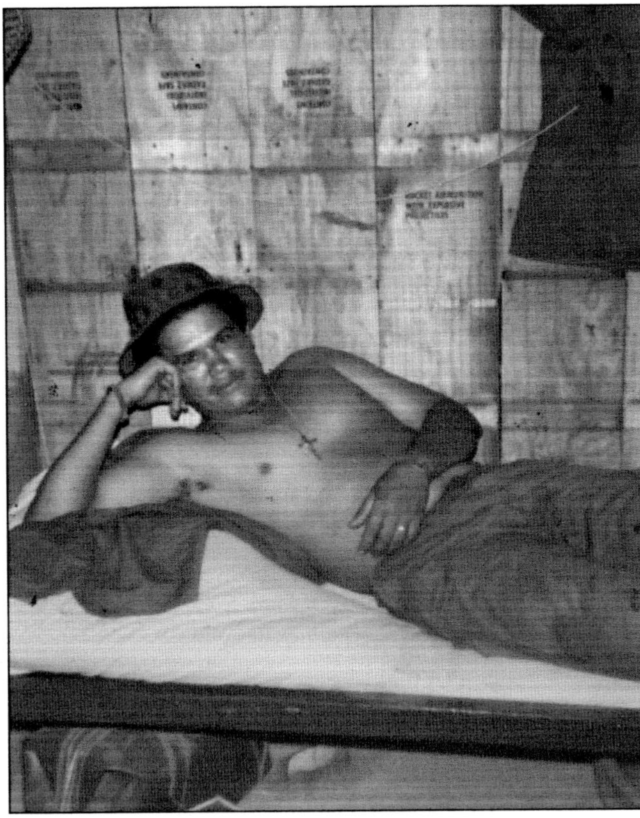

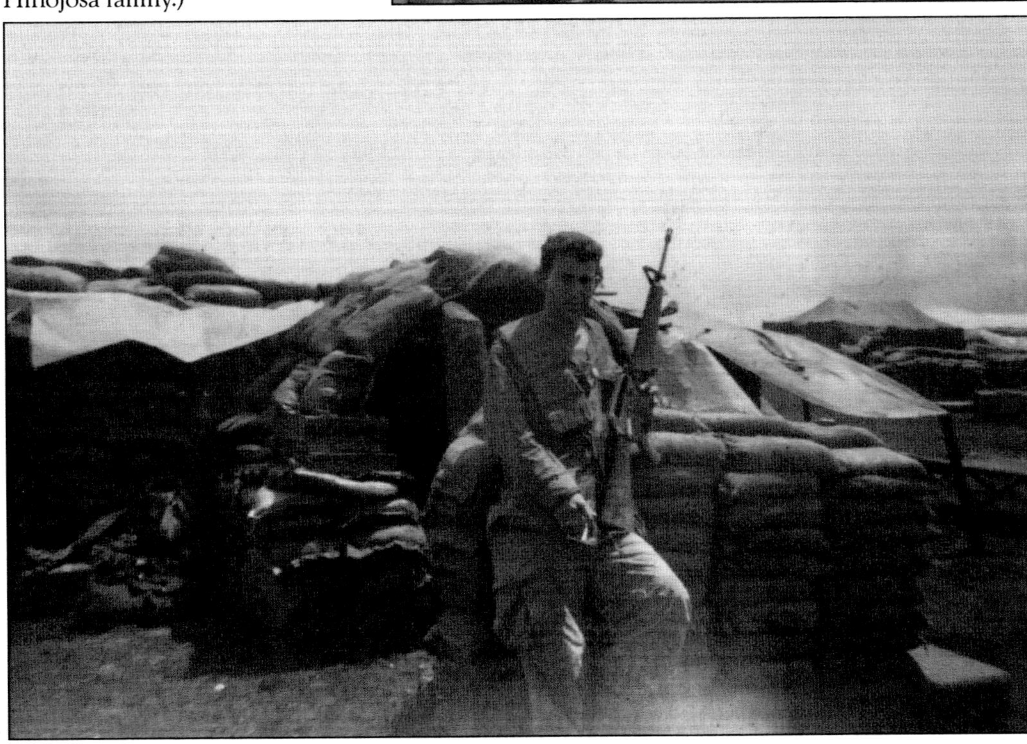

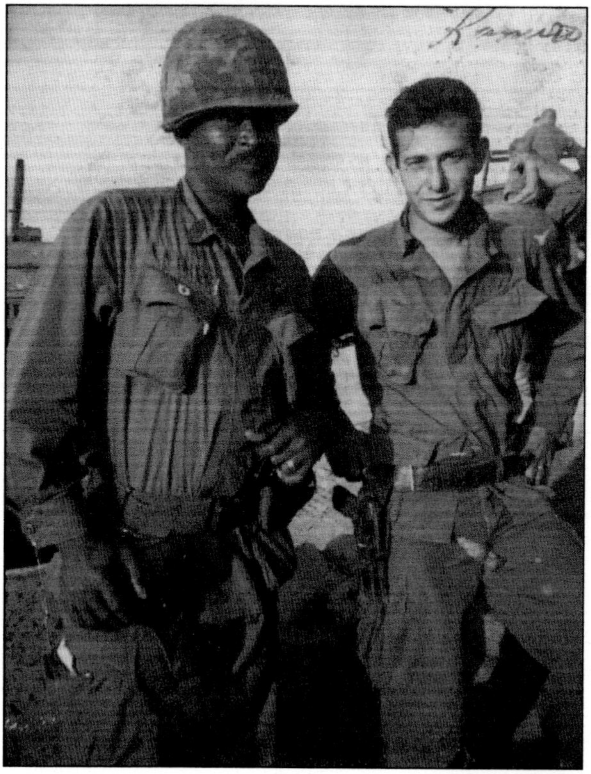

Ramiro's first firefight was chaos; he felt tree bark hitting his face and, falling to the ground, began shooting randomly in many directions. According to Ramiro, after every mission it was obligatory to party. Ramiro also recalls that he must have been ambushed at least 10 times, the result of incompetent platoon or company leaders. Ramiro is pictured at left with his company's first-sergeant. In his time in Vietnam, Ramiro indicates he developed strong bonds with several of his fellow soldiers. He saved the life of his best friend, Jim Kline. As a reward, Kline's wife sent him a recorded message extending her appreciation and gratitude. Of course, the military would also recognize Ramiro's heroism. Ramiro is pictured below (far right) with two of his closest friends. (Courtesy Ramiro Hinojosa.)

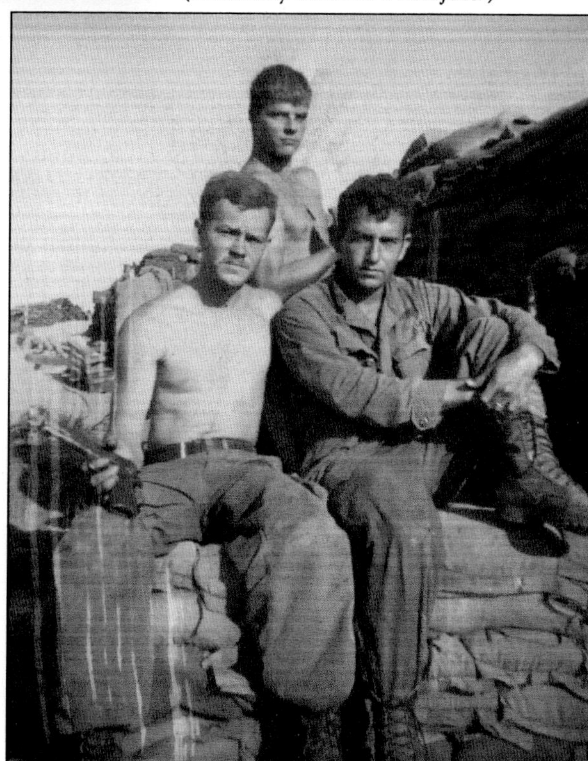

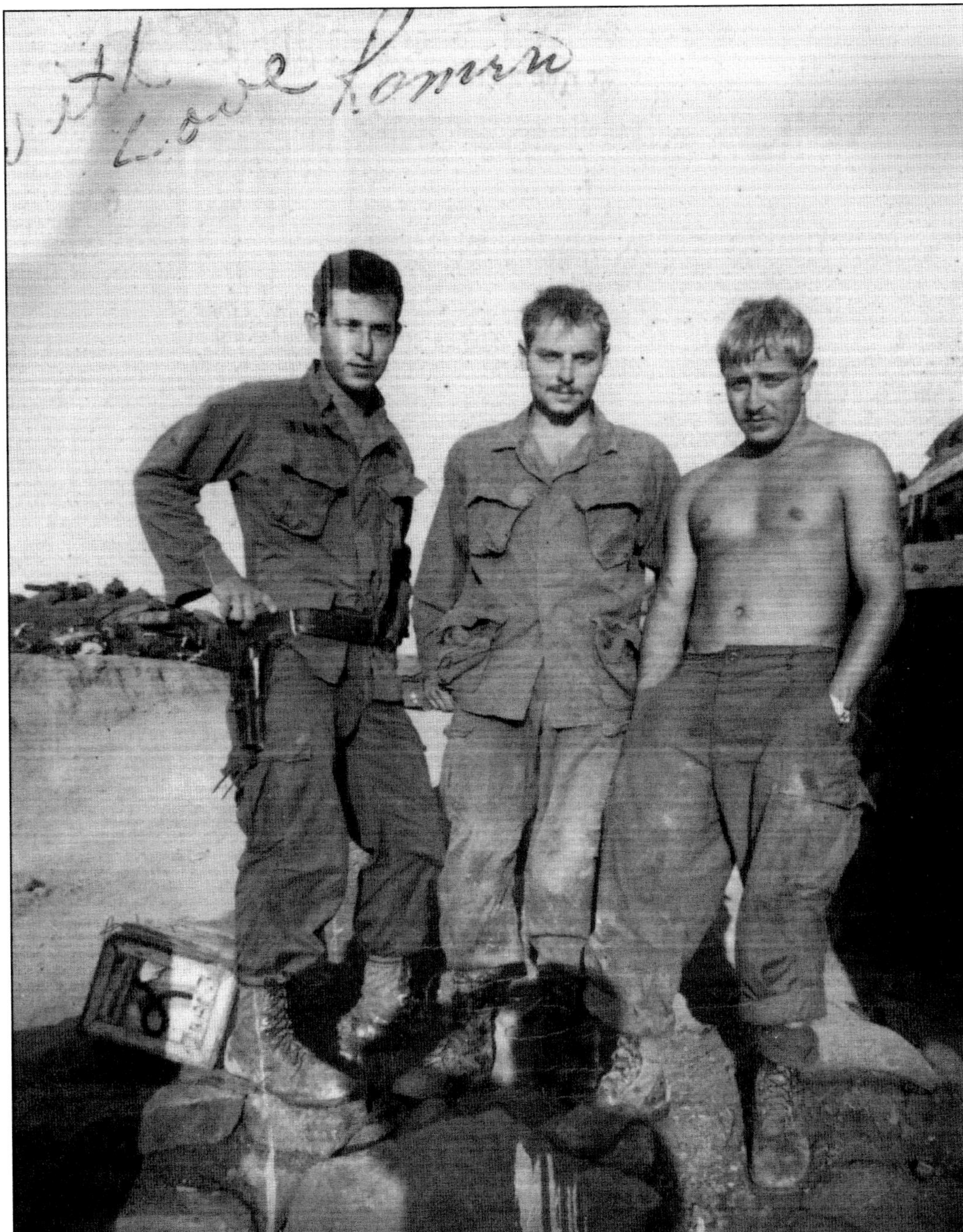

After two tours in Vietnam, participating in the invasion of Cambodia, and seeing many friends die or get wounded, Ramiro returned to the United States in 1971. For saving the lives of 18 soldiers and gallantry above and beyond the call of duty, Ramiro (left) was awarded the Bronze Star, Vietnam Gallantry Cross with Palm Device, Vietnam Campaign Medal, Vietnam Service Medal, National Defense Medal, and Good Conduct Medal. Ramiro sums up his experience in Vietnam by saying, "When I die I'll go to heaven because I spent my time in hell already in Vietnam." Ramiro is pictured in Vietnam with comrades-in-arms. (Courtesy Ramiro Hinojosa.)

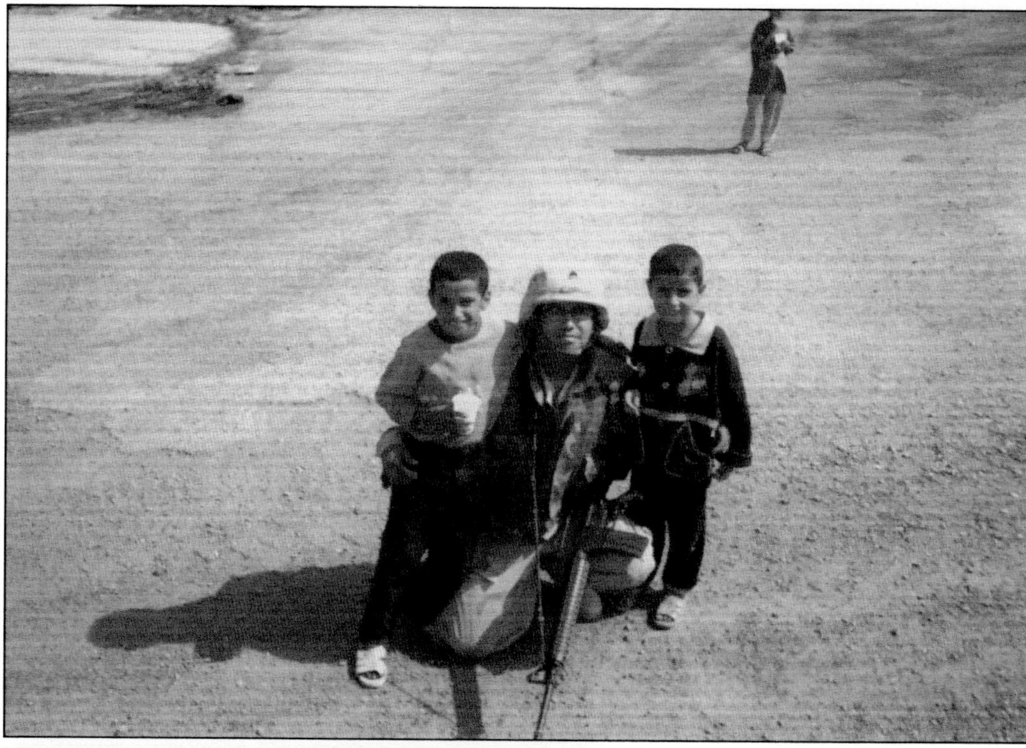

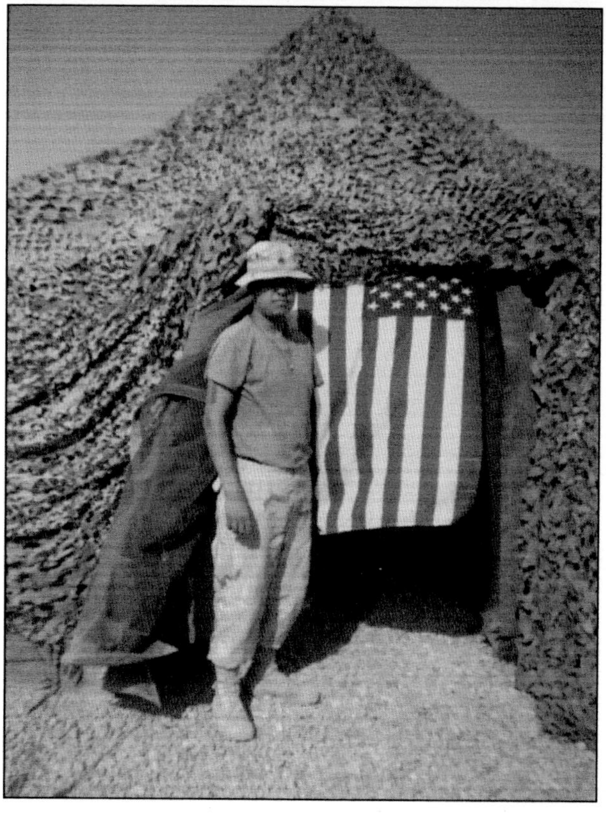

Ricky Garces, like his father and grandfather before him, served in the U.S. Army. Ricky served in the regular army and National Guard from 1996 to 2004. His Washington State National Guard experience took him to Iraq to serve in Operation Iraqi Freedom. Ricky initially served as a Patriot missile crew member and while in Iraq was assigned to transportation support. For serving his country, Ricky received two army Meritorious Service Medals, National Defense Medal, and Iraqi Freedom Medal. The top picture shows Ricky in Iraq near the rail yards in Baghdad with two Iraqi children. The photograph at left is at base camp near the Baghdad Airport on Flag Day. (Courtesy Ricky Garces.)

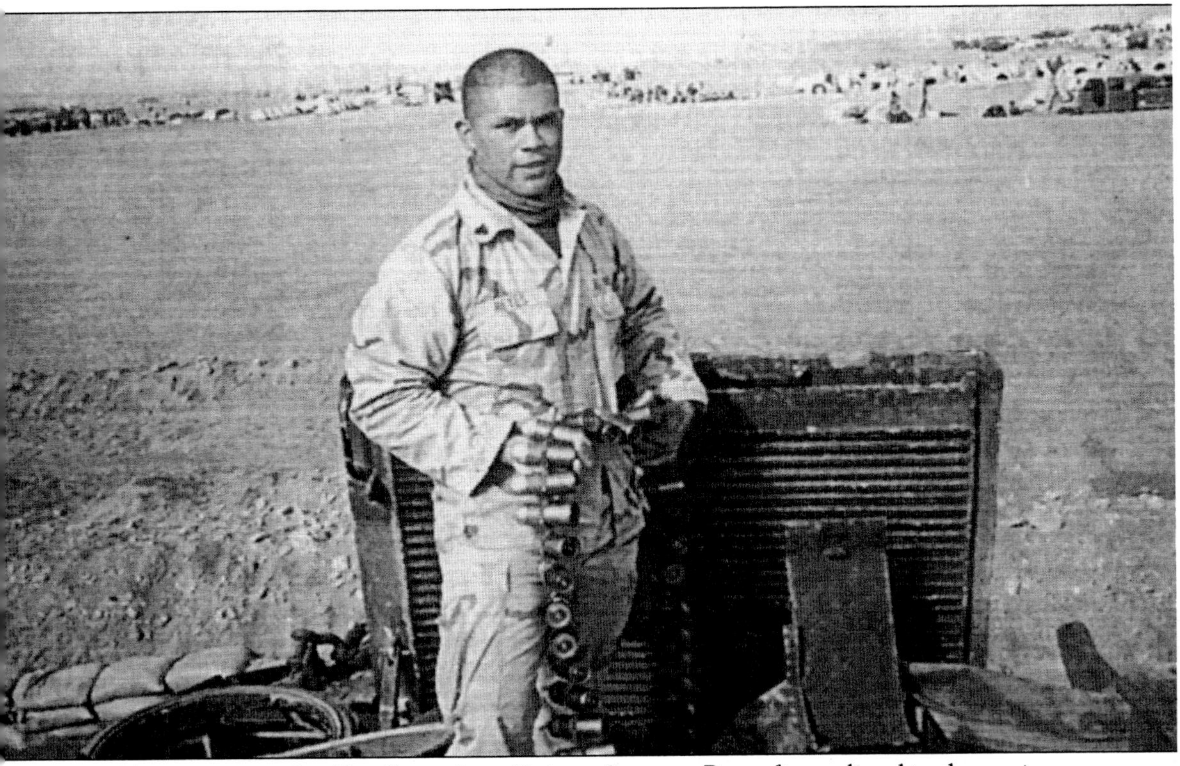

Pictured here is marine Sgt. Ben Reyes from Quincy. Sergeant Reyes first enlisted in the marines in 2000. He participated in military combat operation in Afghanistan and Iraq. Ben is a third-generation Mexican American from the Columbia Basin. His parents, Debbie and Tony Reyes Jr., are the children of Tony and Tomasita Mora and Rebecca and Antonio Reyes Sr., respectively. Tony Reyes Jr. is also a military veteran, having served in the U.S. Army, and Tony Mora Sr. is a World War II veteran. These families are longtime residents of North Central Washington and represent the roots of the Mexican American community in the region. In Iraq, Sgt. Ben Reyes was involved in heavy combat operations when the war began. As a crew chief of an armored assault vehicle, Reyes saw military action in An Nasiriyah and other regions of the country. In this photograph, taken in 2003, Sergeant Reyes is performing maintenance on his AAV and loading ammunition. (Courtesy *Quincy Post-Register.*)

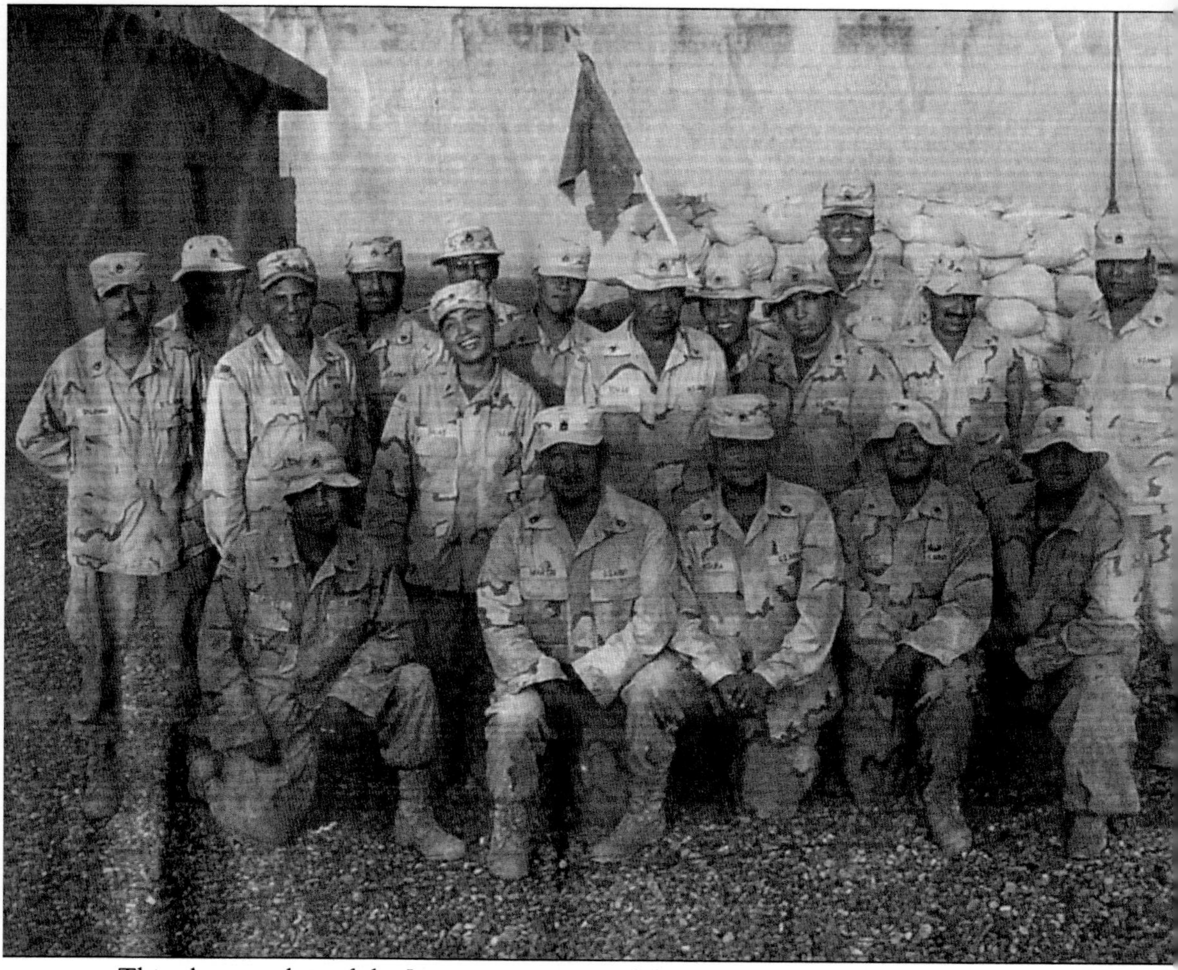

This photograph is of the Latino contingent of the 1161 Transport Company of the National Guard in Ephrata. Of the 100 members of the company, over 20 are Latinos. This company was deployed to Iraq in 2003 as part of Operation Iraqi Freedom. Based at the Baghdad Airport, the main mission of the company is to transport materials up and down the supply lines to combat troops and support personnel. Unfortunately not every Latino from North Central Washington could be mentioned, but there are literally thousands of Latinos from the region serving the United States throughout the globe. And, like the Mexican American warriors of the past, they are all serving with strength and honor. (Courtesy *El Mundo*.)

Nine

Sports and Leisure

What would a community be without sports and leisurely activities? Readers will recognize most of the sports depicted in the following photographs because they are the same ones played by all regardless of ethnic background, with one exception. Furthermore, most of the sports played by ethnic Mexicans were the invention of Europeans or Americans, such as soccer and baseball. However, ethnic Mexicans have heightened the awareness of some sports like soccer, while simultaneously introducing new ones to the communities of North Central Washington. For example, *beísbol* (baseball), *fútbol* (soccer), boxing, and cockfighting are as much about culture and identity as they are about the sports themselves. The national pastimes such as *beísbol* and *fútbol* provide participants and spectators a space to practice their culture of origin without ridicule or shame. For many Mexicans, sports such as *fútbol* and cockfighting are a connection to their Mexicanness and to a land left behind.

The photographs in the following pages will show ethnic Mexicans in NCW participating in organized sports such as Little League, Babe Ruth, boxing, soccer, and American football. The pictures will show leisure activities such as salmon fishing, running, and softball leagues. On the other hand, there is one sport that most people will be unfamiliar with regardless of ethnic background, and that is cockfighting. Ironically this sport was not introduced to NCW by Mexicans, but by Anglo migrants from the American South in the 1930s. This sport, illegal except in New Mexico and Louisiana, was originally introduced to the Americas by the British and Spaniards and became very popular in their respective Colonial empires. By the modern period, cockfighting became part of American Southern culture as well as Mexican. Via migration and immigration, cockfighting has been in NCW for at least 80 years and is practiced by Anglos and Mexicans alike. However, because of its illegality, it remains an underground sport and is practiced by only a small segment of the Mexican population. Overall, the photographs were chosen to depict integration and change but also a sense of cultural continuity through the participation in sports.

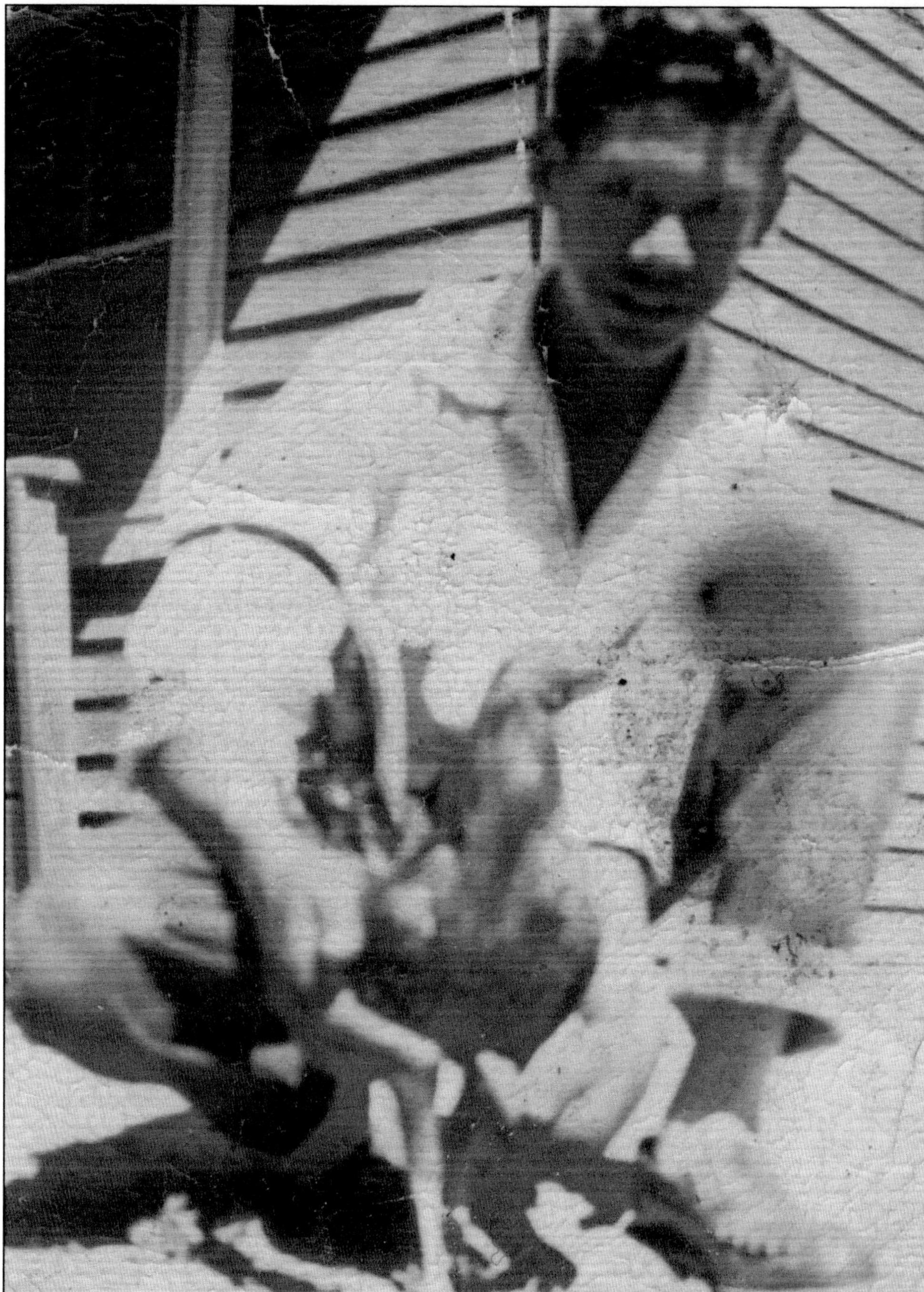

Pictured here is a longtime resident of the Columbia Basin, Don Roberto, when he was 14 years of age and with his first rooster. He recalls, like a dream, of going to his first cockfight when he was five. At age 14, he won his first match against a veteran cockfighter and was hooked for life. When this family emigrated from Mexico and then migrated to the Pacific Northwest in the 1950s, this usual form of culture came along. When this family arrived in the lower Yakima Valley, Anglos had already introduced cockfighting to the region. (Courtesy R. Garcia.)

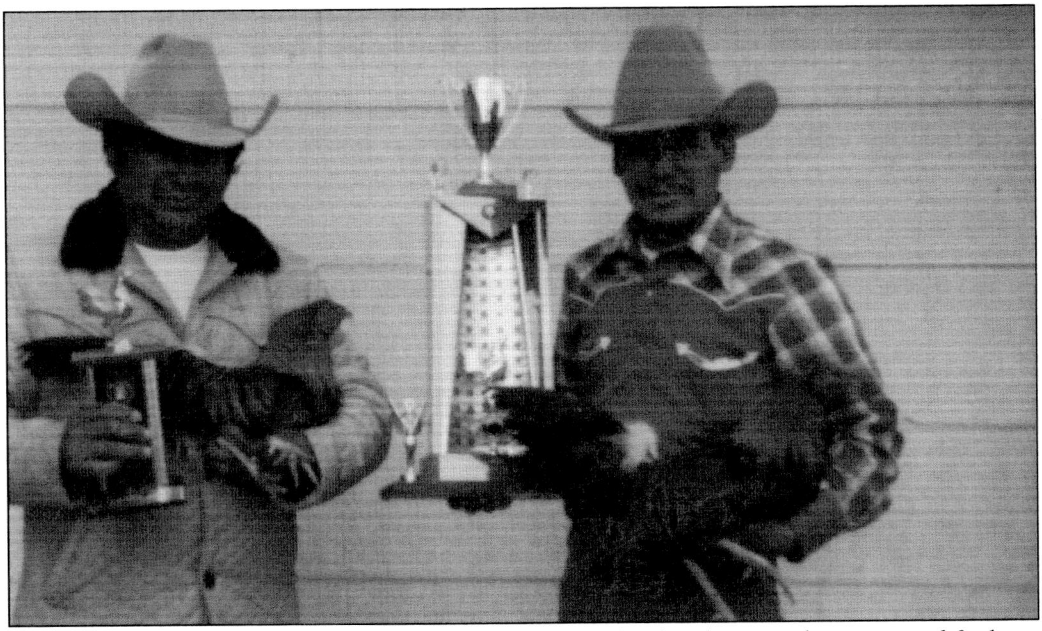

Twenty years later, Dons Roberto (left in both images) and Ruben become champion cockfigthers. As first-generation immigrants, these two brothers achieved success not in the workplace, but in the arena of cockfighting. Although each is known as having a strong work ethic, neither achieved the kind of success nor received the accolades as they did for being expert cockfighters. These two brothers are regionally and nationally known for their skills in this underground sport. These two photographs, shot in the 1970s, were taken shortly after the brothers had won a regional competition. (Courtesy R. Garcia.)

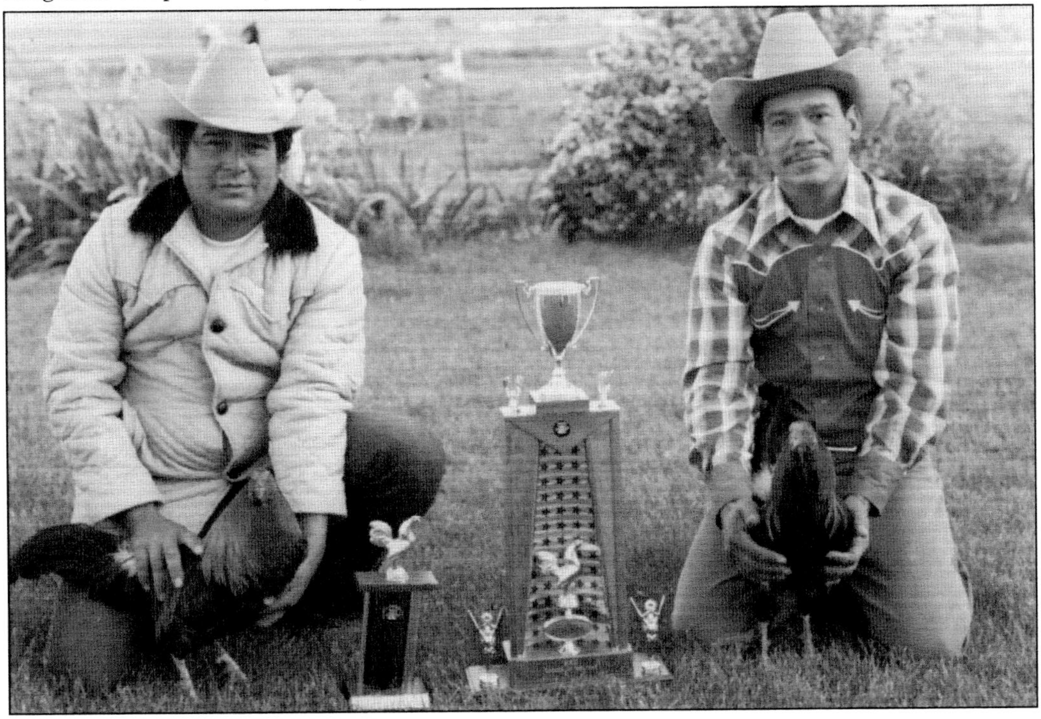

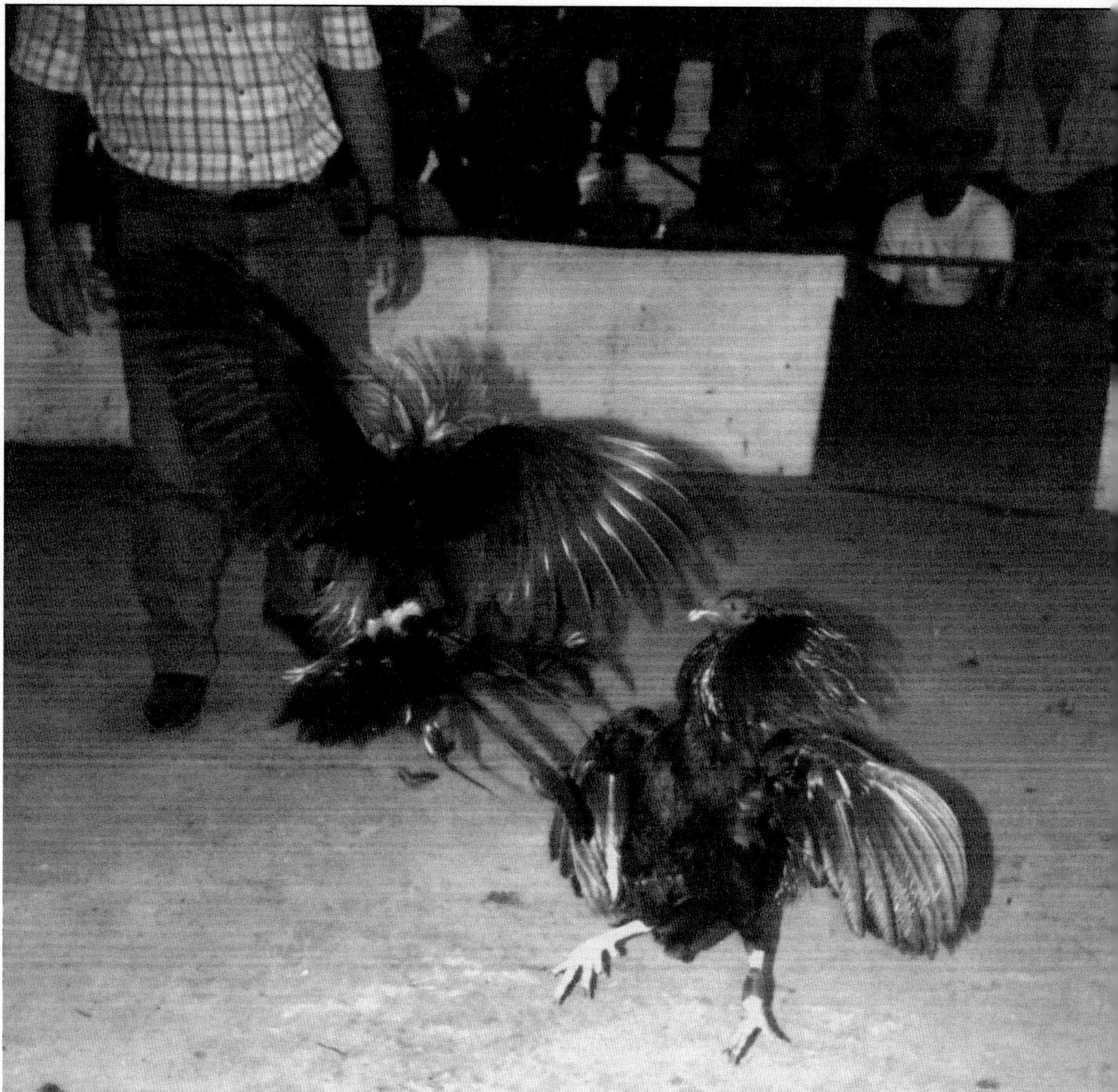

As more Mexicans arrived directly from Mexico, cockfighting expanded in the region and took on a Mexican flavor. This photograph is of a contemporary cockfight in an undisclosed location in NCW. Cockfighting, in general, cannot be completely explained by the fights themselves. There is an unusual cultural affirmation taking place and a form of Mexican masculinity not often seen by the public. (Courtesy R. Garcia.)

Early Mexican Americans in NCW also took up local and regional sporting or leisure activities. In the photograph at right, taken in the 1960s, three Garcias brothers, from left to right, Roberto, José Juan, and Ruben, are pictured in a field somewhere in the Columbia Basin after an outing of pheasant hunting. The bottom image is of Ruben Garcia after catching a king salmon near the Columbia River in 1968. (Courtesy Jerry Garcia.)

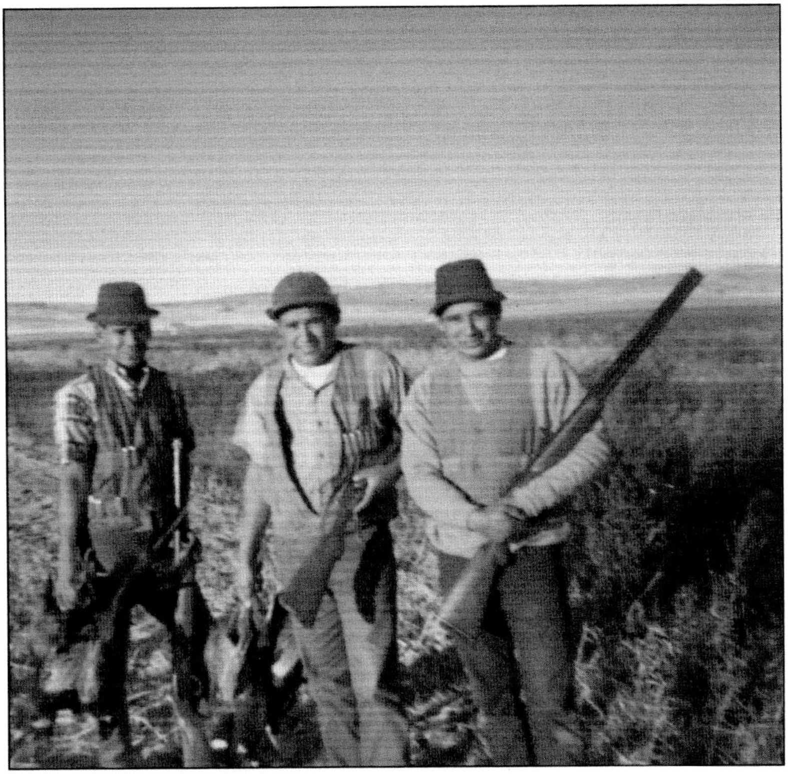

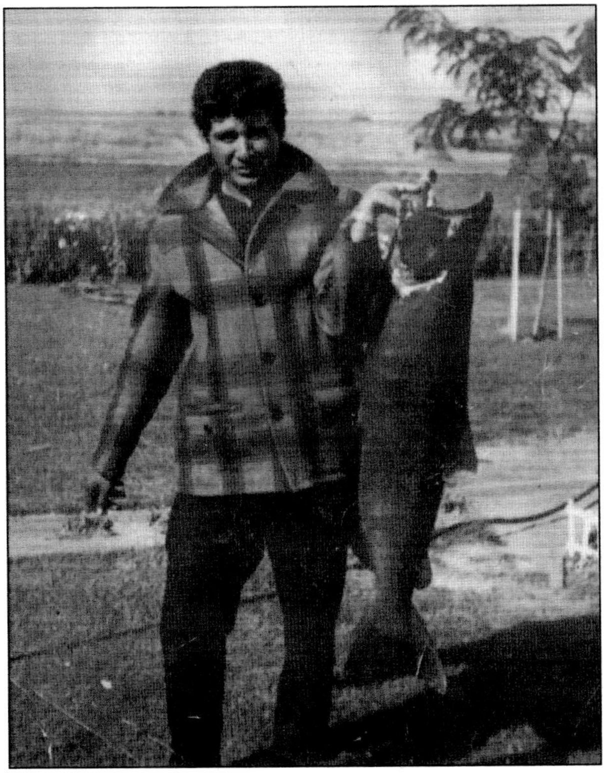

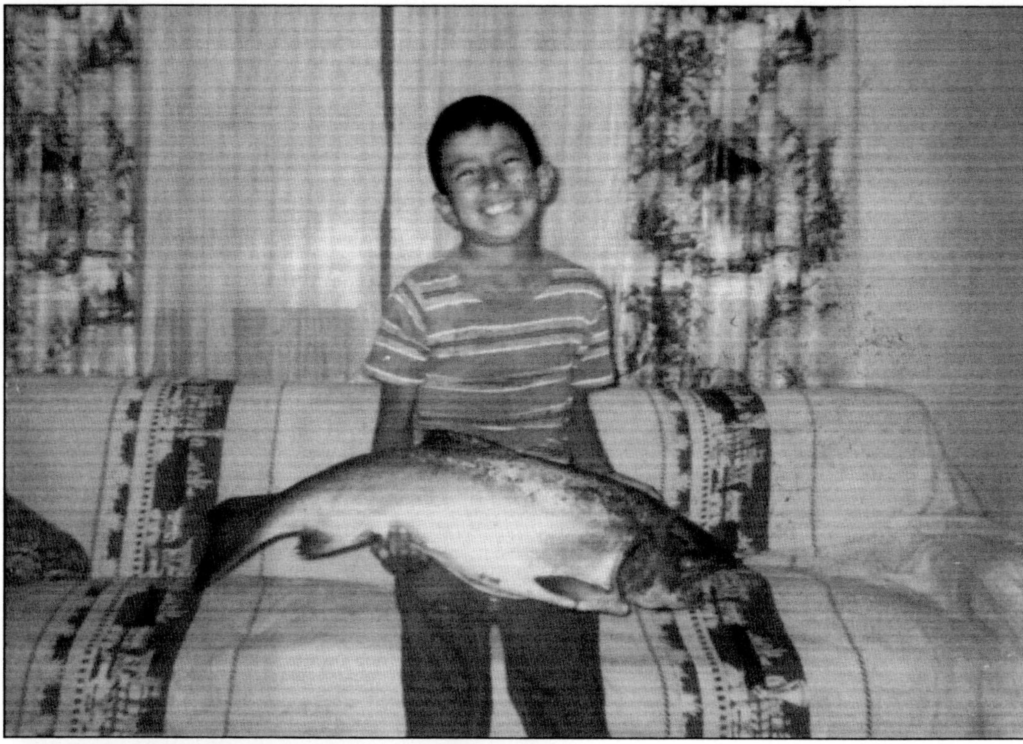

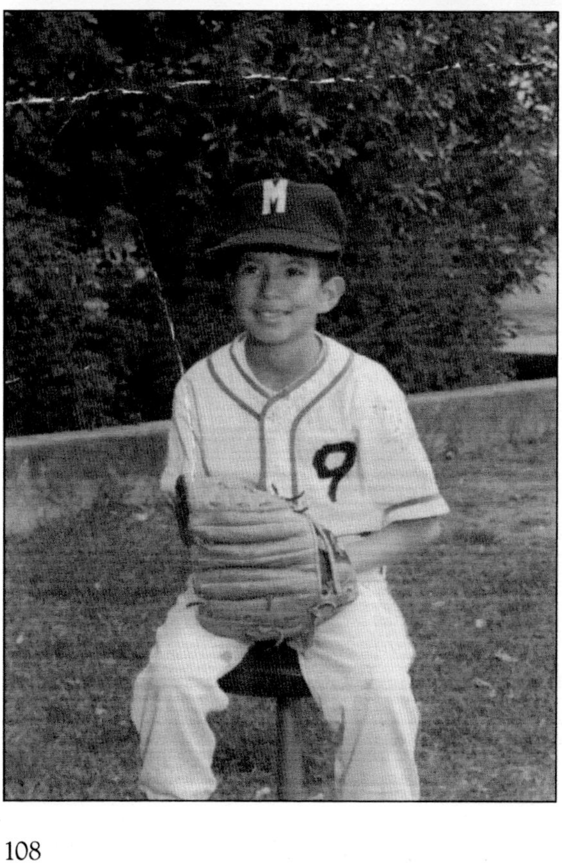

The children of the early Mexican families of the region also participated in a variety of activities in order to help them acclimate to the region and experience the pleasures of the Pacific Northwest. In these two photographs, taken in the late 1950s, Ruben Garcia Jr. is pictured at the top with a salmon he caught on the Columbia River. The bottom picture is his Little League photograph. (Courtesy Jerry Garcia.)

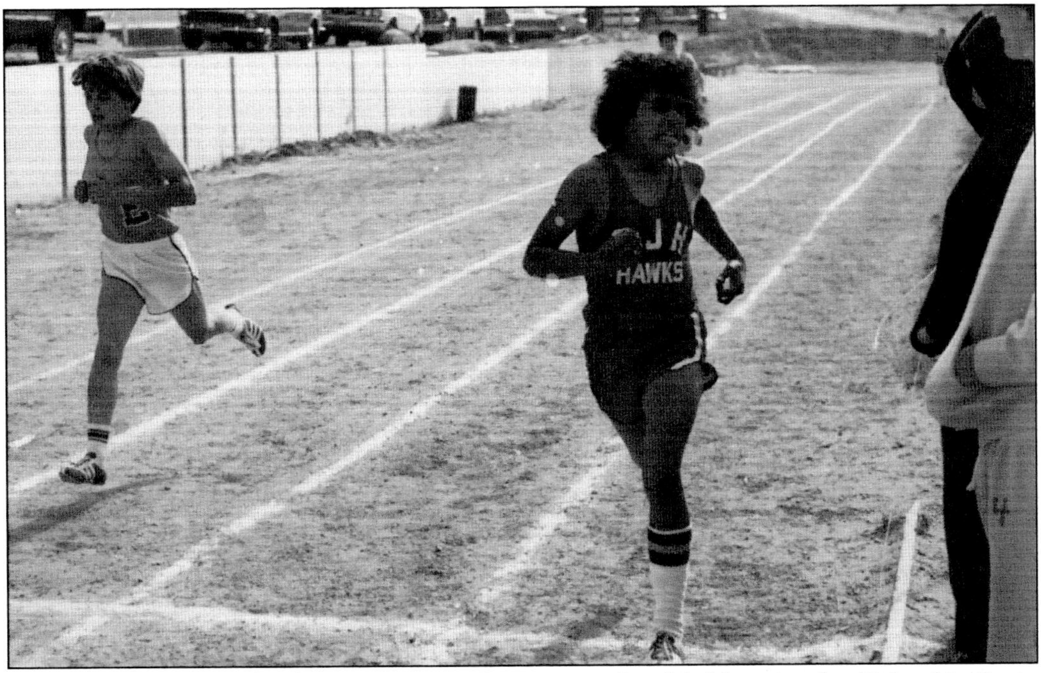

These two photographs depict Mexican American schoolchildren in the Columbia Basin participating in organized sports. The top image is of the author when he was in middle school winning his first race and in pain. The bottom image is of the 1981 Quincy High School wrestling team. More than half the team was of Mexican origin. The Mexican Americans pictured are, from left to right, (first row) Pat Medrano, unidentified, Fred Ybarra, unidentified, Ernie Sepulveda, Silver Flores, unidentified, John Martinez, and Julian Arredondo; (second row) Wally Medrano, Roberto Marroquin, Ed Bews, unidentified, Henry Luna, unidentified, and Jerry Garcia. Not pictured but also on the team were Gilbert Garcia, Johnny Garcia, and Alberto Rivera. (Courtesy Jerry Garcia.)

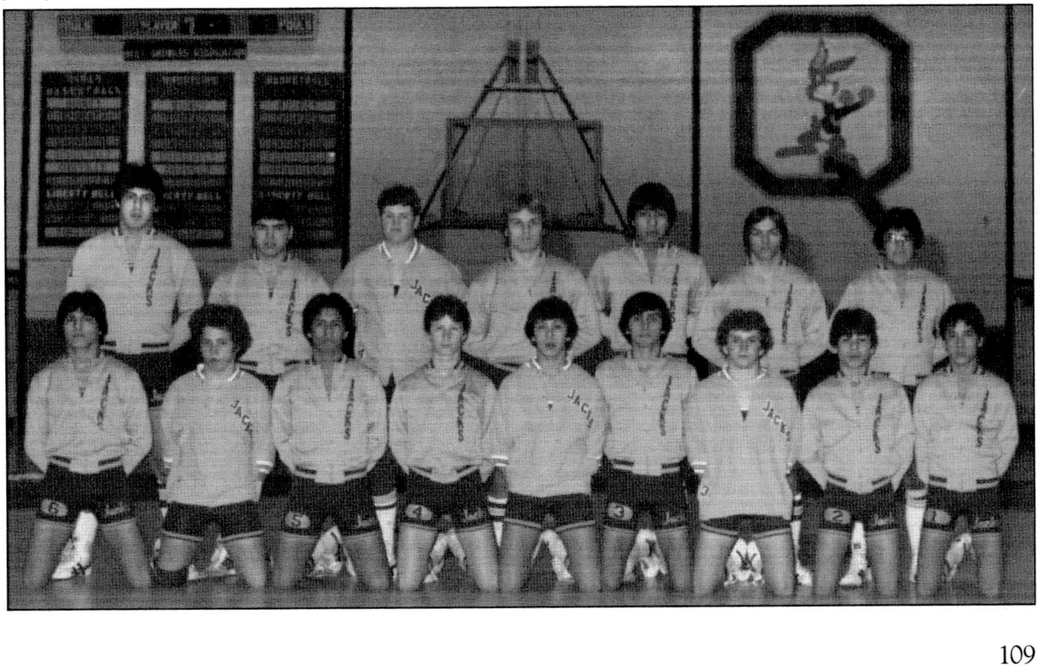

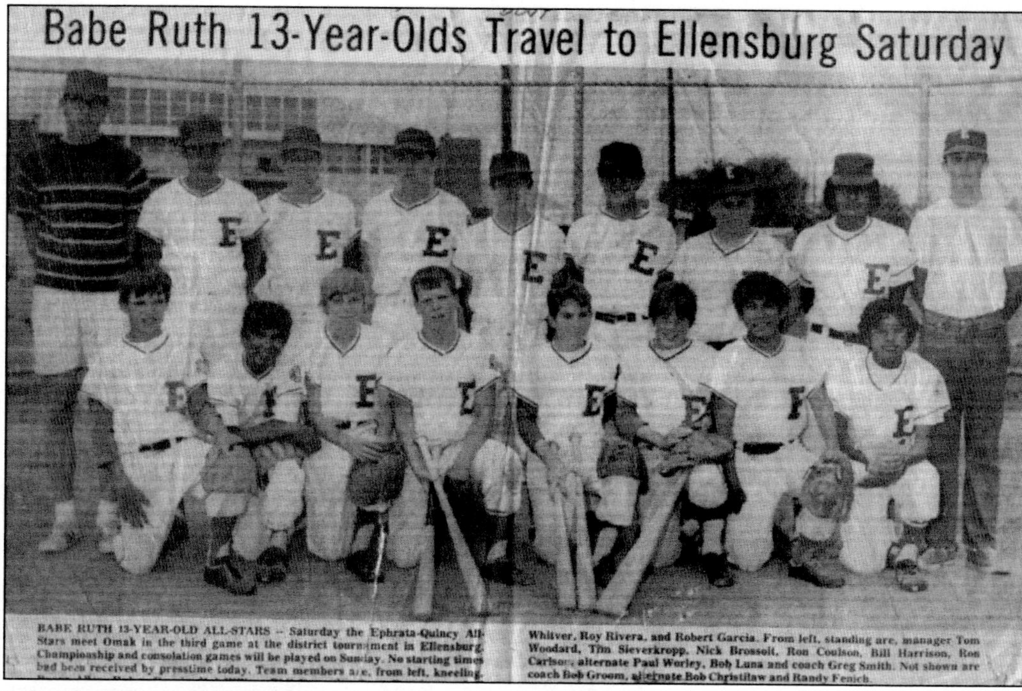

Babe Ruth 13-Year-Olds Travel to Ellensburg Saturday

BABE RUTH 13-YEAR-OLD ALL-STARS – Saturday the Ephrata-Quincy All-Stars meet Omak in the third game at the district tournament in Ellensburg. Championship and consolation games will be played on Sunday. No starting times had been received by presstime today. Team members are, from left, kneeling, [illegible] Whitver, Roy Rivera, and Robert Garcia. From left, standing are, manager Tom Woodard, Tim Sieverkropp, Nick Brossolt, Ron Coulson, Bill Harrison, Ron Carlson, alternate Paul Worley, Bob Luna and coach Greg Smith. Not shown are coach Bob Groom, alternate Bob Christilaw and Randy Fenich.

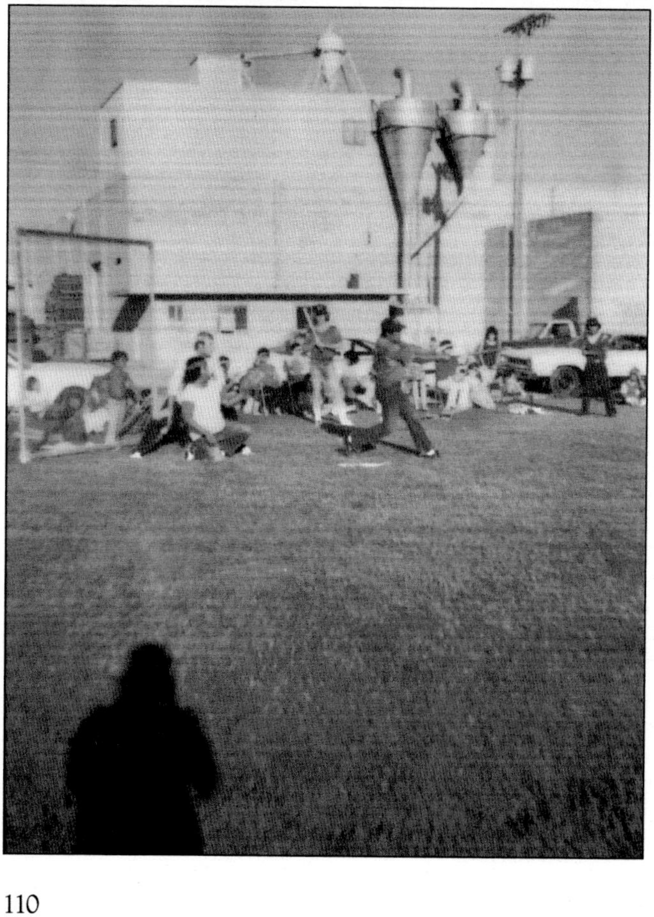

As depicted by some of the photographs, so far many of the Mexican American children participated in traditional sports or other activities. This was all part of the integration process and influence of the school system. In the end, activities such as baseball, football, and wrestling helped many of these children navigate the complexities of school as minorities during this era with acceptance. The top photograph depicts a young Babe Ruth team of the early 1970s. Many Mexican schoolchildren excelled in sports, as shown from the All-Star team made up of Mexican and Anglo students. The bottom image is of a Chicano softball tournament in the Columbia Basin. For many Mexican Americans, softball leagues have played an important role in leisure, friendly competition, and recognition. (Courtesy Jerry Garcia.)

Like cockfighting, boxing in Mexican culture is highly honored and respected as a form culture, self-determination, courage, and strength. Indeed, many Mexican men see themselves as human cockfighters. The photograph at right, taken in the 1940s, depicts a young Roberto Garcia shadow boxing and showing his form. To individuals such as Roberto, boxing helped maintain a sense of discipline and focus in and out of the boxing ring. This is also illustrated in the bottom photograph of the Quincy Boxing Club. The sport taught many of these young children the importance of self-discipline, good health, honor, and courage. (Right, courtesy R. Garcia; below, courtesy *El Mundo*.)

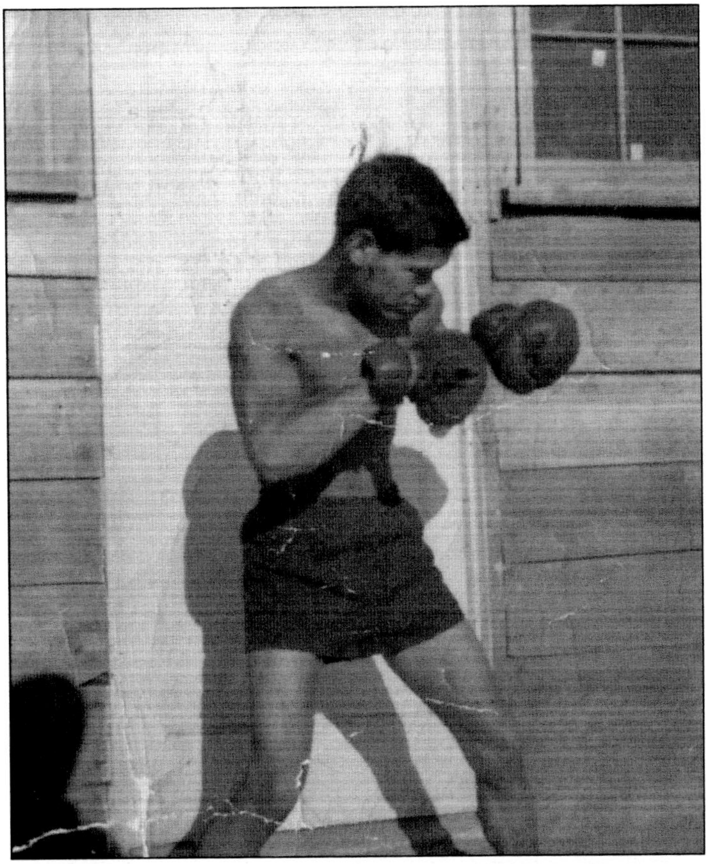

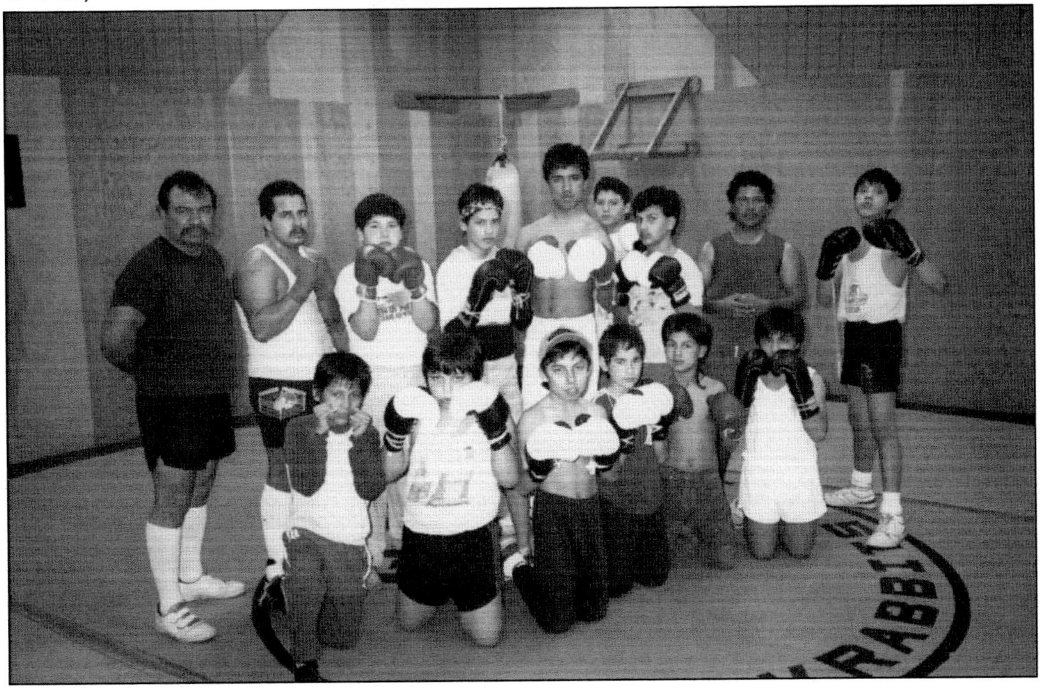

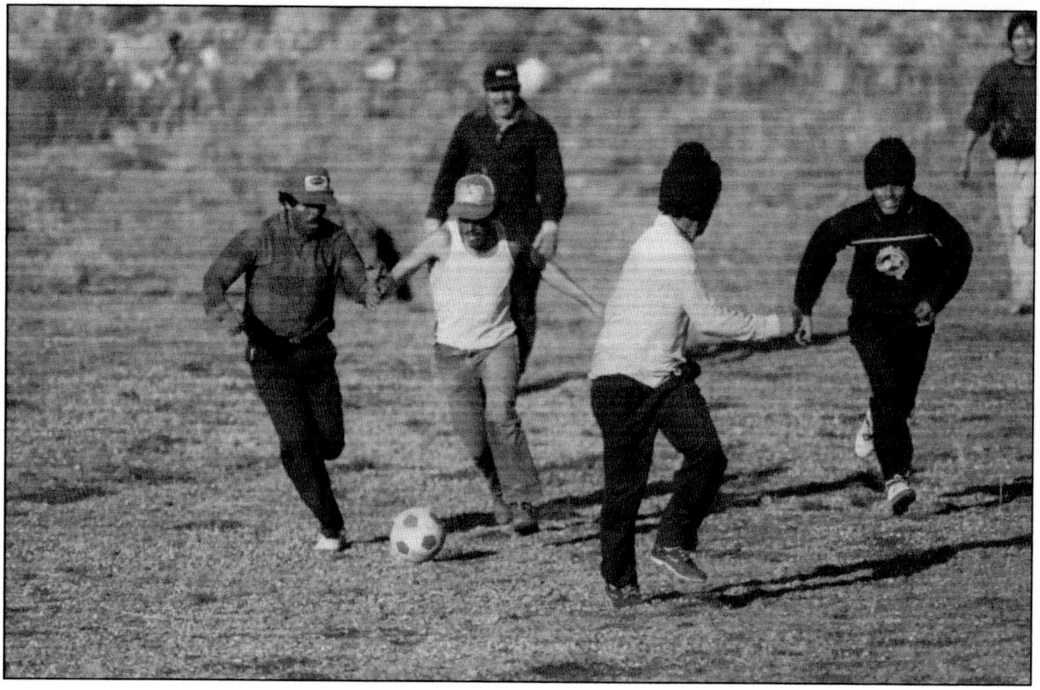

Although *fútbol* (soccer) has been played in NCW forever, it took on a new dimension and flavor when Mexican immigrants brought the passion for the sport to the region. Initially, as seen in the top photograph, soccer matches were often played during lunch breaks at work or impromptu matches were organized. Later, as more Mexican immigrants arrived and made places such as Wenatchee permanent homes, organized teams and leagues were developed. From the bottom picture, it is evident Mexicans in NCW take their *fútbol* very seriously and play the game at a high level. (Courtesy *El Mundo*.)

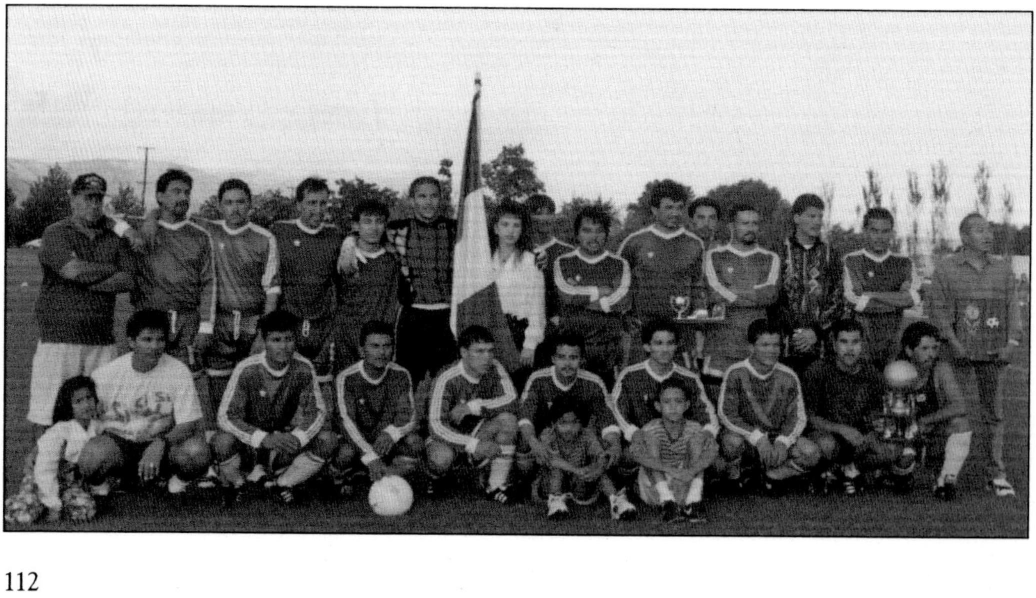

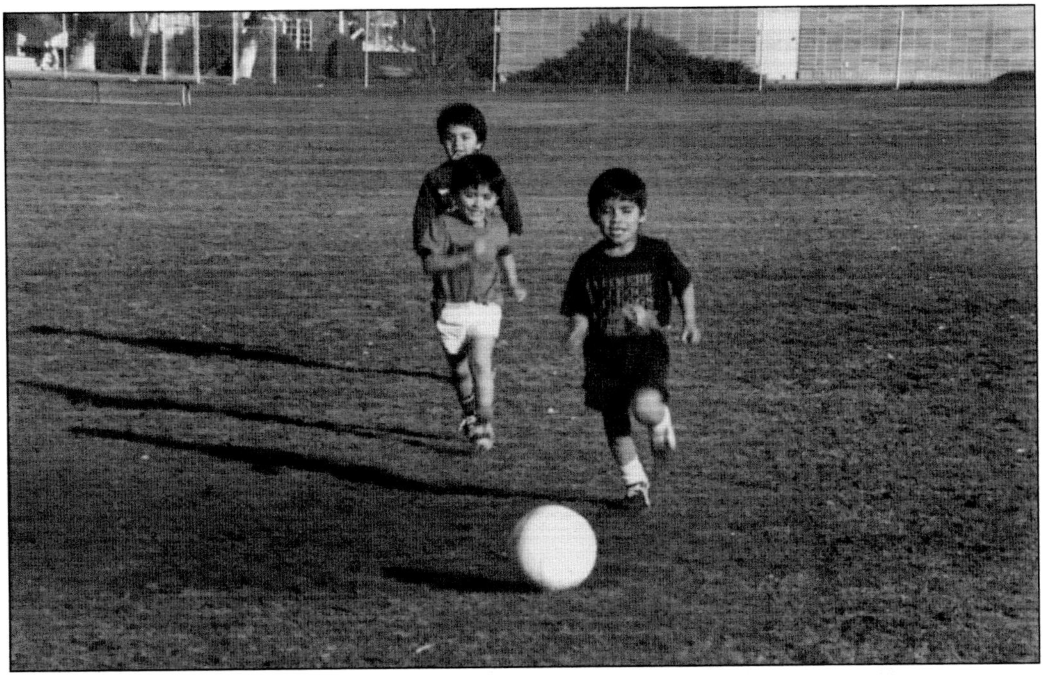

Similar to Little League or Babe Ruth baseball, indoctrination to *fútbol* arrives at an early age and is part of that continuity of the game and culture of *fútbol*. These two photographs were shot in Wenatchee depicting Mexican children playing the game. In the top photograph, what might appear as just three children playing soccer is actually a well-organized match between two teams. The bottom image shows one of the teams from a youth league. (Courtesy *El Mundo/ Wenatchee World.*)

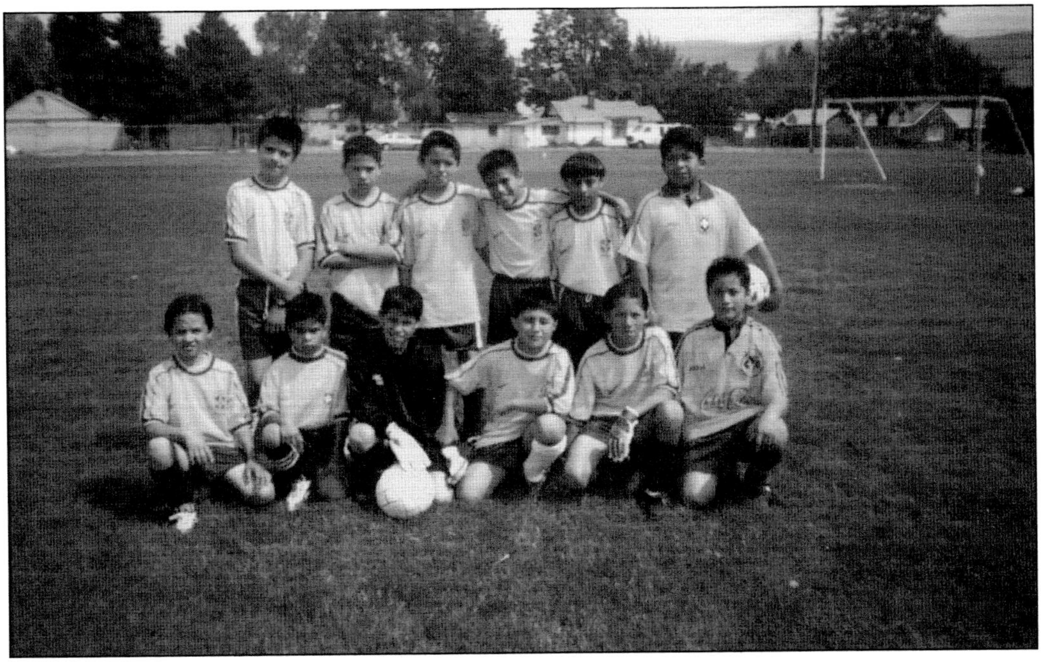

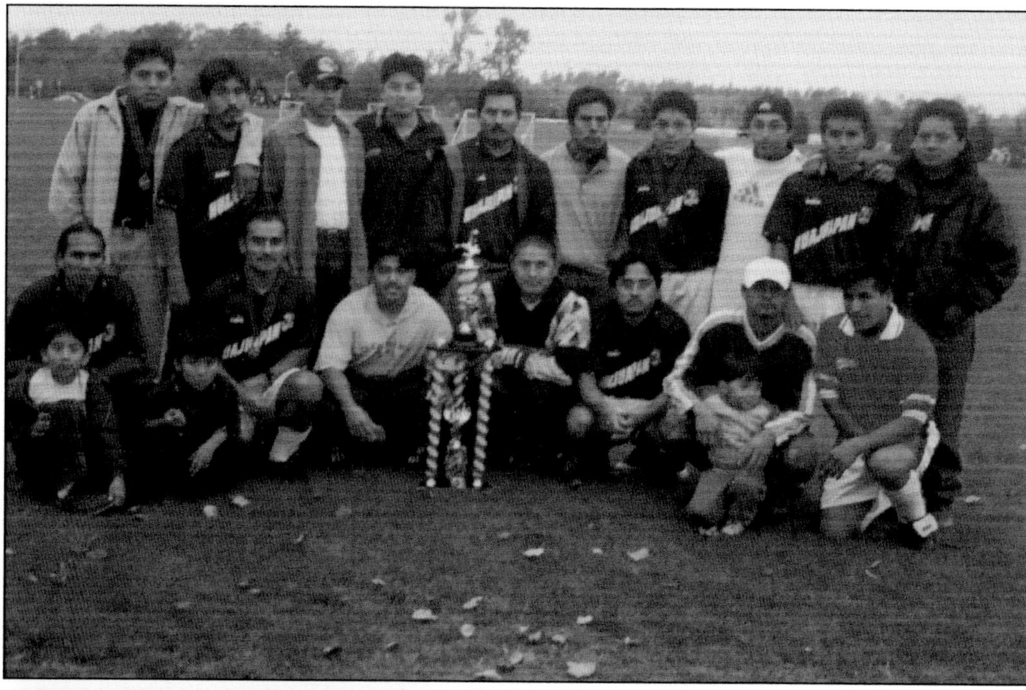

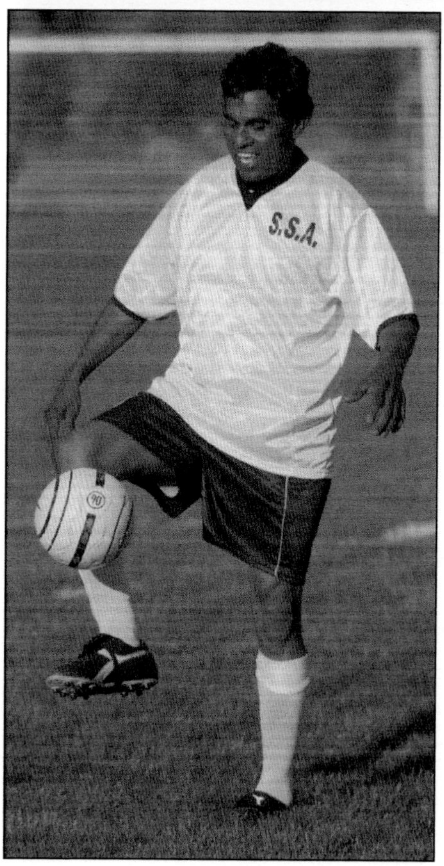

For Mexican participants, *fútbol* symbolizes not only culture, but a home left behind. Throughout NCW, Mexican soccer leagues have formed and have been organized and constructed to resemble their homeland. In the top picture, a Mexican team from Wenatchee has taken on the name Huajuapan, the name of the home town in Oaxaca where many of these players emigrated from. The photograph at left is of José Joya warming up before a match in Cashmere. At age 58, he is still active in the Hispanic Soccer League. (Courtesy *Wenatchee World*.)

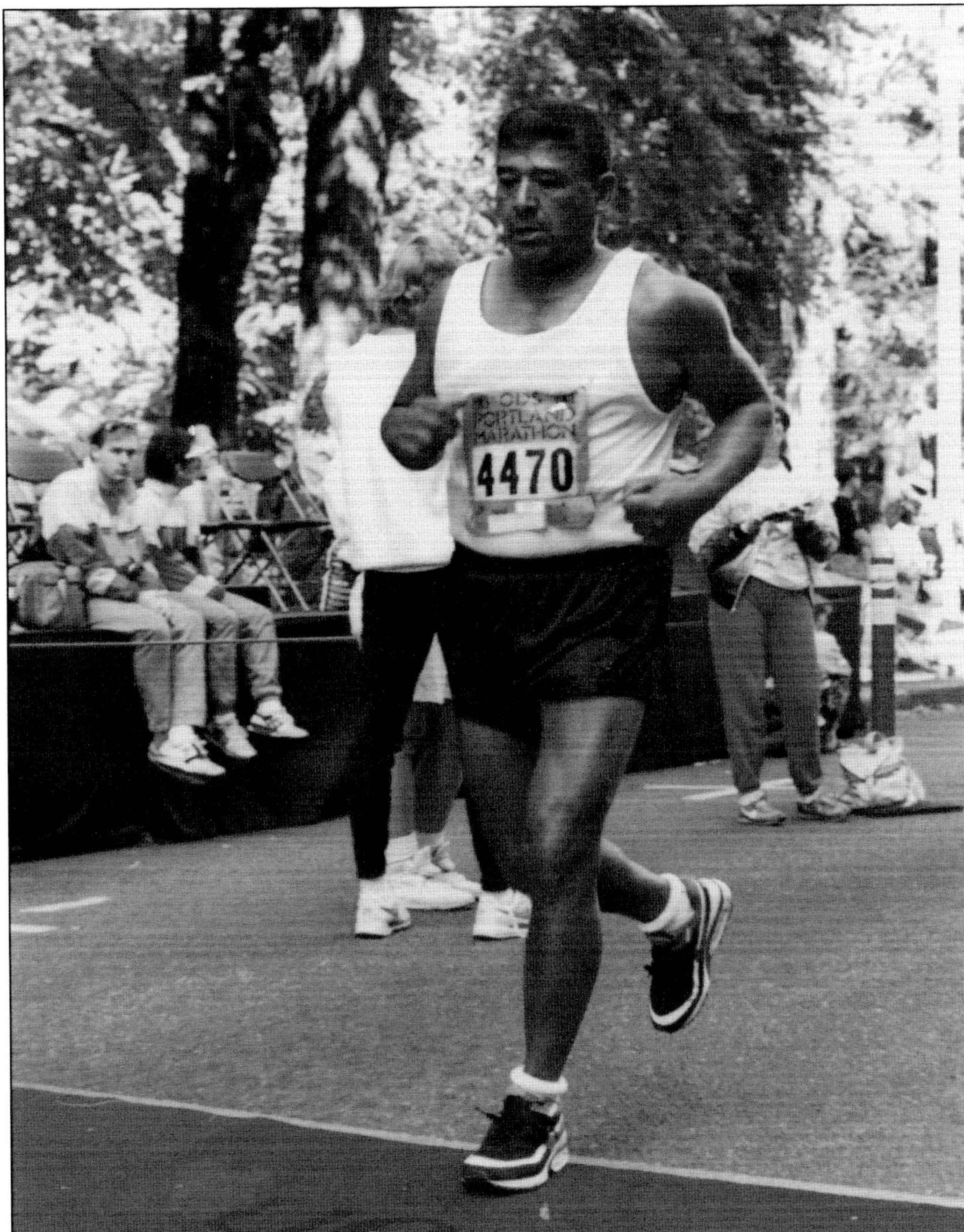

Running as a form of endurance continues with many ethnic Mexicans now living in the United States. The most famous runners from Mexico are the Tarahumara Indians from northwestern Mexico, who have a tradition of long-distance running dating back thousands of years. In this photograph is Ruben D. Garcia, a longtime resident of the Columbia Basin. Ruben is shown running the Portland Marathon. (Courtesy Jerry Garcia.)

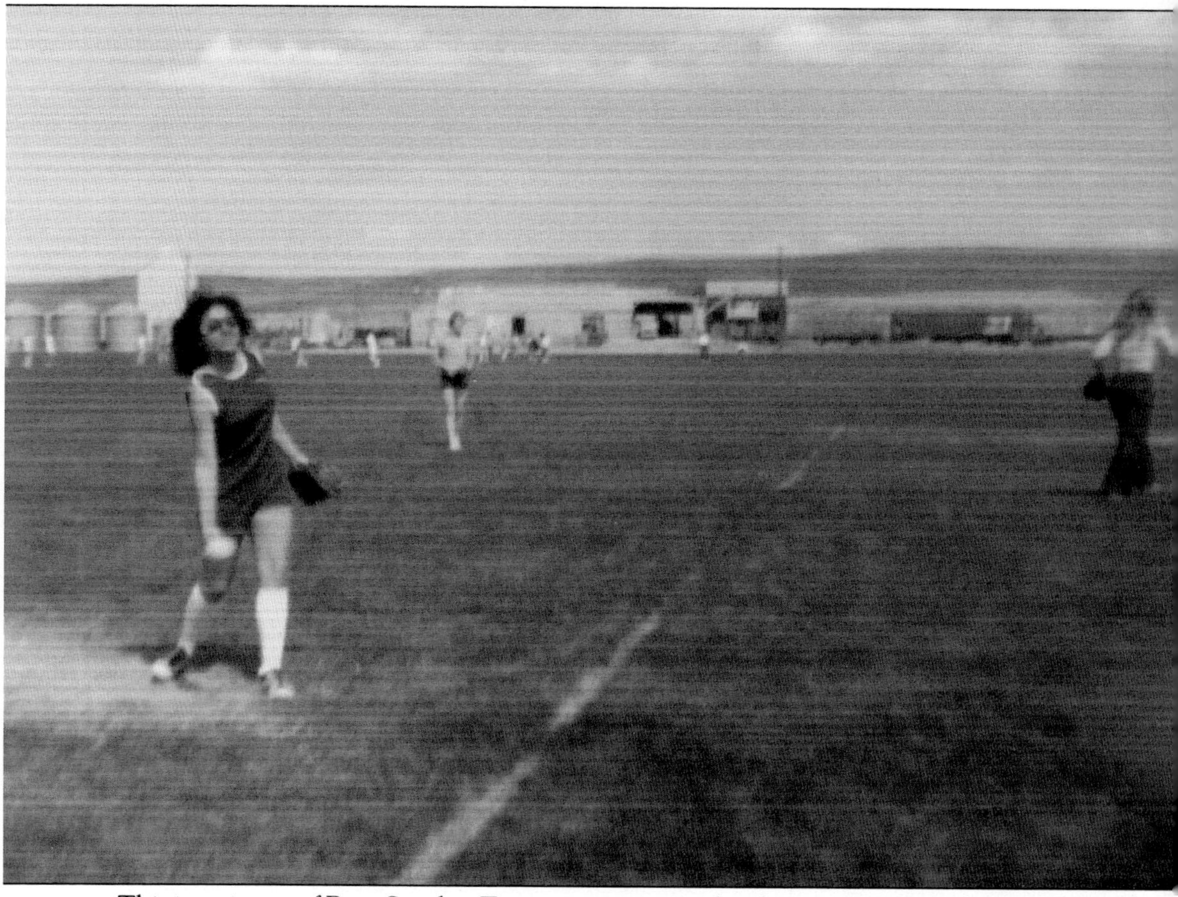

This is an image of Dora Sanchez Treviño running in a local race in NCW. Beyond the physical benefits from running, Dora indicates that she is able to relax and relieve stress when running. She picked up the sport/leisure activity in the 1980s. For ethnic Mexicans, young and old alike, running is an ancient sport, but it represents elements of modernity when analyzed from the contemporary perspective. (Courtesy Dora Treviño.)

Ten

The Changing Face of NCW

What has occurred demographically in North Central Washington (NCW) in the past 15 years can only be described as phenomenal. The 140 percent increase in the Latino population of NCW from 1990 to 2000 is being felt in almost every economic, social, and political sector. To put this in perspective, in 1970, Chelan County counted a total of 248 people of Spanish origin. In 2004, there were over 14,000 people of Spanish origin in Chelan County, and the city of Wenatchee has 6,156. Yet these are not even the largest increases! The largest concentration of Mexicans in NCW is located in Mattawa, where Mexicans represent almost 90 percent of the community. These types of numbers were unheard of even a decade ago. This pattern is replicated throughout NCW. What were some of the causes for this dramatic increase? One of the causes can be traced back to the Immigration Reform and Control Act of 1986. When almost 6,000 Latinos were given legal residency, this allowed them to sponsor other relatives to enter the United States under the process of family reunification. The increase was also fueled by the labor markets in NCW and family networks in place for decades. Of great importance is that most of the new arrivals are coming as permanent immigrants settling and establishing roots in NCW.

The expansion of the Mexican population has also diversified it. In communities throughout NCW, Mexicans who work in professional fields and are teachers, business owners, and owner-operators of their own orchards can be found. Perhaps the educational system provides the best illustration regarding the change, growth, and future of the Mexican communities in NCW. As in any decade or period, the future and well-being of the communities are in the hands of the children. The strong value ethnic Mexicans place on education will ensure a bright future for all in NCW. The following photographs illustrate the change, growth, and future for North Central Washington.

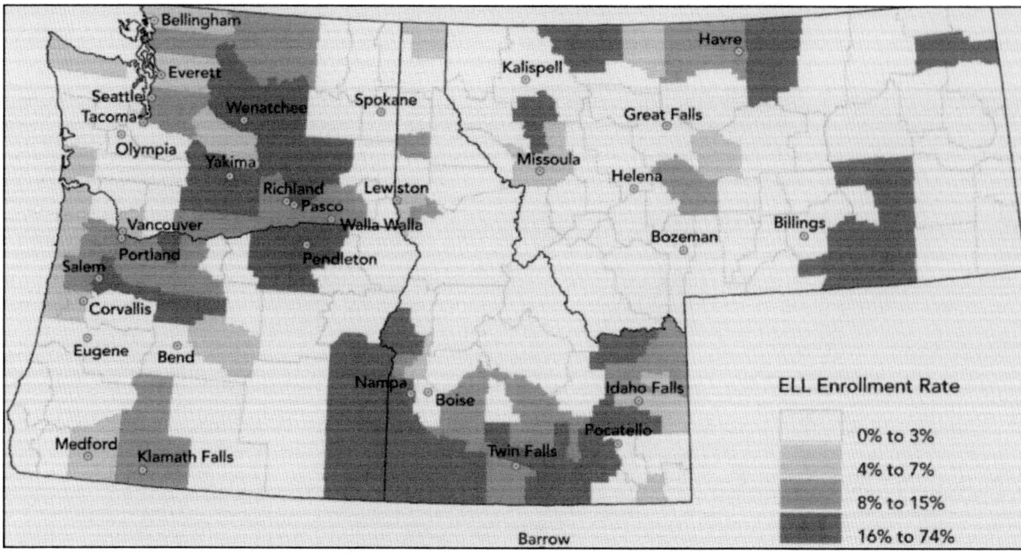

This map of the Pacific Northwest illustrates the impact of the growth of the Mexicans population. Wenatchee and North Central Washington has some of the largest percentages of schoolchildren enrolled in ELL (English Language Learners) programs. What this signals is a rise of recent arrivals from various places, but Mexican immigration is high on the list. Population trends also tell us that the recent Mexican population of NCW is here to stay, which means that the Mexican children in these programs and attending local schools are part of the area's future. The bottom photograph is of Rosemary Tiffany, who is a bilingual kindergarten teacher at Lewis and Clark Elementary in Wenatchee. Rosemary grew up in the Yakima Valley and was a migrant child. After struggling through school, she eventually overcame some of the barriers and went on to earn bachelor's and master's degrees and was recognized as the North Central ESD Regional Teacher of the Year. (Courtesy Northwest Education.)

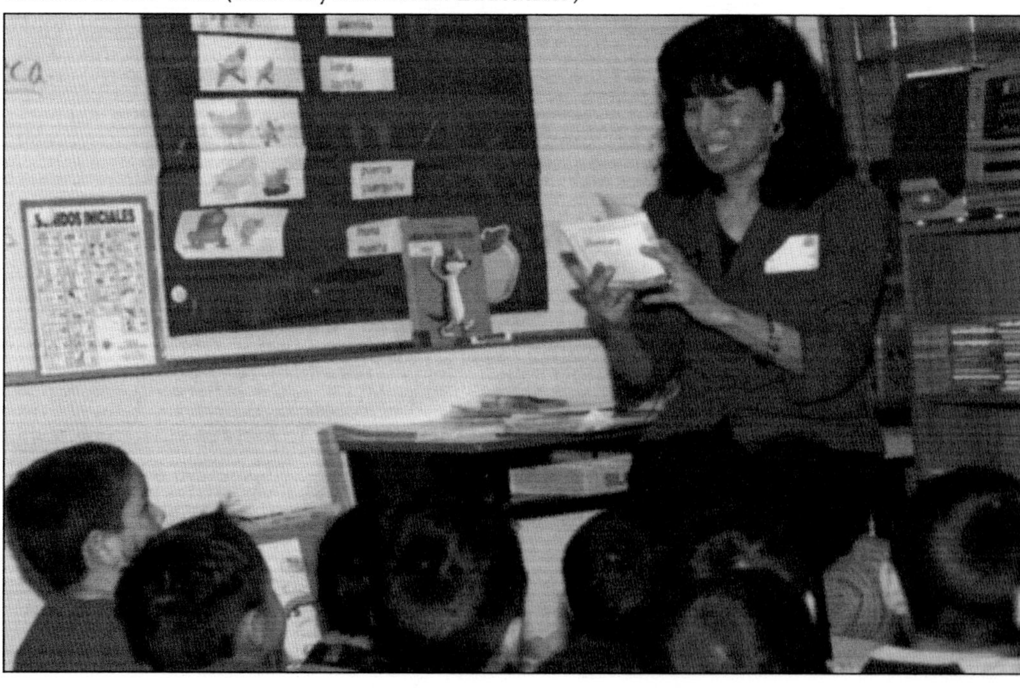

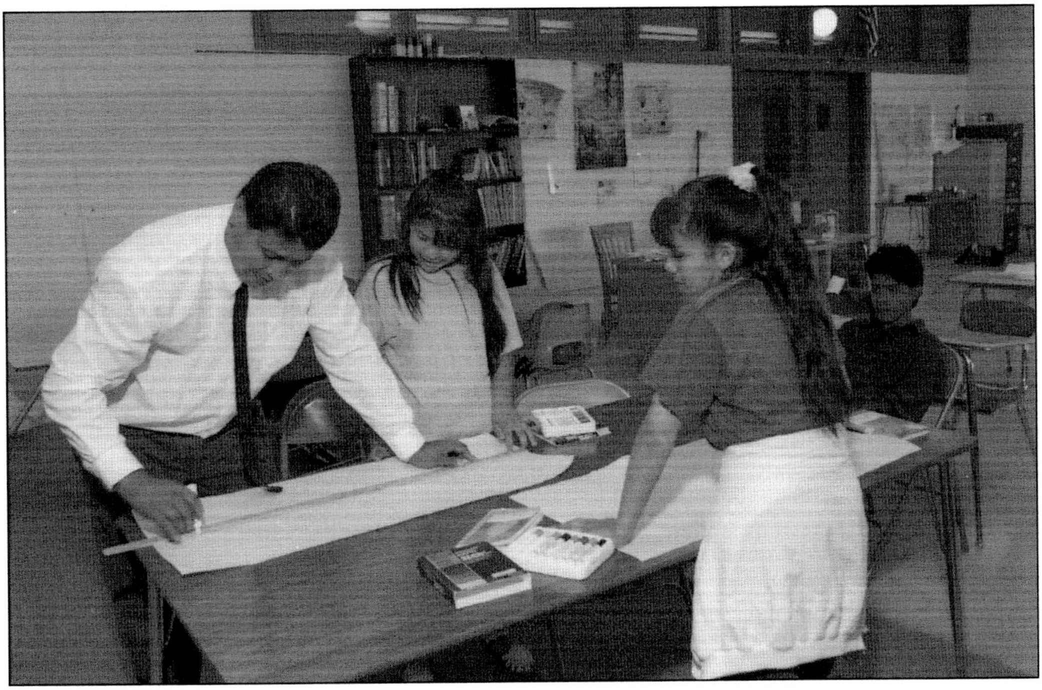

The above photograph is of Fred Martinez, who taught in Quincy when this photograph was taken. The Quincy School District has the one of the highest percentages of Latino students, but it has struggled to develop a cadre of teachers to meet the needs of those students. One of the great successes has been the life of Lewis and Clark Elementary principal Alfonso Lopez. From his humble beginnings in Oaxaca to the fields of NCW, and eventually to a teaching position in Wenatchee, Alfonso has brought needed skills and knowledge to the region. An award-winning teacher, Alfonso was appointed principal of Lewis and Clark in 2006. Principal Lopez is shown greeting people at the beginning of the school year (below). (Courtesy *Wenatchee World*.)

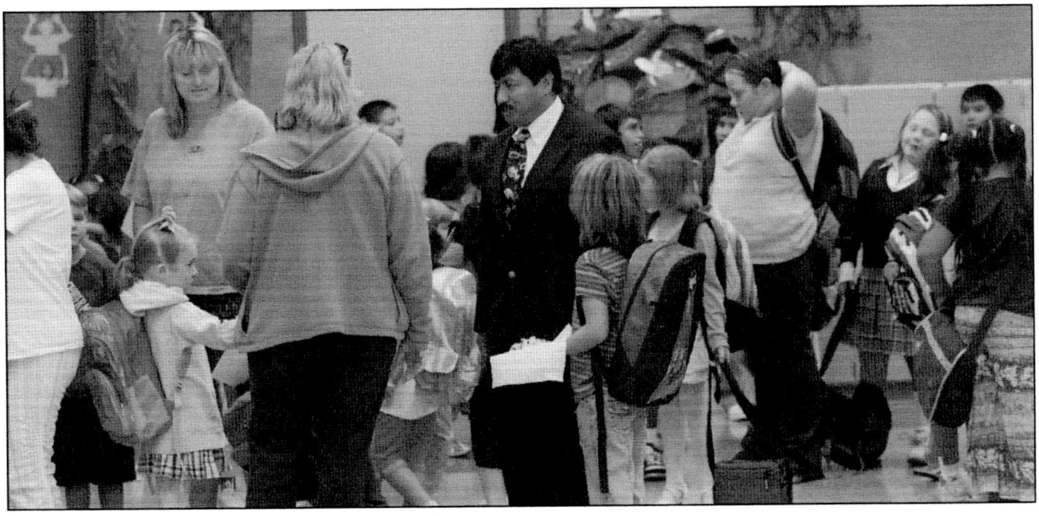

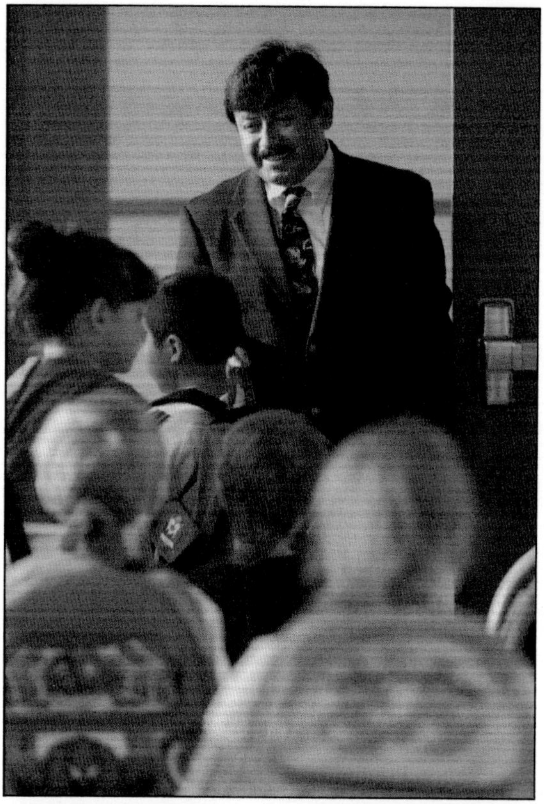

The first photograph on this page depicts Principal Lopez greeting students, faculty, and parents. These photographs, although different, truly represent the demographic change of NCW. As the Mexican population in places such as Wenatchee was integrated into the community, Mexican culture became more visible and open. These two images are examples of the process of integration and acceptance. In the bottom image are three Mexican princesses during the 1999 Washington State Apple Blossom Festival Grand Parade, representing Holy Apostles Hispanic community. (Courtesy *Wenatchee World*.)

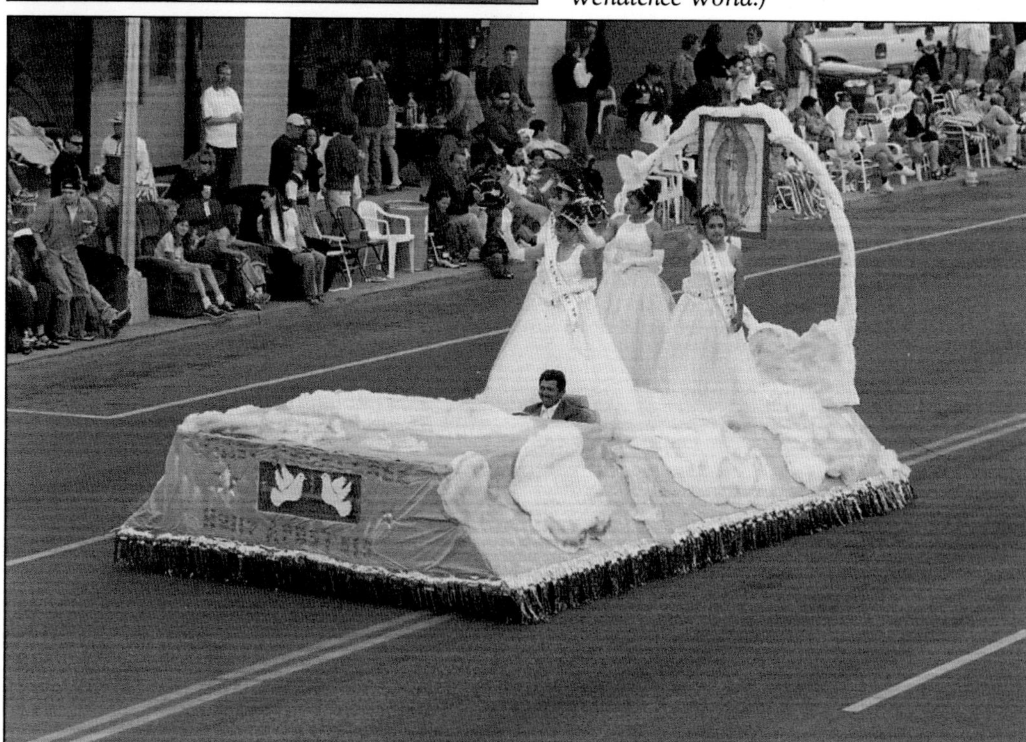

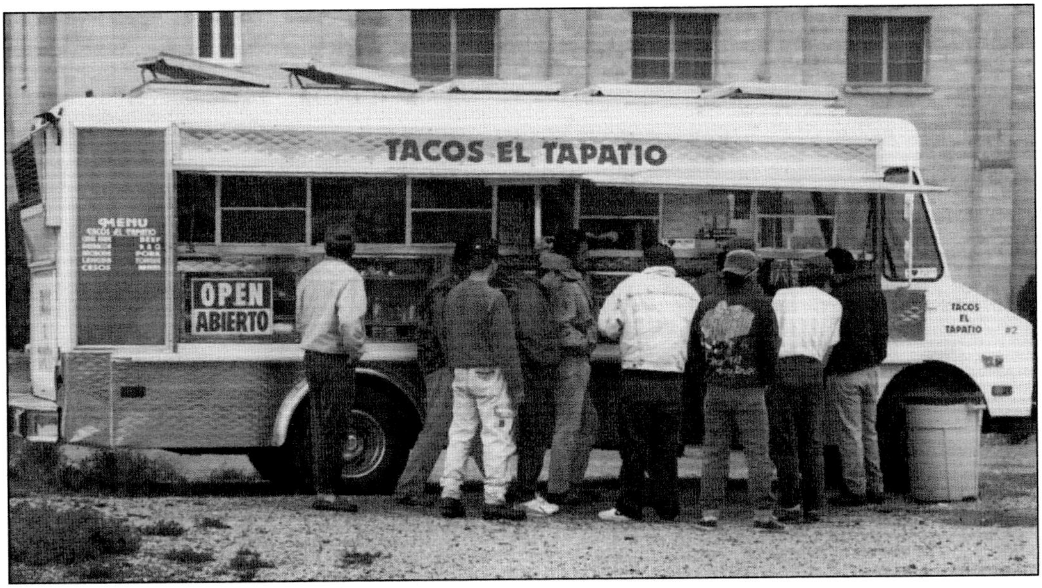

The top image is a "taco van" serving Mexican tacos. These taco vans are very popular throughout NCW and are frequented by all ethnicities. In 1986, the Immigration Reform and Control Act (IRCA) was passed by Congress, and nationally over three million undocumented individuals came forward. In NCW, almost 6,000 individuals applied for residency and received it. The image below, taken in 1986, shows Mexican immigrants attending a meeting concerning the impact of IRCA. Although some called the 1986 act amnesty, most of the individuals and families had earned the right for legalization through their hard work and contributions to the various communities in NCW. The issue of immigration will reemerge in the early 21st century. (Courtesy *Wenatchee World*.)

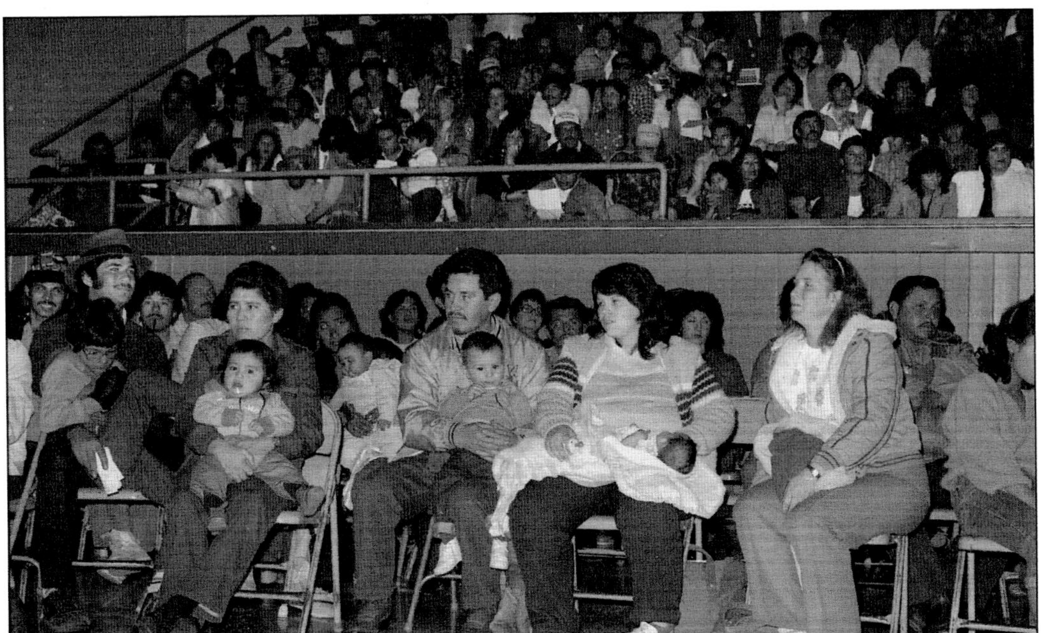

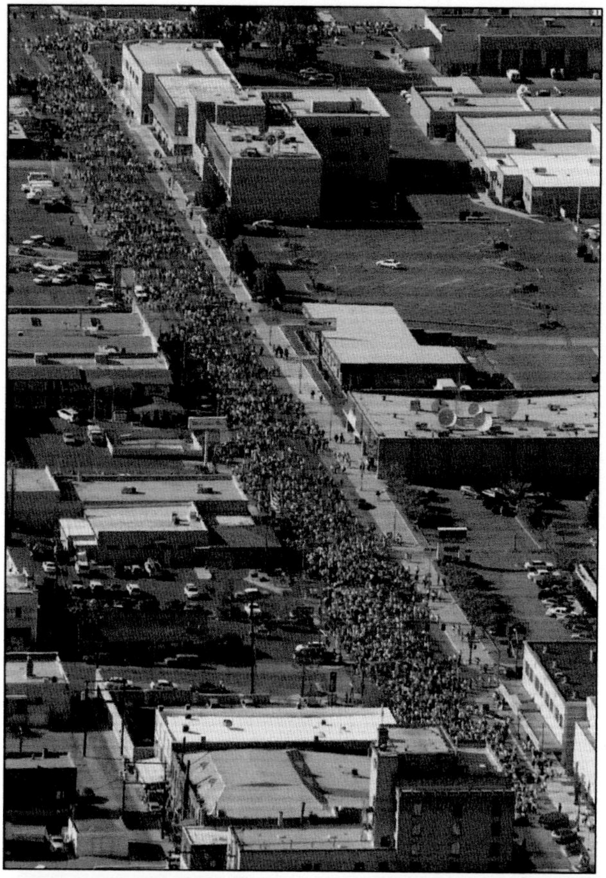

The full affects of the political economy of the nation and NCW were felt in the spring of 2006 when nationwide millions marched in the streets for the fair treatment of undocumented immigrants in the United States. Those unfamiliar with immigration and individuals with xenophobic tendencies viewed immigration through a narrow lens. Locally NCW followed the national trend by holding marches throughout the region. These two images depict rallies in Wenatchee with over 4,000 marching in the top photograph. The second photograph depicts a close-up of the march and details of the many symbols carried that day, which include La Virgen, U.S. and Mexican flags, and protest sign against HR4437, the Border Protection, Anti-terrorism, and Illegal Immigration Control Act of 2005. This marches included children, teenagers, adults, and those from many ethnic backgrounds. (Courtesy *Wenatchee World*.)

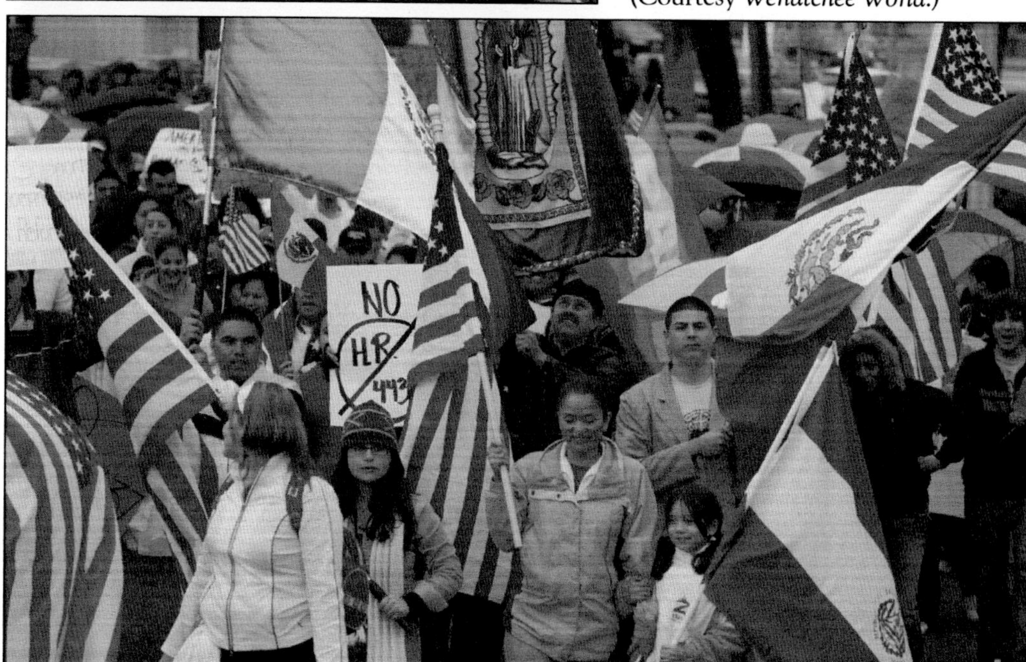

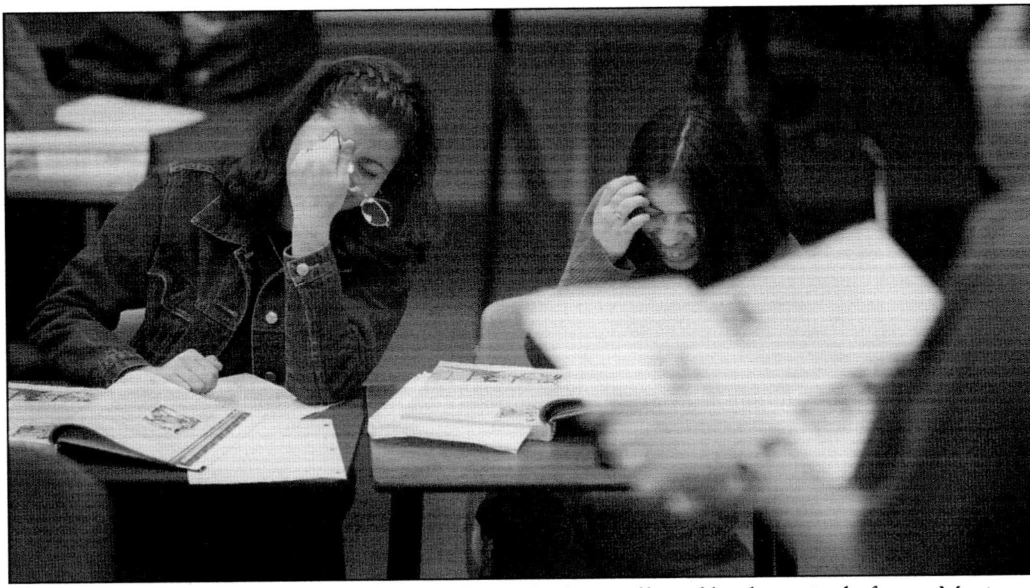

Secondary education and higher education have also been affected by the arrival of more Mexicans to the region. One misunderstanding about the educational system in the United States is that it is not a privilege, but a right for all children K–12 to receive an education. Even undocumented children have the right to an education based on the 1982 Supreme Court decision *Pyler v. Doe*. These two images show Latinos in high school and registering for English classes. The top image is of Patricia Hernandez (left) and Carolina Mendez, students in Enrique Sanchez's Spanish for Spanish Speakers class at Eastmont High School, 2004. In the bottom photograph, Latino students wait in line to fill out registration forms to get into English as a second language (ESL) classes at Wenatchee Valley College. (Courtesy *Wenatchee World*.)

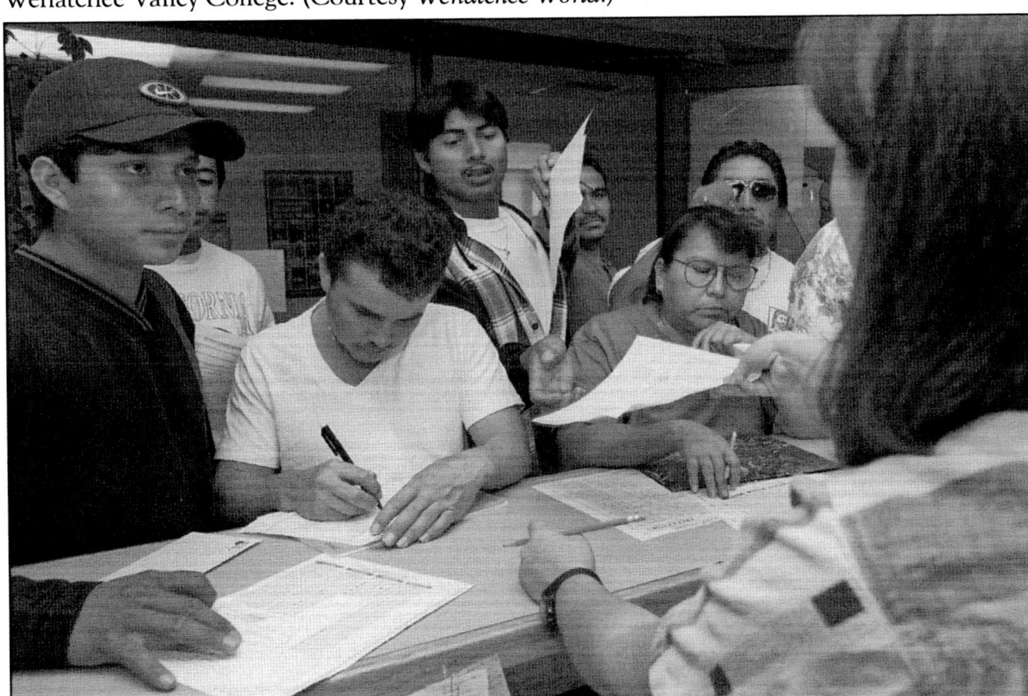

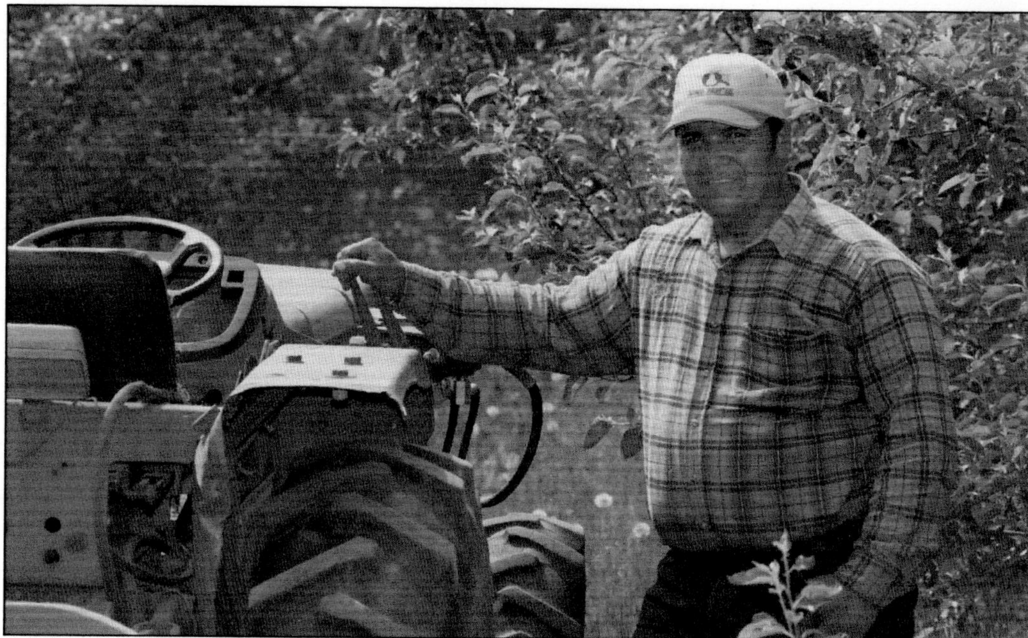

By the end of the 20th century, some Mexican laborers had gained enough experience and found capital in order to purchase and operate their farms or orchards. Since the arrival of ethnic Mexicans to the region, some of the biggest obstacles for economic independence have been discrimination, an unfamiliarity navigating the economic and financial infrastructure that is required to efficiently operate a farm or orchard, and a lack of experience and credit history for loans as seed money for operations. However, by the late 1990s, a shift was occurring throughout NCW where many Latinos were purchasing and operating their own businesses. One of the individuals who has broken through those barriers is José Límon, pictured above in 2001. In 1988, Límon purchased 10 acres of land and planted his first orchard. In 1998, he was able to quit his job for Auvil Fruit Company and farm full-time on his own land. Max Campos, pictured below in 2004, operated a Baker Flats Orchard. (Courtesy *Wenatchee World*.)

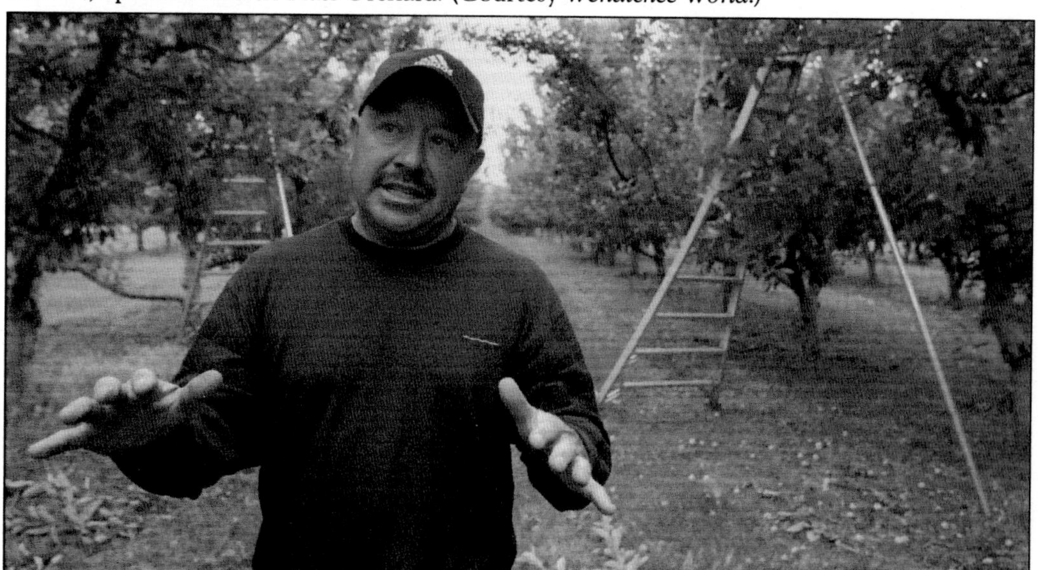

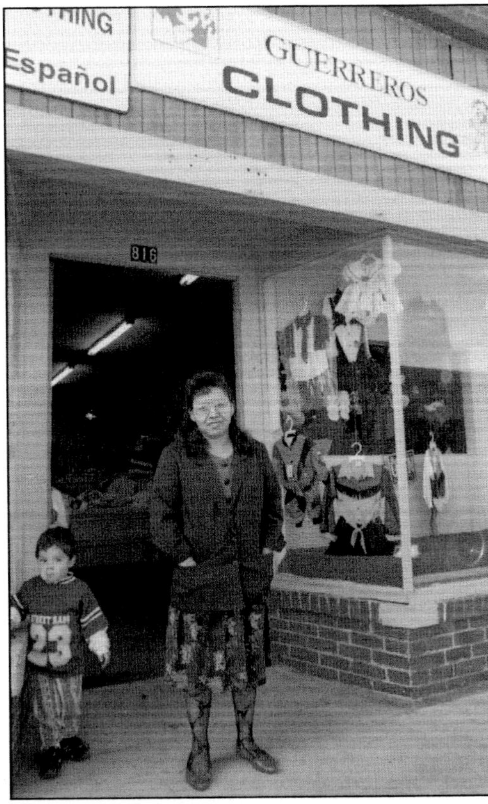

Beyond orchards and farms, many Mexicans have opened up retail businesses throughout NCW. They range from restaurants, grocery stores, tax and immigration services, law offices, and clothing stores. These two images depict two of the hundreds of Mexican-owned and -operated stores throughout NCW. Pictured in front of her store in 1993, Maria Guerrero went from the orchards' packing sheds to opening her own retail business in south Wenatchee. Below, Socorro Madrigal opened her Mexican bakery La Espiga in the 1990s. In this photograph, she is pictured with Martin Romero. (Courtesy *Wenatchee World*.)

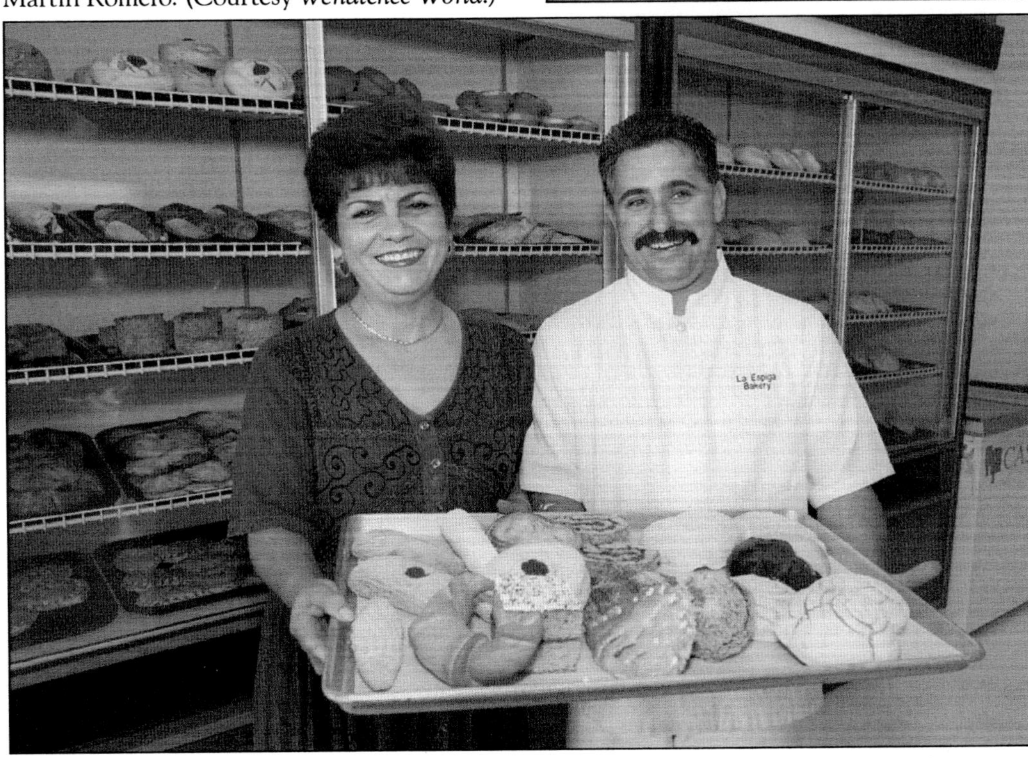

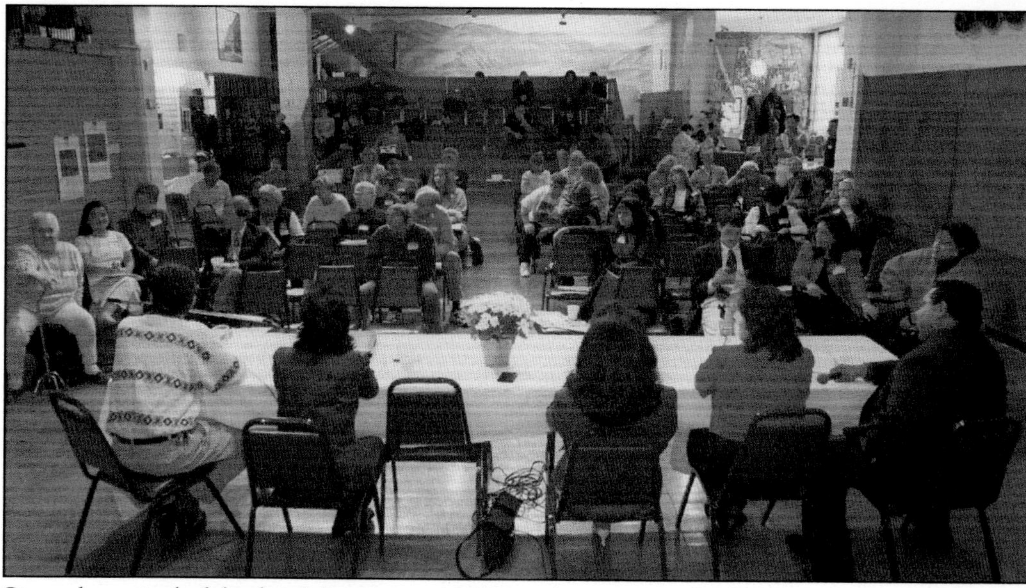

Since the arrival of the first Mexicans to NCW in the 1940s, some in various communities have struggled with differences and changing demographics. In NCW, where an established Mexican American community has been in place for decades, there is also a very young and vibrant Mexican immigrant community. Very few people understand the complexity of various cultures coexisting together and navigating each others nuances. Yet NCW has been a sociologist's dream come true with Anglos, Mexican Americans, Mexican immigrants, Japanese Americans, Native Americans, and blacks living within the social sphere. These two images show disparate views of the Mexican community. In the top image, community members have come together to discuss Anglo and Latino concerns and issues affecting the Wenatchee area. The lines of communication are open. In the image below is a "Jim Crow" sign Mexican style. This photograph was shot by Jim Tiffany of *El Mundo* as he was driving in the Okanogan area. This attitude and position is rare but not unheard of in NCW. (Above, courtesy *Wenatchee World*; below, courtesy *El Mundo*.)

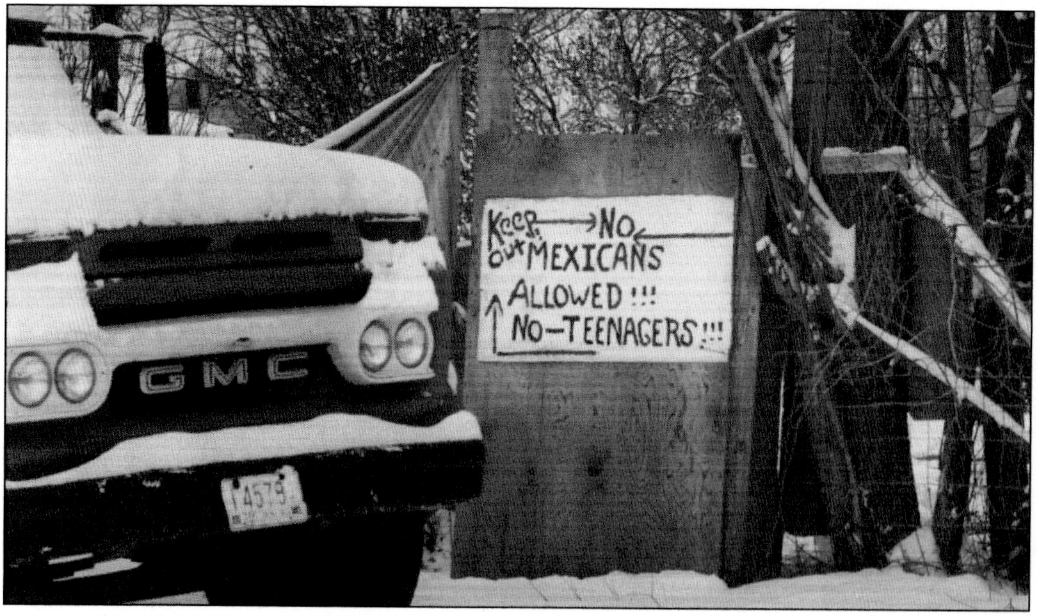

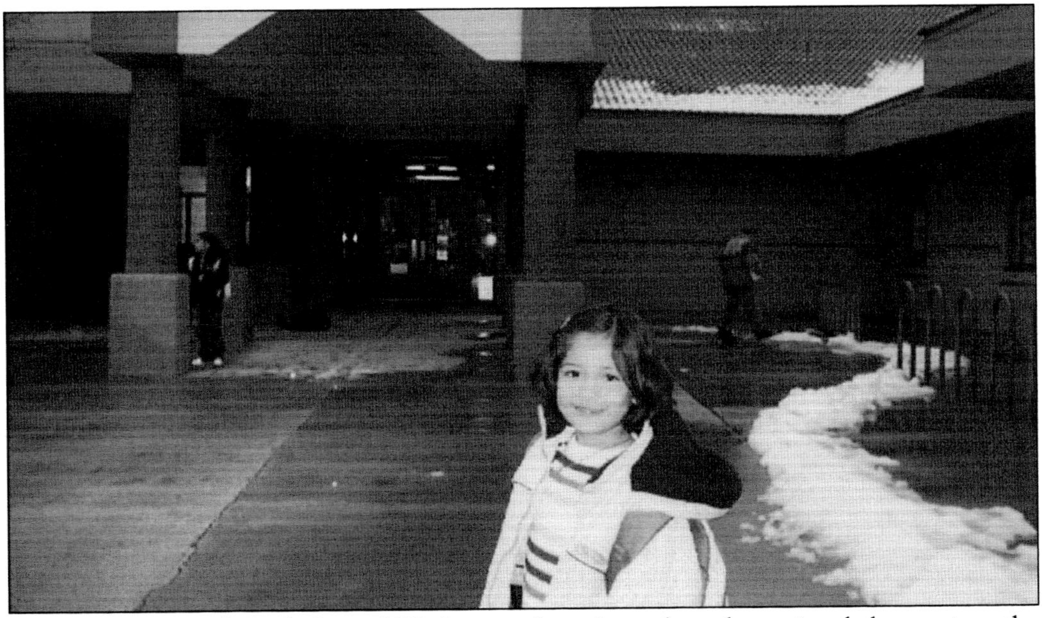

The communities of North Central Washington have been through continual change since the development of the region. And there is very little doubt that the evolution of the region continues. The arrival and settling of ethnic Mexicans is no different from previous groups that have come to the region as migrants dating back to the arrival of the first Europeans. Although sometimes difficult to see, the common values all groups share in NCW include the importance of family, self-determination, and seeking better opportunities for their children. These two photographs epitomize why Mexicans have traveled thousands of miles from their homeland: a better life for their children such as Natalia D. Alonso, pictured above, and the ESL class of Cheri Dudek at Mission View Elementary. (Above, courtesy Shanna Alonso; below, courtesy *Wenatchee World*.)

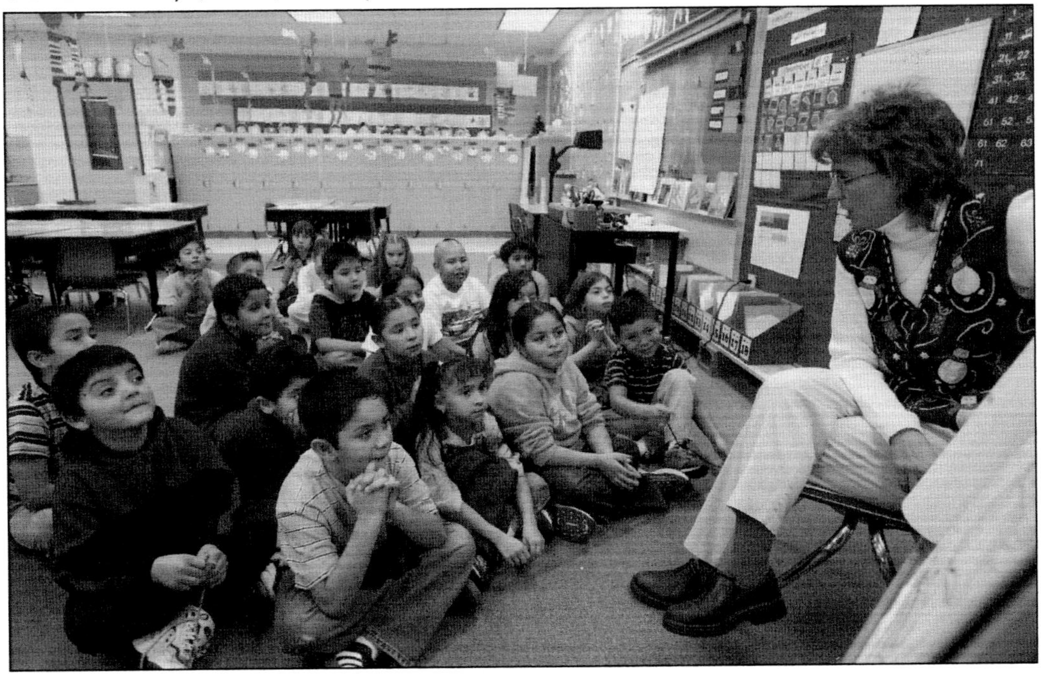